U0148914

魯迅越界跨國新解讀
Lu Xun: A Cross-Cultural Readings

◎王潤華 著

by W.Y. Wong

教育部頂尖大學
元智大學人文通識與倫理計劃

文史哲出版社印行

國家圖書館出版品預行編目資料

魯迅越界跨國新解讀=Lu Xun:A Cross-Cultural
Readings / 王潤華著. 初版. -- 臺北市：文
史哲, 民95.
頁： 公分
部份內容為英文
ISBN 957-549-698-2 (平裝)

1.周樹人－作品研究

848.4 　　　　　　　　　95026301

魯迅越界跨國新解讀

著　　　者：王　　潤　　華
倡 印 者：元　　智　　大　　學
　　　　　桃園縣中壢市內壢遠東路一三五號
　　　　　電　話：886-3-4638800
出 版 者：文　史　哲　出　版　社
　　　　　http://www.lapen.com.tw
登記證字號：行政院新聞局版臺業字五三三七號
發 行 人：彭　　正　　雄
發 行 所：文　史　哲　出　版　社
印 刷 者：文　史　哲　出　版　社
　　　　　臺北市羅斯福路一段七十二巷四號
　　　　　郵政劃撥帳號：一六一八〇一七五
　　　　　電話886-2-23511028・傳真886-2-23965656

實價新臺幣三四〇元

九十五年（2006）十二月初版

自　序

　　魯迅在 1904 年 9 月 13 日早上八點第一次步入仙台醫專（現稱東北大學）的第六教室。由於他是當時仙台醫專最早也是唯一的中國留學生，教務處特別安排一位書記總助次郎陪同魯迅進入教室，並且向同學介紹：「這是從中國來的學生！」大講堂的長條木板座位從左到右，共分成三排，魯迅的座位在中間的第三排的最右邊（面向台下）的座位。由於當時學生座位每天固定的，現在大學把這個座位貼上紀念魯迅的說明文字。為了紀念魯迅，目前東北大學特意保留了醫專魯迅時代的這棟大課室。

　　九十年後的 1994 年 9 月 6 日，我和其他十四位外國及日本研究魯迅的學者，一起走進魯迅習醫時最常用的第六教室。魯迅留學仙台九十周年紀念國際研討會主席阿部兼也教授，也模仿當年的情形，向日本學術文化界 ── 介紹我們。譬如輪到我的時候，他說：「這是來自新加坡的王潤華教授。」然後邀請我上台在古老的黑板上題字留念。我上台在古老的黑板上題字留念。我隨手寫上：「當南洋還在殖民地時代，魯迅已是我們的導師。」魯迅在五、六十年代的新加坡與馬來西亞，由於中國左派思想之流行，被華人文化知識界奉為思想導師。這是促使我研究魯迅的起因。

　　我在馬來西亞小學畢業那一年，從來沒有讀過魯迅的作品，但我們同學在畢業紀念冊互相題字的時候，就會用「橫眉冷對千夫指，俯首甘為孺子牛」或是「地上本沒有路，走的人多了，也變成了路」這一類魯迅的名言來互相勉勵。到了中學，我大量閱讀魯迅，開始寫有關魯迅的文章，其中一篇刊〈魯迅與木刻運動〉刊登在新加坡出版的《萌芽》（1958 年 10 月 1 日出版，第三期，頁 15）這期是紀念魯迅逝世 22 周年特輯）雜誌上。1962 年秋天到臺北就讀國立政治大學，我所攜帶魯迅、郁達夫及其他五四作家的書籍卻被臺北松山國際機場的海關全部沒收，當時臺灣嚴禁魯迅及其他五四作家，我便只好跟着大家寫現代派的詩歌。

1968 秋天到了美國威斯康辛大學修讀碩士與博士，我的指導老師是當時非常重要的、權威的英文《五四運動史》（*May Fourth Movement*， *Intellectual Revolution in Modern China*. Harvard University Press，196）的作者周策縱，於是又引起我對五四作家的興趣，我的第一篇學期報告便是魯迅小說人物的分析，這引導我後來在 1990 年出版的《魯迅小說新論》（上海學林/臺北東大圖書）的研究。

今年（2006）爲魯迅逝世 70 周年，爲了紀念這位現代文學大師，在中國與世界各地，官方與民間機構，有不少相應的活動。爲配合在香港舉行的「2006 香港魯迅週『魯迅是誰』展覽」，香港中文大學逸夫書院也舉辦了「2006 香港魯迅論壇」，2006 年 9 月 8 日邀請了周海嬰、周令飛、李歐梵、王宏志、千野拓政與我，在香港中央圖書館演講廳辦了一場講座，再度思考在現代語境下「魯迅是誰」？

爲了配合「魯迅是誰」？的主題，我撰寫主題演講〈魯迅越界跨國新解讀〉，我重新閱讀自己與世界各國學者的論著。我特別重視西方與日本漢學與「中國學」研究典範下論述魯迅的黑暗面、東歐學者強調魯迅傳統與現代的整合精神，西方學者在科際研究的下所洞見魯迅豐富的思想文化資源，還有海外華人研究所看見魯迅在中心與邊緣之間定位錯亂而產生的對話，我認爲是現代魯迅論述很重要的一部分，可彌補中大陸、臺灣、香港魯迅研究的不足。

　　從西方漢學到中國學、文學分析到政治閱讀、比較文學到近期的文化研究（cultural studies），各種方法典範下的魯迅研究，開拓了許多創新的視野與方法，建構了很多理論。最特別的地方，是比較文學、文學分析、訓詁考據學、歷史語言學、再加上社會科學（政治學、史學、思想史等）的方法，跨越區域與學科疆界的文化視野，因此開創魯迅研究新方向與方法，帶來全新的詮釋與世界性的意義。這種魯迅學術思考與分析，完全著眼於客觀事實，很少涉及道德的判斷或民族的感情偏向，或政治意識的論調，維持客觀的、科學化的史學的思考。很多複雜的問題，在他們的眼前，只是一個客觀體，這是奉科學爲典範下的人文研究。

　　這些魯迅學者就像魯迅自己，善於利用世界性的文化與思想資源，但沒有被任何一種文化思想資源勞役。就因爲擁有與使用豐富又深刻的參考架構，他們對魯迅及其作品具有集體感應及特殊感。

　　我生長於中華文化邊緣的東南亞，經常越界跨國，站在邊緣思考與觀察魯迅。當魯迅遇到東南亞受英文教育的華人的如林文慶，魯迅以衝突作爲對話，當魯迅到了南洋華人社會，魯迅被支持者神話化，從反殖民變成文學殖民者。郁達夫進入新馬華文後殖民文壇，爲什麼對魯迅在海外影響產生反感與不滿？重返日本仙台醫學專現場解剖周樹仁棄醫從文的原因，我們發現幻燈事件的神話意義。這些域外的、邊緣的魯迅論述，都是我在 1990 年出版的《魯迅小說新論》（上海學林/臺北東大圖書）以後所進行的研究。這本書中，我也順便將英文的論文及數首寫魯迅的詩收集在書内。爲這個時期的魯迅研究畫上結束的句號。

王潤華

2006 年 10 月 31 日臺灣元智大學

魯迅越界跨國新解讀

目　錄

魯迅越界跨國新解讀

一、「越界跨國」的定義

我所要說的「越界跨國」，不單指跨越民族國家的區域界限，也指跨越學科、文化、方法的、視野的邊界，同時也超越文本，進入社會及歷史現場，回到文化/文學產生的場域，突破傳統中國文學的詮釋典範去解讀魯迅及其文學作品。種種跨越，為的就是要設法貼切的去解讀魯迅及其文學作品。

遠在進入網路社會、知識整合時代，還沒有為了因應轉型為創新知識驅動型的全球化經濟，歐洲與北美一流大學與學者，早已開始大力拆除大學院系與學科間的圍牆。人才不設圍牆，概念不設圍牆，思維不設圍牆，知識不設圍牆。知識一旦不設圍牆，知識的發現，知識的轉移，知識的應用，不但能善用資源，集思廣益，知識也成為實用性很強的文化了。

中國現代文學研究在六、七十年代開始在西方，尤其美國，發展迅速蓬勃，就因為一大群來自不同學科的學者，包括社會、歷史、政治、哲學、西洋文學的學者，進入中文文學的領域，知識整合所帶來的綜合效應（synergies），使得中文文學具有國際的視野，走向多學科、多方法。[1]

1　王潤華〈中國現代文學研究的新方向〉《越界跨國文學解讀》（臺北：萬卷樓，2004），頁 3-32；James Liu, "The Study of Chinese Literature in the West: Recent Developments,

二、西方漢學與「中國學」研究典範下的魯迅

突破傳統思考方式，去思考中國文化現象的多元性的漢學（Sinology）傳統，是許多海外學者探討研究中國文化的重要傳統。傳統漢學的強點是一門純粹的學術研究，專業性很強，研究深入細緻。掌握普通學科的基礎理論，通曉多種語言，研究中國文學的人對西洋文學有深入的認識，能運用人文與社會學的治學方法。[2]往往窮畢生精力去徹底研究一個小課題，而且是一些冷僻的，業已消失的文化歷史陳跡，和現實毫無相關。因此傳統的漢學研究在今天，也有其缺點，如研究者不求速效，不問國家大事，所研究的問題沒有現實性與實用法，其研究往往出於奇特冷僻的智性追求，其原動力是純粹趣味。[3]傳統漢學比較忽略純文學，尤其現代文學。但是把漢學治學的方法用來研究文學，其突破與創新是難於想像的。

美國學術界自二次大戰以來，已開發出一條與西方傳統漢學很不同的研究路向，這種研究中國的新潮流叫中國學（Chinese Studies），它與前面的漢學傳統有許多不同之處，它很強調中國研究與現實有相關，思想性與實用性，強調研究當代中國問題。這種學問希望達致西方瞭解中國，另一方面也希望中國瞭解西方，對西方有所反應。[4]

中國研究是區域研究（Area Studies）興起的帶動下，從邊緣走向

Current Trends, Future Prospects", *The Journal of Asian Studies*, Vol. XXXV, No.1（Nov. 1975），pp. 21-30。

2 周法高《漢學論集》（臺北：正中書局，1965），頁 8-16；James Hightower, "Chinese Literature in the Context of World Literature", *Comparative Literature*. Vol. V （1955），pp. 117-124，中譯見《英美學人論中國古典文學》（香港：香港中文大學出版社，1973，頁 253-265。

3 杜維明《漢學、中國學與儒學》見《十年機緣待儒學》（香港：牛津大學出版社，1999），頁 1-33。

4 同上，頁 1-12。關於中國學在美國大學的發展與研究方法，參考 Paul Sih （ed.）, *An Evaluation of Chinese Studies* （New York: St. John's University, 1978）。

主流。區域研究的興起,是因為專業領域如社會學、政治學、文學的解釋模式基本上是以西方文明為典範而發展出來的,對其他文化所碰到的課題涵蓋與詮釋性不夠。對中國文化研究而言,傳統的中國解釋模式因為只用中國文明為典範而演釋出來的理論模式,如性別與文學問題,那是以前任何專業都不可單獨顧及和詮釋。在西方,特別美國,從中國研究到中國文學,甚至縮小到更專業的領域中國現代文學或世界華文文學,都是在區域研究與專業研究沖激下的學術大思潮下產生的多元取向的學術思考與方法,它幫助學者把課題開拓與深化,創新理論與詮釋模式,溝通世界文化。[5]本文所討論的魯迅研究,都是在西方漢學與中國學,或近期的文化研究(cultural studies)思考典範下的產品。

在美國第一、二代的研究中國文學的華人學者中,他們幾乎是從別的學科轉行過來的,而且經常往返於中國古典現代文學之間。像周策縱為紅學、古文字、古典文學、現代文化/文學研究大師,是最好的例子。他原是密芝根大學的政治系博士,成名作《五四運動史》(The May Fourth Movement: Intellectual Revolution in Modern China,1960)為博士論文[6]其改寫與出版都在哈佛大學的中國學(Chinese Studies)的治學方法與學術思潮中進行,完全符合中國研究與現實有相關,思想性與實用性,強調研究當代中國問題的精神。另一方面,區域研究思潮也使本書超越以西方文明為典範而發展出來的專業領域如社會學、

5　關於以哈佛為中心的漢學、中國學區域研究的發展,參考杜維明〈漢學、中國學與儒學〉,見《十年機緣待儒學》(香港:牛津大學出版社,1999 年),頁 1-33;余英時〈費正清的中國研究〉及其他論文,見傅偉勳、歐陽山(邊)《西方漢學家論中國》(臺北:正中書局,1993),1-44 及其他相關部分。

6　Chow Tse-tsung ,*The May Fourth Movement: Intellectual Revolution in Modern China* (Cambridge ,Mass: Harvard University Press,1960; Stanford: Stanford University Press, 1967.)

政治學、文學的解釋模式，同時更突破只用中國文明為典範而演繹出來的傳統的中國解釋模式。所以《五四運動史》成為至今詮釋五四對權威的著作，成了東西方知識界認識現代新思想、文化運動的一本入門書，也是今天所謂文化研究的典範。[7]

《五四運動史》對中國社會、政治、思想、文化、文學和歷史提出系統的觀察和論斷。本書奠定了作者在歐美中國研究界的大師地位。這本書使用大量原始史料，包括中、日、西方語文的檔案資料，這是窄而深的史學專題（monograph）思想文化專題的典範著作。另外不涉及道德的判斷或感情的偏向，凸顯出客觀史學（現實主義史學）的特質。周教授在密之根大學念的碩士與博士都是政治學，因此社會科學（政治、社會、經濟學等）建構了他的現實客觀的歷史觀 這正是當時西方的主流史學，這點與費正清的社會科學主導的客觀史學很相似。[8]而且被奉為在中國研究中，跨越知識領域研究、文化研究最早的研究典範。西方中國現代文學研究，尤其魯迅研究，以《五四運動史》這本書開始，具有象徵的意義。

他最近的新書《棄園古今語言文字考論集》（2006），也說明周教授是當今的把古文字的名物訓詁，文字考釋，歷史語言學、社會科學、西方漢學、區域研究中的中國學轉向全面用來做名物訓詁，文字考釋、文學經典考證的關鍵性大師。他認為我們知道除了對中國的古文字、

---

7 國際漢學大師周策縱教授在一九六三至一九九四年期間，擔任威斯康辛大學的東亞語文系與歷史系的教授，周教授的教學與研究範圍，廣涉歷史、政治、文化、藝術、哲學、語言、文字、文學。1941 年中央政治學校學士，一九四八年離開中國前已對中國社會、歷史、文化，包括古文字學有淵深精深的造詣。獲密芝大學政治學碩士（1950）與博士（1955）。1955-1962 在哈佛大學擔任研究員，正是西方漢學（Sinology）轉型成中國研究（Chinese Studies）的重要發展時期，也是區域研究，特別是亞洲研究的成熟期。見王潤華，〈國際漢學大師周策縱學術研究新典範〉，周策縱《棄園古今語言文字考論集》（臺北：萬卷樓，2006），237-255。

8 參考余英時〈費正清的中國研究〉，見上引《西方漢學家論中國》，pp.1-44.

歷史文化、經典文獻深厚的知識（這是目前東西方年輕學者的致命傷），更重要的是治學的方法。他採用涵蓋面很廣的詮釋模式，多元的分析方法：「凡古今中外的校勘、訓詁、考證之術，近代人文、社會、自然科學之理論、方法、與技術，皆不妨比照實情，斟酌適可而用之。」[9]

而對研究魯迅有新見解的學者，也是如此。夏志清是耶魯大學的英文系博士，以文本細讀、比較文學大解讀現代與古代小說。夏志清在 1961 年已出版的《中國現代小說史》，恐怕是最早以文學論文學，以「文學分析」（literary analysis）或稱文本細讀（scrutiny）來研究中國現代文學的典範之作。他的《現代中國小說史》中的魯迅，廣泛運用比較文學、新批評的文本細讀的文學分析法，因此發現魯迅及其他被忽略的沈從文、張愛玲等人作品中的藝術結構。另外李維斯（Leavis）文學爲人生各種現象象徵的大傳統理論也同時出現其論述的架構中，魯迅及其同代人感時憂國，對社會關懷與人生的道德感，成爲現代中國文學的新傳統。夏志清獨排當時左派神話魯迅的論述，引起重讀魯迅及其他作家的學術風氣與方法，影響一直到今天。[10]

李歐梵從台大到哈佛，讀的是西方文學、國際關係及中國文化思想史，最後以思想文化研究給現代文學帶來全新的詮釋。[11]他的《魯迅的遺產》（The Legacy of Lu Xun）[12]，《鐵屋子的聲音》（Voices from

---

9　周策縱《棄園古今語言文字考論集》（臺北：萬卷樓，2006）。頁 1-29。

10　C.T.Hsia, *A History of Modern Chinese Fiction*（New Haven: Yale University Press, 1961）。

11　Leo Lee, *The Romantic Generation of Modern Chinese Writers*（Cambridge, Mass: Harvard University Press, 1973）, *Voices From the Iron House: A Study of Lu Xun*（Bloomington: Indiana University Press, 1987），《中西文學的徊想》（香港：三聯書店，1986 年）；《徘徊在現代和後現代之間》（臺北：正中書局，1996 年）；《現代性的追求：李歐梵文化評論精選集》（臺北：麥田出版社，1996 年）；*Shanghai Modern: The Flowering of a New Urban Culture in China, 1930-1945*（Cambridge, Mass: Harvard University Press, 1999）。

12　Leo Lee(ed.), Lu *Xun and His Legacy*(Berkeley: University of California Press, 1985)。

the Iron House）[13]，前者帶引現代思想、政治、歷史等十二位不同領域的專家,以跨學科的研究，從各個層面解剖魯迅作品藝術與政治、思想的的意義，評估非神話魯迅對文學與社會的影響。《鐵屋子的聲音》（Voices from the Iron House），通過魯迅內在的吊詭、矛盾、與絕望的黑色語言，對魯迅的人生經驗與作品細緻的分析，對魯迅小說現代性的技巧（technique of modernity）的論述，如個人抒情性（personal lyricism）與象徵敘事（symbolic narrative），突破過去馬克思與現實主義的思想性與政治性的閱讀，帶動了去神話化魯迅的人文工程。

　　中國現代歷史與文化思想學者林毓生，帶著《中國思想意識的危機》（The Crisis of Chinese Consciousness,1979）[14]的研究經驗與視野，一旦進入魯迅文學小說與文學作品中，發現魯迅在理性與道德上，都有傳統和反傳統的不可調和的信念系統在互相衝突，正如文學作品所表現，徹底反傳統的思想通常是意識的、顯示的，傳統思想通常是潛藏的意義、隱示的。從李文蓀（Joseph Levenson）的中國知識分子由西方價值與民族傳統造成分裂性的緊張[15]到林毓生所建立的中國知識分子傳統與反傳統的分裂性緊張，無論理論如何形成，因新舊文化衝突，而形成魯迅思想與人格上的緊張，對閱讀魯迅的散文與小說有絕對創新的視野。周昌龍曾運用這個理論來析讀魯迅的《吶喊》與《彷徨》，呈現出許多複雜的，可以吶喊與彷徨兩種精神為象徵的內涵。[16]

---

13 Leo Lee ，*Voices From the Iron House: A Study of Lu Xun*（Bloomington: Indiana University Press, 1987）

14 Lin Yu-Sheng, *The Crisis of Chinese Consciousness*（Madison: University of Wisconsin Press,1979）.,中譯本林毓生，《中國意識的危機》，穆善培譯（貴州：貴州人民出版社，1988）。

15 Joseph Levenson, Confucian China and Its Modern Fate（Berkeley: University of California Press,1964）.

16 周昌龍,〈魯迅的傳統與反傳統思想〉《新思潮與傳統》（臺北：聯經，1995），頁 101-160。

三、東歐漢學的魯迅研究

在東歐學者中，也多數是跨越本行學科，偶然走進來的局外人，後來都成爲大師級的學者。普實克（Jaroslav Prusek，1906-1980）就是一個典範。他本來也是非文學的學者，原本在布拉格查理大學文學院，開始研究世界古代民族如拜占庭的歷史文化。1928 到 1930 年，他師從瑞典哥德堡大學的漢學教授高本漢（Bernard Karlgren）學漢語。1930 年，他獲得查理大學歷史專業文學博士學位，1932 年，捷克東方研究所派他到中國學習了三年，他在北京的民族大學（民族學院）學的是經濟歷史，不是文學。[17]但是最後他的魯迅研究不但是東歐也是全世界歐最具獨特成就的典範。

當英美學人注重文學作品內在語言藝術結構的作家的同時，在 1960 年代開始，東歐以普實克爲首的布拉格學派（Prague School），注重研究革命文學的理論與歷史發展，不像英美地區學者，只強調文學分析。普實克也進行文學分析，但不停止於分析，嘗試向前探討其文學源流的傳統。他發現魯迅的小說具有強烈的懷舊與抒情性，考證現代中國革命文學的根源在更早期的中國古典文學裏，不是英美很多學人所強調的全是受西方的影響。中國現代文學在理論上是相對於傳統古典文言文的文學，但古典文學中詩詞的抒情性與懷舊，影響了在現代小說抒情的情境，它不是來自西方現代文學，雖然相似，而是中國古典詩詞主體性的表達，所以對普實克而言，魯迅的《吶喊》、《彷徨》中的〈故鄉〉，甚至更早的〈懷舊〉都是結合文學、歷史、社會情

17 普實克的唯一女兒卡特瑞娜·馬爾莎科娃　KaterinaMarsalková 的自述，見 http://www.chinesezj.com/asp/zhuce/tougao/CASE/viewarticle.；高克利（M，Galik）〈普實克：傳奇與現實〉《二十一世紀,》，1993 年 5 月號，頁 120-127；August Pakit, Leo Lee 等人的回憶文章，尤其前者對普實克的學歷研究敍述詳細，見 Archiv Orientalni, Vol. 59 , No 2（1991），pp.105-121.

懷的抒情史詩。

懷舊與抒情性乃中國的古典文學的基本精神，因此這代表擁抱傳統的傾向，由於這種精神，魯迅不像表面的觀察所見，他的作品不是十九世紀西方的寫實主義傳統，而像兩次世界大戰期間文明受到破壞後，歐洲現代文學所表現出的抒情傳統，魯迅擁抱中國古典文學中懷舊與抒情性，因爲中國發現西方的新價值，但中國社會人群人困在黑暗絕望中，無能走向光明，再回頭中國傳統的鄉土人情和寧靜的生活又消失了[18]。這種論述與上面提到美國的林毓生的看法，因新舊文化衝突，形成魯迅思想與人格上的分裂性緊張思相符合的[19]，而且與本文後面會提到的更早的竹內好與夏濟安的黑暗面形成一個理論系統。

1960 到 1970 年代歐洲的共產國家的魯迅研究方向有共同的方向，如俄國學者謝曼諾夫（V.I Semanov）的《魯迅和他的前驅》20也是建構研究魯迅時向內往前進入中國古典文學的研究典範。他探索魯迅的小說敍事技巧與其他結構的形成，發現清代末年譴責小說的作者，是魯迅小說的前驅。謝曼諾夫的學術研究以清代章回小說開始，後來才跨入魯迅研究領域，因此才能看見思想反傳統，小說形式西化的魯迅小說，是在傳統小說裏尋找他的小說範本。這種特別的眼光，

---

18 我在〈沈從文：中國現代小說的薪傳統〉曾討論沈從文肯定魯迅肯定自己的書寫被物質文明毀滅的鄉村小說的傳統，見南京大學中國現代文學研究中心編《中國現代文學傳統》（北京：人民文學出版社，2002），頁 417-428。

19 他的魯迅著作見解 Jaroslav Prusek, *The Lyrical and the Epic*, Leo Lee （ed.）（Bloomington: Indiana University Press, 1980）；中譯本：普實克《普實克中國現代文學論文集》（長沙：湖南文藝出版社，1987 年）。普實克特別重要的論魯迅的文章是 "Lu Hsun's 'Huai Chiu' : A Precursor of Modern Chinese Literature",見 *The Lyrical and the Epic*，pp. 102-109.李歐梵在《我的哈佛歲月》（南京：江蘇教育出版社，2005 ）。多處回憶普實克在哈佛擔任訪問教授時與他的來往。

20 V.I. Semanov, *Lu Hsun and his Predecessors*，tr. Charles Alber（New York: M.E. Sharp1980）;中譯本：　謝曼諾夫，李明濱譯《魯迅和他的前驅》（長沙：湖南文藝出版社，1987）。

有深度的爲魯迅小說解讀，也更準確的給魯迅定位。

四、科際研究的魯迅

前面說過，中國研究是在區域研究（Area Studies）興起的帶動下，從邊緣走向主流。區域研究的興起，是因爲專業領域如社會學、政治學、文學的解釋模式基本上是以西方文明爲典範而發展出來的，對其他文化所碰到的課題涵蓋與詮釋性不夠。對中國文化研究而言，傳統的中國解釋模式因爲只用中國文明爲典範而演繹出來的理論模式，如性別與文學問題，那是以前任何專業都不可能單獨顧及和詮釋。在西方，特別是美國，從中國研究到中國文學，甚至縮小到更專業的領域中國現代文學或世界華文文學，都是在區域研究與專業研究衝激下的學術大思潮下產生的多元取向的學術思考與方法，它幫助學者把課題開拓與深化，創新理論與詮釋模式，溝通世界文化。[21]

這種趨勢一直發展到今天，不少原來非研究中國現代文學的人，進入這一研究區域，主要是受學科與學科間的科際研究（Interdisciplinary Studies）之學術風尚之影響。這些學者將文學與人類生活上如哲學思想、宗教、歷史、政治、文化銜接起來，給我們帶來廣面性的方法，幫助我們從各種角度來認識古今文學，使文學研究不再是片斷和孤立的學問，甚至可以將研究中的真知灼見和結果，文學與非文學的學科互相運用。由李歐梵編，1985 年出版的論文集《魯迅及其遺產》（*The Legacy of Lu Xun*），[22]所收集的文章都很專門，所有十一位作者中，竟有六位原來不是專攻純文學的學者：

---

21 杜維明〈漢學、中國學與儒學〉，見《十年機緣待儒學》（香港：牛津大學出版社，1999 年），頁 1-33；余英時〈費正清的中國研究〉及其他論文，見傅偉勳、歐陽山（編）《西方漢學家論中國》（臺北：正中書局，1993），1-44 及其他相關部分。

22 Leo Lee(ed.), *Lu Xun and His Legacy*(Berkeley: University of California Press, 1985).

1、李歐梵：臺大外文系畢業，先到芝加哥讀國際關係，後來轉哈佛大學專攻中國近代思想史，得碩士及博士學位。

2、林毓生：芝加哥大學歷史系博士。

3、亨特（Theodore Huters）：史丹福大學政治系博士。

4、何大衛（David Holm）：耶魯大學東南亞及蘇聯史博士。

5、戈曼（Merle Goldman）：哈佛大學遠東史博士。

6、愛博（Irene Eber）：克爾蒙學院亞洲研究（思想史）博士。

我在上面說過，李歐梵自己所走的學歷道路，從外文系到國際關係，再從近代思想史到中國現代文學與文化研究，正代表跨越科系的學術發展趨勢。他的著作《浪漫的一代》、《鐵屋子的聲音：魯迅研究》、《中西文學的徊想》、《徘徊在現代和後現代之間》、《現代性的追求》、《上海摩登》是文學、社會、文化和思想史，代表了多元文化跨領域的研究方向。他主編的《魯迅及其遺產》更集合了一批學術背景與他相似的學者而寫的一部多種途徑、多種觀點，探討魯迅的著作。林毓生的論文〈理知的道德與政治的不道德：論知識分子魯迅〉（The Morality of Mind and Immorality of Politics: Reflections on Lu Xun, the Intellectual）[23]，論證魯迅對政治的悲觀絕望，但他始終維持一個知識分子應有的高道義與前衛思想.他參加左翼聯盟是道義行為，當那暗藏的政治黑手暴露後，他拿出勇氣，抗拒政治壟斷。儒家把政治道德化，法家把政治弄成不道德的東西，魯迅雖然徹底反傳統，他接受這種傳統政治觀。他左傾，那是道德的行動，當他的聲望與作品被政治人士利用與操縱，他認為那是不道德的政治。在極端神化魯迅的時代，這種冷靜客觀的分析及其史實的考證，是難能可貴的。

---

23 Leo Lee（ed.）, *Lu Xun and His Legacy* ,pp. 107-128；.後來林毓生自譯（也是改寫），〈魯迅政治觀的困境〉，收入《政治次序與多元文化》（臺北：聯經，1989），頁253-275。

　　由於林毓生對現代中西方意識形態有專門的研究，他研究魯迅的文章，[24]幫忙我們認識到魯迅固然用整體主義的方式來反傳統，把傳統劃為單一體，必須將它打倒，但在許多層面，不得不承認傳統文化的複雜性，因而產生了很大的矛盾。他跟傳統的中國文化精神乃有很強的正面聯係。另一方面，魯迅思想資源很複雜，但他善於使用豐富的思想資源，並沒有被資源勞役。如他的思想有很多存在主義的因素，但不能用存在主義來理解他，更不能從他在意識形態層次上攻擊傳統的做法來理解他。

　　林毓生魯迅學術研究最重要的貢獻，就是認識這種複雜性的存在，探討這個矛盾的意義。在中國大陸的魯迅論述中，以前很多學者，即使現在還是不少沒有看見或故意看不見。所以林毓生說：「他的深刻性在於它體會了整個文化解體後產生的一些基本矛盾，這些矛盾代表了時代精神，而他是這個時代的巨人」[25]

　　超越文本，進入社會及歷史現場，回到文化/文學產生的場域，突破傳統國文學的詮釋典範去解讀魯迅及其文學作品。這種跨學科的研究帶來驚人的透視力，我的範列就是對魯迅棄醫從文的考古新發現。我曾寫過〈回到仙台醫專，重新解剖一個中國醫生的死亡：周樹人變成魯迅，棄醫從文的新見解〉與〈從周樹人仙台學醫經驗解讀魯迅的小說：重新解剖周樹人仙台經驗的小說〉[26]，因此下面僅作簡單的概述。

---

24 包括上註〈魯迅政治觀的困境〉、〈魯迅思想的特質〉，收入《政治次序與多元文化》，頁 235-252、《中國現代意識的危機》、〈五四時代–元式反傳統思想〉《文化超現代》鄭培凱、馬家輝編（香港商務，2000），頁 19-32，以及其他論現代思想史的文章。
25 〈五四時代一元式反傳統思想〉《文化超現代》，頁 25。
26 見王潤華〈回到仙台醫專，重新解剖一個中國醫生的死亡：周樹人變成魯迅，棄醫從文的新見解〉，及〈從周樹人仙台學醫經驗解讀魯迅的小說:重新解剖周樹人仙台經驗的國際會議〉，《越界跨國文學解讀》（臺北：萬卷樓，2004），頁 257-292。

　　1994 年 9 月 6 日至 9 日，日本仙台東北大學的語言與文化學院以小田基與阿部兼也二教授為首，主辦了「魯迅留學仙台 90 周年紀念國際學術與文化研討會」。會場設立在東北大學醫學院（前身即仙台醫專），集合了仙台東北大學教職員與當地文化界，各國文學、社會學、醫學學者重新解剖周樹人仙台經驗，理解他棄醫從文，變成作家魯迅的重要原因，把魯迅棄醫從文背後隱藏著的奧秘揭開。仙台東北大學教職員、當地文化人士與學者，考古似的分析大學附近的環境，強調當時仙台是一個軍國主義思想很強烈的城市，藤野「過於熱心」修改解剖學筆記，引起魯迅的反感與消極的影響。檢查魯迅的成績單，發現分數算錯，匿名信告發考試作弊，純是因為當時大日本主義者不相信中國人的能力的污蔑與猜忌，因為藤野所教的解剖學是七科中唯一不及格的，魯迅只得 59.3 分。仙台的軍國主義社會環境強化他對中國的危機感的認識。不如過去學者，單靠《吶喊》的〈自序〉及〈籐野先生〉幾篇文章的文學印象，把幻燈事件簡化成是唯一的重要原因。

　　其實藤野「過於熱心」修改解剖學筆記，引起魯迅的反感與消極的影響。過去由於魯迅在〈藤野先生〉中，表示對他一年級解剖老師的尊敬，因為在軍國主義與種族歧視的環境中，藤野是唯一例外，自動提出要幫忙魯迅修改解剖學筆記，因為怕他沒能力做筆記，因此遭來同學之猜忌，甚至造謠說藤野在他筆記中做了暗號，故意洩露考題。從這篇文字開始，中日學者便大做文章，把他們二人的關係加以神話化。最後藤野不但是魯迅在醫專的守護神，魯迅現代學術思想之形成之導師，甚至成為中日關係友好的象徵性人物。

　　可是至今沒有人詳細檢查過藤野修改過的魯迅解剖學筆記（魯迅說失落了，後來 1951 年才找到，現存北京魯迅博物館）。現任仙台附近的福井縣立大學看護短期大學泉彪之助醫學教授，在 1993 及 1994 兩次詳閱這本筆記，這次在研究會中把他的調查報告《藤野教授與魯

迅的醫學筆記》發表了。他不但匯報了真實的內容，而且坦白大膽的
發表他的看法。泉彪之助先生說，藤野的修改加筆處，有時幾乎滿滿
一頁，他說：「從藤野的修改加筆之中，或許會產生魯迅的醫學筆記錯
誤很多的感覺。」其實對一個醫科一年級，日語只學了二年的學生來
說，「筆記的內容似乎還是很正確的」，許許多多的地方，都沒有改動
的必要。〈藤野先生〉文中所說：「你將這條血管移了一點位置了」。這
句話，泉先生說是魯迅表示有所不滿而說的。藤野很多批語，泉先生
與他的醫學教授同事討論，都覺得矯枉過正，甚至不正確的。

　　所以泉先生十分驚訝的：「在調查魯迅的筆記以前，我從未認為藤
野嚴九郎用紅筆修改的魯迅的筆記一定會對魯迅產生什麼消極的影
響，然而，看了藤野所修改的魯迅筆記後，我不禁想到修改加筆之處
常常過多，是否偶爾也會引起魯迅的反感呢？」解剖學是醫學的基礎，
也是第一年唯一屬於醫學的科目，魯迅竟不及格（59.3 分），偏偏又
是藤野的課（其實與敷波合教），對魯迅的信心是一大打擊！泉彪之助
責藤野「過於熱心修改」，那是含蓄客氣的話，我總覺得他有大日本主
義的心態，要不然怎麼許多像「這裏的錯誤很多」的批語，泉先生及
其醫生同事都說「不正確」？

　　當時日本人對魯迅的偏見很多。渡邊襄教授小心檢查現存當年周
樹人的成績記錄表，一年級的「學年評點表」中，居然有二個錯誤：
生理學應是 65 分（60＋70÷2＝65），不是 63.3 分。七科成績總平均應
是 65.8 分（458.6÷7＝65.8），不是 65.5 分。另外在「第一年學年試驗
成績表」上倫理學等級為丙，這是錯誤的，應是乙等，因為在「評點
表」上倫理學得 83 分。[27]這麼簡單的數學，怎麼竟犯了三個錯誤？身
為仙台市居民及魯迅仙台留學記錄調查委員會的重要委員渡邊襄不禁

---

27 魯迅在仙台記錄調查委員會編《魯迅在仙台記錄》（東京：平凡社，1978 年）。

感嘆：[28]

　　但我認為，此事至少對魯迅來說是件極為不快的事。儘管在試題洩漏一事上遭到了同學們的偏見和中傷，但及格完全是依靠魯迅自身實力的。少計了考試成績也不給予糾正，魯迅對醫專和教官到底怎麼看的呢？

　　上述的仙台經驗，不但是導致周樹人變成魯迅棄醫從文的原因，而且也構成以後魯迅文學創作中，特別他的小說的重要藝術與思想結構。[29]

五、海外華人研究的魯迅：邊緣還是中心？

　　王賡武是歷史家，尤其海外華人研究。王賡武的〈魯迅、林文慶和儒家思想〉（ "Lu Xun, Lim Boon Keng and Confucianism"）[30]。他有歷史家的冷靜，遠離當時政治意識鬥爭，從海外華人文化來看魯迅與林文慶的衝突，他難於理解兩位具有現代文化與科技背景的人的不和諧。魯迅土生土長，反對傳統，從內追求西方現代性；林文慶在殖民地生長與受教育，企圖以西方科技結合傳統文化，兩人都努力建立現代中國。但兩個背景迴異的人無法對話，因為他們之間因別人的流言而還存在許多障礙：如魯迅誤會林文慶尊孔、瞧不起沒有文化深度而有錢的海外華僑的心態，而林文慶擁有的西方優越感，作為廈門大學校長需要用英語講演，尤其在 1926-1927 年，難於被中國人接受。紹

---

28 渡邊襄的分析意見《魯迅仙台留學九十周年紀念國際學術文化研討會論文集》（仙台：東北大學語言文化學院，1994 年）續集，頁 18。

29 詳見上註及這次會議的論文集《魯迅留學仙台 90 周年紀念國際學術與文化研討會報告論集》（仙台：東北大學語言文化部，1994）。

30 wang Gungwu,"Lu Xun, Lim Boon Keng and Confucianism, "*China and the Chinese Overseas*（Singapore: Times Academic Press,1991）, pp.147-165. 王賡武〈魯迅、林文慶和儒家思想〉,《中國與海外華人》（臺灣：臺灣商務印書館，1994），頁 173-194。

興話與英語的這一場對話註定完全失敗。

　　過去中國國內都過度簡單的詮釋為反傳統的魯迅攻擊林文慶尊孔的事件。史學家以不涉及感情的偏向，凸顯出客觀史學，所以王賡武敢指出，過去中國學者不敢說的事實：魯迅多少具有中國文人瞧不起海外華僑有錢而沒有中國文化的心態：

> 回顧起來，似乎魯迅也沒有脫離開中國文人學士歷來的成見，瞧不起沒有受過文化教育的、通過個人奮鬥而成功的富人，認為它是利用金錢為自己樹碑立傳。對於林文慶這樣的人，生在英國殖民地，受的是西方教育，還在渴望學習中國的東西，要同中國認同，不管是何用意，對此他肯定沒有好感。在魯迅看來，顯然這位中國的「局外人」，對經書不過是一知半解卻在那裏指手劃腳，較重年輕人。[31]

　　我在〈林文慶與魯迅/馬華作家與郁達夫衝突的多元解讀：誰是中心誰是邊緣？〉一文中，也嘗試從新馬華人與中國人，中心與邊緣的角度來思考魯迅與東南亞的華人文化對話。[32]在 1926 年，尋求西方科技與華族文化結合的新馬華人林文慶與追求現代性、反舊傳統的中國作家魯迅在中國的土地上發生衝突。原因是林文慶擔任廈門大學校長時，聘請魯迅擔任國學研究所的教授，魯迅有所不滿，只做了四個月零十二天就辭職了。多數學者過於簡單的解讀為，那是魯迅反林文慶尊孔的事件，代表新與舊，傳統與現代的衝突。[33]

---

31 同上，頁 187。

32 〈林文慶與魯迅/馬華作家與郁達夫衝突的多元解讀：誰是中心誰是邊緣？〉中國文學與馬華文學：中心與邊緣的對話國際研討會論文，2003 年 10 月，吉隆坡新紀元學院。

33 關於中國早期的論述見薛綏之（編）《魯迅生平史料彙編》第四輯（天津：天津人民出版社，1983），尤其俞荻、俞念遠、陳夢韶、川島的文章。我曾指導一篇碩士論文，把這場"爭論"從所有發表過的文章中，給予分析，見莫顯英《重新解讀魯迅與林文慶在廈大的衝突》（新加坡：新加坡國立大學中文系，2001。關於事件有

　　以前我們稱他們之間發生爲「衝突」,「對」與「不對」來解讀,那是單元的思考,那是中國從文化思考中心或本土中心單元的解釋模式的話語。在今天多元文化,多元思考的後現代後結構時代,我們應該把衝突解構,改稱爲「對話」,也需要重新思考與解讀。從這二宗中國與馬華文化/文學的爭論中,可釋放出許多有關中國與馬華文化/文學有關中心與邊緣的新意義。

　　中國人與海外華人,誰是中國文化中心誰是邊緣?林文慶與魯迅這兩位醫生分別處於半殖民地的中國與英殖民地的馬來亞權政中心之外的邊緣地帶的知識份子,同是被權力與中心文化霸權放逐的人,他們都是邊緣人。對林文慶來說,他前往中國廈門出任夏大校長時,更是在邊緣之邊緣。魯迅被自我放逐到中國政治文化的邊陲地帶廈門,具有文人古代被貶放南方的落魄情懷。同是身爲邊緣思考的人,他們又怎麼會衝突呢?另外因爲林文慶自小接受英國教育,深受維多利亞時代英國文化的氣魄與眼光所影響,有膽識、有領導改革的才華,年輕時就被英國接受,肯定爲優秀的英國海外子民。對民族主義思想日愈強大、本土化的中國人來說,林文慶的背景甚至被誤看成是殖民者的代言人。魯迅土生土長,追求現代性,以五四反傳統的革命精神出發,追求現代性,他的革命容納不了傳統。遇見「尊孔」、講英文的殖民主義的強人、上流社會的校長,自己更感邊緣化,更把對方看成中心。因此「尊孔」,假想的敵人(舊社會,加上殖民主義代言人)妨礙了對話。他們的不和,主要是當時單元的政治文化論述所造成。學者總是把他們看作現代與傳統,中心與邊緣對立的衝突。[34]

　　很多人不知道郁達夫與魯迅在南洋發生過衝突。郁達夫於 1938

　　關的資料,可見 該論文完整的參考書目。

34 莫顯英對兩種不同的看法都有分析,見《重新解讀魯迅與林文慶在夏大的衝突》(本人指導的碩士論文,新加坡國立大學中文系,2002),pp. 11-68.

年 12 月 28 日抵達新加坡，受《星洲日報》之聘，擔任副刊編輯。1939
年一月 21 日，他在《星洲日報》與檳城的《星檳日報》同時發表〈幾
個問題〉的文章。這是他在檳成與文藝青年對話後的所想到的問題。
這篇文章引起最大的爭議，是郁達夫批評南洋文藝界盲目跟隨中國文
壇，他要求南洋作家去中國化，他更要求去魯迅化。[35]

　　自我放逐南洋後，郁達夫擁抱新馬華人邊緣文化，在 1939 與擁抱
中國文學傳統的新馬中國僑居作家與本土華文作家發生衝突，甚至反
對魯迅所代表的中國現代文學的戰鬥傳統。[36]這一場被稱爲郁達夫與
魯迅在南洋的衝突，説明走出中國的文化中心，郁達夫具有雙重視野
（double vision）他代表本土化情緒高漲的，魯迅的影響力變成殖民文
化。

　　從這二宗中國與馬華文化/文學的爭論中，可釋放出許多有關中國
與馬華文化/文學有關中心與邊緣的新意義。

六、新馬華文文學中的魯迅：文學殖民主義

　　我研究的東南亞華文文學，也提供有用的參考架構。從這個角度，
我又看見其他視野無法看見的魯迅的文學從影響走向政治行動殖民意
義。魯迅如何走進新馬後殖民文學中，及其接受與影響，然後再產生
的文學殖民意義，是一個錯綜複雜的問題。1999 年我第一次在東京大
學提出，來自中國大陸的學者，表示似乎很難接受。[37]其實即使今天

---

35 方修（編）《馬華新文學大系》（新加坡：星洲世界書局，1971），理論批評第二集，
　　pp. 444-448。
36 鬱達夫與當時作者討論的論文收集于方修編《馬華新文學大系》，理論批評第二集，
　　（新加坡：星洲世界書局，1971）。楊松年〈從鬱達夫〈幾個問題〉引起的論爭看
　　南洋知識分子的心態〉《亞洲文化》23 起（1999 年 6 月），pp.103-111; 鄒慧珊、李
　　秀萍、黃文青〈魯迅與鬱達夫在新馬的論爭－華文後殖民文學情境的解讀〉，2002
　　在王潤華《中國現代文學專題》（新加坡國立大學中文系）的報告。共 13 頁。
37 從反殖民到殖民者：魯迅與新馬後殖民文學 東亞魯迅學術會議，1999 年 12 月

在新馬的作家，也有不肯接受的。

魯迅以其經典作品引起新馬華人的注意後，接著又被移居新馬的左翼文化人用來宣揚與推展左派文學思潮。除了左派文人，共產黨、抗日救國的愛國華僑都盡了最大的努力去塑造魯迅的神話。有的爲了左派思想，有的爲了抗日，有的爲了愛中國。魯迅最後竟變成代表中國文化或中國，沒有人可以拒絕魯迅，因爲魯迅代表了中國在新馬的勢力。1939 年郁達夫在新馬的時候，已完全看見魯迅將變成神，新馬人人膜拜的神。從文學觀點看，他擔心「個個是魯迅」，人人「死抱了魯迅不放」。他說這話主要是「對死抱了魯迅不放，只在抄襲他的作風的一般人說的話」。可是郁達夫這幾句話，引起左派文人的全面圍攻，郁達夫甚至以《晨星》主編特權，停止爭論文章發表。攻擊他的人如耶魯（黃望青，曾駐日本大使）、張楚琨在當年不只左傾，也是共黨的發言人。反對魯迅就等於反對「戰鬥」，反對抗戰，反對反殖民主義，最後等於反對中國文化。[38]高揚就激昂的說死抱住魯迅、抄襲他的作風都無所謂，「因爲最低限度，學習一個戰士，在目前對於抗戰是有益」。[39]

魯迅在新馬 1930 年以後的聲望，主要不是依靠對他的文學的閱讀所產生的文學影響，而是歸功於移居新馬的受左派影響的中國作家與文化人所替他做的非文學性宣傳公在這些南下的中國作家中，尤其一些左派文藝青年如張天白（丘康），往往成爲把魯迅神話移植新馬的大功臣。[40]他甚至高喊「魯迅先生是中國文壇文學之父」的口號。[41]這些

14-16，東京大學山上會館。此論文現收集在王潤華《越界跨國文學解讀》，頁 201-232。

38 這些文章收集於《馬華新文學大系》第 2 集，頁 444-471。

39 同上，頁 461。

40 章翰（韓山元）的論文〈張天白論魯迅〉認爲張天白（常用馬達、丘康、太陽等筆名）在三十年代，爲文崇揚魯迅最多，見章翰《魯迅與馬華新文學》，頁 50-56。

來自中國的作家及文化人宣揚魯迅的文章，有些收錄在《馬華新文學大系》的第一、二（理論批評）及十集（出版史料）。[42]

魯迅被政治化最好的例子，就是各種非文學的社團，尤其教育程度很低的勞工團體，為了團結以來反殖民主義，經常辦群眾大會時，以魯迅為號召。如 1932 年 10 月 19 日舉行的魯迅逝世一周年紀念，居然有二十五個團體參加。章翰在〈魯迅逝世在馬華文藝界的反應〉及〈馬華文化界兩次盛大的魯迅紀念活動〉二文中詳細分析了這些追悼魯迅逝世的文章。[43]當時新馬文化人對魯迅的推崇，特別強調魯迅的戰鬥精神，民族英雄形象，年青人的導師、抗日救亡的英雄。從下面常出現的頌詞，可瞭解當時左派文化人所要塑造的魯迅英雄形象及其目的，這些都是非文學的：

> 一員英勇的戰士，一位優良的導師。（劉郎）這位為著祖國爭取自由，為著世界爭取和平的巨人，……他曾衝破四周的黑暗勢力；他為中國文化開闢了光明的道路；他領導了現階段的抗日救亡的文化陣線……在抗敵救亡的文化陣線裡指揮作戰……。（曙明）魯迅先生是一個偉大的戰士……。（陳培青）偉大的人群的導師。（辛辛）新時代戰士的奮鬥精神……肩擔著人生正確的任務。── 以魯迅先生為榜樣。（紫鳳）魯迅先生可以說是真正的民族文藝家，普羅文藝英雄了。（二克）魯迅不但是中國新文學之父，而且是一個使我們可敬畏的「嚴父」。

張天白論魯迅的文章，分別收集在方修主編《張天白作品選》（新加坡：上海書局，1979 年），有二篇附錄在《魯迅與馬華新文學》，4-5；張天白其他文章可見《新馬新文學大系》，第一及二集。

41 丘康《七七抗戰後的馬華文壇》，《魯迅與馬華新文學》頁 11；又見《馬華新文學大系》，第 1 集，頁 505。

42 陵〈文藝的方向〉，《星洲日報·野苑》（副刊），1930 年 3 月 19 日，又見方修編《馬華新文學大系》（新加坡：世界書局，1971-1972 年），第 1 冊，頁 69-70。

43 章翰（韓山元）《魯迅與馬華新文學》，頁 11-35；頁 44-49。

（陳祖山）我們要紀念我們英勇的導師。（俠魂）

從戰士、巨人、導師、嚴父，甚至「新文學之父」，都是政治化以後盲目的吹捧，其目的不外是製造一個萬人崇拜的神像。

共產黨在新馬殖民社會裏，爲了塑造一個代表左翼人士的崇拜偶像，他們採用中國的模式，拿出一個文學家來作爲膜拜的對象。這樣這個英雄才能被英國殖民主義政府接受。所以魯迅是一個很理想的偶像，他變成一把旗幟、一個徽章、一個神話、一種宗教儀式，成爲左派或共產黨的宣傳工具。

魯迅在 1936 逝世時，正是馬來亞共產黨開始顯示與擴大其群眾力量的時候，而新馬年青人，多數只有小學或初中教育程度，所以魯迅神話便在少數南來中國文化人的移植下，流傳在新馬華人心中。

所以反殖民主義的魯迅，到了新馬文學/文化界，他變成殖民文化，被人利用以達到各種政治的目的。

七、結論：從漢學到文化研究典範下的魯迅

本文只討論了幾個例子，其他可見於收集在樂黛雲編的《國外魯迅研究論集》[44]與 Irene Eber 編 的〈西方語言魯迅論著選書目〉的研究中[45]，都是在西方漢學與中國學思考典範下的產品。

除了歐美、其實像日本的中國現代文學研究，至今還是以研究魯迅爲重鎮，全國性重要的學者，成就要被承認，學術地位的建立，必先在魯迅研究上有突出的表現。[46]從竹內好、竹內實、丸山昇、到現

---

44 樂黛雲編《國外魯迅研究論集》（北京：北京大學出版社，1981）。

45 Irene Eber, " A Selective Bibliography of Works by and about Lu Xun in Western Languages", *Lu Xun and His Legacy* ,Leo Lee （ed.）, pp.242-274.

46 從一般的現代文學研究書目就可表現出來，如孫立川、王順洪編《日本研究中國現當代文學論著索引 1919-1989》（北京：北京大學出版社，1991）；日本目前的魯迅學者以魯迅論集編集委員會所編的論文作者爲中心，見《魯迅與同時代人》與《魯

在籐井還是繼續維持這個傳統。日本的魯迅研究在「鏡子理論」強調研究與現實有相關，思想性與實用性，絕對不可忽視[47]。像竹內好，就如代田智明指出，他早在 1944 的《魯迅》及 1953 年的《魯迅入門》就已在魯迅作品與思想中看見濃厚的黑暗，通過這黑暗意識的分析和思考，他繪出了一幅他自己的魯迅像，很親近他的學生代田智明指出：

> 他認爲這黑暗面就是解釋魯迅文學的關鍵，也推測這黑暗的根本在於魯迅對一些人生上的失敗或貽誤的悔恨。竹內描寫的魯迅無疑是遠遠的離開英雄的所謂「啓蒙主義者」或「戰士」。但理所當然魯迅的屈折或罪意識不會個人的，而都是和中國傳統社會有關的，竹內也知道這一點，就是說，竹內提出的魯迅像是內心緊緊被傳統社會束縛，有罪自我……他認爲自己是舊的人，自己背上的「過去」太多，捨不得這些東西使他備受折磨……[48]

這個論點，過了很久，後來在美國夏濟安的〈黑暗的閘門〉[49]、李文蓀、林毓生的魯迅傳統與反傳統思想緊張論述中再度獲得呼應與發展。

近十多年年來，文化研究（cultural studies）成爲主流[50]，這個思

迅研究之現在》（東京：東京汲古書院，2002）。

47 參考王潤華〈中國現代文學研究在日本〉，《越界跨國文學解讀》，頁 233-256。

48 代田智明發表兩篇論文〈竹內好與他的魯迅〉及〈論竹內好：關於他的思想、方法、態度〉，這是東京大學 1999 年 12 月 14-16 日舉辦《東亞魯迅學術會議：戰後日本的魯迅經驗》的論文。前者共 6 頁；後者已發表在《世界漢學》，第一期（1998），127-136。

49 Hsia Tsi-an, "Aspects of the Power of Darkness in Lu Hsun", *The Gate of Darkness: The Studies on the Leftist Literary Movement in China* (Seattle: University of Washington Press, 1968) ,pp.146-162. 中文翻譯見樂黛雲（譯）,〈魯迅作品的黑暗面〉，樂黛雲編《國外魯迅研究論集》（北京：北京大學出版社，1981）頁 366-382。

50 有關文化研究的發展趨向，參考李歐梵〈文化史跟「文化研究」〉，《徘徊在現代和後現代之間》，頁 182-186；及王德威《小說中國》（臺北：麥田出版社，1993 年）

考典範下的產品也有很多突破性的研究。例如具有爭論性的劉禾論魯迅阿 Q 小說人物所象徵的國民性性格的書寫，受了殖民話語的影響論。簡單的說，劉禾在〈國民性理論質疑〉[51]中指出，魯迅是根據根亞瑟‧史密斯的著作的日譯本，將傳教士的中國國民性理論，翻譯到阿 Q 小說人物中。所以《阿 Q 正傳》的生成經過是：亞瑟‧史密斯的《中國人的氣質》；其人物原型是源于波蘭顯克微支的小說《勝利者巴泰克》的主人公；澀江保的日譯本《支那人之氣質》。這樣便對中國人展現了一個殘酷的事實：原來被文學史捧為經典之作，也不過是被西方殖民者東方主義化後產生的醜陋中國人之後的產物。雖然這是文化考古出土的事實證據，許多中國大陸的學者作家讀者，仍然難於接受。事實上，魯迅許多小說人物的產生，包括〈狂人日記〉的狂人，都有西方文學中的人物與思想的影響。[52]

在西方漢學與中國學，或近期的文化研究（cultural studies）的方法典範下的魯迅研究，開拓了許多創新的視野與方法，建構了很多理論。最特別的地方，是比較文學、文學分析、訓詁考據學、歷史語言學、再加上社會科學（政治學、史學、思想史等）的方法，跨越區域與學科疆界的文化視野，因此開創魯迅研究新方向與方法，帶來全新的詮釋與世界性的意義。這種魯迅學術思考與分析，完全著眼於客觀事實，很少涉及道德的判斷或民族的感情偏向，或政治意識的論調，維持客觀的、科學化的史學的思考。很多複雜的問題，在他們的眼前，只是一個客觀體，這是奉科學為典範下的人文研究。

一書中「批評的新視野」一輯中的三篇論文，尤其〈想像中國的方法〉及〈現代中國小說研究在西方〉，頁 345-407。

51 原是英文專書 Lydia Liu , *Translingual Practice*（Stanford: Stanford University Press,1998）的第二章，中文翻譯有宋偉傑等譯《跨語際實踐：文學、民族文化與被譯介的現代性》（北京：三聯，2002），頁 75-108。

52 王潤華《魯迅小說新論》（臺北：東大圖書，1992），頁 89-112。

　　這些魯迅學者就像魯迅自己，善於利用豐富的思想資源，但沒有被思想資源勞役。就因爲擁有與使用豐富又深刻的參考架構，他們對魯迅及其作品具有集體感應及特殊感，如林毓生對現代意識形態有專門的研究，精通 Edward Shils 的《論意識形態》、熟讀 Michael Polanyi 的知識論，研究過中國意識的危機，才能深入的寫出〈魯迅思想的特質〉、〈魯迅政治觀的困境〉等文章[53]。也因爲有了魯迅傳統與反傳統的精神緊張論、普實克的懷舊與抒情性古典文學主體論、竹內好與夏濟安等人對魯迅思想與作品的黑暗面的考釋，有了理論性的架構，對純文學研究的人做文本分析時，就有解剖刀，更有透視力，找出隱藏與象徵的意義。

　　上述的每一項的魯迅研究，都是一個個超文本（hypertext），互相連接，譬如竹內好與夏濟安等人的黑暗面論點，與傳統與精神緊張論，同時也跟東歐學者如普實克的懷舊與抒情性古典文學主體論，謝曼諾夫的魯迅以舊譴責小説爲典範的論述互相關聯。同時強調純文學的文本分析的魯迅研究，基本上也與那些思想性的研究緊緊聯係在一起。有了魯迅反傳統與傳統的複雜思想情懷理論，基於魯迅的懷舊與抒情說，周昌龍才能在〈酒樓上〉裏找到深層的内涵：跑遍天下的「我」，重返家鄉的小酒樓，被深冬廢園中雪裏的梅花與火紅的茶花的風景迷住：超越了對實際景觀的描述，變成作者懷舊情懷的抒發，象徵的話語説明了魯迅對傳統本土文化的再興與期待。[54]

---

53 關於林毓生的學問，參考丘慧芬編《自由主義與人文傳統》：林毓生先生七秩壽慶論文集》（臺北：允晨，2005），尤其丘慧芬〈前言〉。
54 周昌龍〈魯迅的傳統與反傳統思想〉《新思潮與傳統》，頁 125-137。

以魯迅爲典範：
日本中國現代文學研究

一、沿著日本中國現代文學研究發展的路線走一趟

日本在中國現代文學研究方面的學術地位，近幾十年來，愈來愈受到世界各國學者的重視。即使在中國大陸，日本學者在這方面的成就，也受到特別的承認。譬如北京大學出版的《國外魯迅研究論集，1960-1981》，選擇的論文中，日本學者的論文占了五篇，美國學者四篇，海外華籍學人三篇，選自捷克的有兩篇，其他國家如蘇聯、荷蘭、澳洲、加拿大各有一篇。書中附錄了近二十年歐、美、亞、澳各大洲的〈近二十年國外魯迅研究論著要目〉，用日文寫的專書或論文共二百種，英文的三十七種，俄文的四十八種。[1]這份目錄可說明日本研究中國現代文學在世界學術界之重要。實際上歐美各國大學的學者很早就重視日本人的中國現代文學研究之學術地位，因此攻讀高級學位的學生，如果研究中國現代文學，一般上都要修讀兩年的日文。歐美學者認爲，研究中國現代文學，而不參考日本有關方面的研究成果，那是不完整的研究。

因此親自到日本了解日本學者研究中國現代文學的情形，一直是我的一大心願。今年（1985）5 月 31 日至 6 月 28 日間，在日本學術

---

1 樂黛雲編《國外魯迅研究論集，1960-1981》（北京：北京大學出版社，1981 年）。

振興會的贊助下，我如願以償的前往日本各大學作交流訪問。我的訪
問目的，主要是要了解日本各大學對中國現代文學在教學與研究上的
情形。在出發前，我曾寫信給東京大學東洋文化研究所所長尾上兼英
教授，向他請教我應該訪問什麼大學，應該跟哪些日本研究中國現代
文學的專家交流。他馬上回信表示衷心歡迎我訪問該所，並稱在東京
研究中國現代文學的學者很多，還開列了以下一張名單：

東京大學：丸山升教授、伊藤敬一教授

東京都立大學：松井博光教授、飯倉照平教授

東京女子大學：伊藤虎丸教授

早稻田大學：杉本達夫教授

京都大學：竹內實教授

大阪外國語大學：相浦杲教授

神戶大學：山田敬三副教授

關西大學：北岡正子教授

大阪市立大學：片山智行教授

九州大學：秋吉久紀夫教授　等等[2]

尾上兼英是東京地區日本研究中國現代文學的重要領袖之一，他
開給我的名單無意中說明一個事實：日本中國現代文學研究已不局限
於東京大學，它已被許多著名的學者傳播到東京各大學及其他地區。
譬如，竹內好（1908-1977）先後在慶應大學及東京都立大學任教，小
野忍（1906-1983）在東大退休後，1967 年轉任和光大學，竹內實於
1968 年離開東京大學後，曾在東京都立大學任教，一直到 1973 年才

---

2 見尾上兼英致本人 1985 年 4 月 23 日信。尾上兼英教授，現任東京大學東洋文化研
　究所所長，爲魯迅、中國三十年代左翼文學及說唱文學專家，主要著作有《幽明錄‧
　游仙窟》及《三十年代中國文藝雜誌》。有關本文內談到之日本學者之生平著作，
　可參考嚴紹璗《日本的中國學家》（北京：中國社會科學出版社，1980 年）。

轉入京都大學。松枝茂夫曾在東京都立大學、北九州大學、早稻田大學任教。武田泰淳（1912-1976）把中國現代文學研究風氣帶到北海道大學，因此北海道現在搞中國現代文學的人實在不少。[3] 增田涉（1903-1977）先後到過大阪市立大學、關西大學及京都大學（兼職）傳播中國現代文學的種子，這跟目前關西地區大學成為東京以外，第二個最重要的中國現代文學研究中心不無關係。

　　所以今天要了解日本的中國現代文學研究，必須沿著研究發展的路線走一趟，才比較容易明白。因此我決定先到東京，而且又以東京大學為中心，然後去橫濱市立大學及北海道大學，接著到關西地區如京都大學、大阪外語大學，再去北九州大學，最後再回到東京。

二、東京地區中國現代文學研究

　　我到東京之後，先拜見了尾上兼英及丸山升教授[4]，他們不但是東京大學最有成就之中國現代文學專家，而且也是東京地區最有影響力的領導人。尾上兼英教授為了讓我更快的掌握日本的中國現代文學的實際情況，他於 1985 年 6 月 13 日假東洋文化研究所舉行一場座談會。

　　下面是當天應邀出席的學者名單：[5]

1、尾上兼英（1927）東京大學

2、伊藤敬一（1927）東京大學

3　北海道大學雖然遠離東京，而在以農業為主的札幌，文學部教員有副教授丸尾常喜（近年現代文學、魯迅），副教授須藤洋一（葉聖陶、魯迅等）；在言語文化部有藤本幸三（許地山、茅盾）、野澤俊敬副教授（瞿秋白、丁玲等）、中野美代子教授（老舍、茅盾等）。

4　丸山升教授和尾上兼英是以前魯迅研究會及現在的三十年代中國文學研究會的重要領導人。丸山升教授被中國肯定為第二代學者中研究魯迅成就最大者，重要著作有《魯迅與革命文學》（東京：紀伊國屋書店，1972 年）及《魯迅：他的文學與革命》（東京：平凡社，1965 年）。

5　上兼英教授說，依日本人之習慣，女性姓名後下列出生年份，杉本達夫教授因事前未肯定出席，故原來沒列入名單中。尾上教授說照順序，應列入第 12 號。

3、伊藤虎丸（1927）東京女子大學

4、蘆田孝昭（1928）早稻田大學

5、立間祥介（1928）慶應大學

6、松井博光（1930）東京都立大學

7、丸山升（1931）東京大學

8、井口晃（1934）中央大學

9、飯倉昭平（1934）東京都立大學

10、木山英雄（1934）一橋大學

11、釜屋修（1936）和光大學

12、前田利昭（1941）中央大學

13、小島久代（　　）學習院大學

14、蘆田肇（1942）國學院大學

15、佐治俊彦（1945）和光大學

16、近藤龍哉（1946）埼玉大學

17、尾崎文昭（1947）明治大學

18、江上幸子（　　）東京大學

19、白水紀子（　　）和光大學

20、代田智明（1952）茨城大學

21、下山鐵男（1952）和光大學

22、加藤三由紀（　　）御茶水女子大學

23、平石淑子（　　）

24、刈間文俊（1952）駒澤大學

25、溝口雄三（1933）東京大學

26、小鹽惠美子（　　）御茶水女子大學

27、佐藤普美子（　　）大東文化大學

28、杉本達夫（1937）早稻田大學

　　可惜那天東京下著狂風暴雨，許多位先生都未能出席，要不然真是集東京地區研究中國現代文學之菁英於一堂，而且是兩代同堂，因爲日本東京地區代表第二及第三代的研究中國現代文學者大都在此了。

　　中國現代文學作品，自從在二十年代末期傳入日本，就廣爲讀者所愛閱讀和研究。像日本中國學專家青木正兒，早在 1920 年出版的《支那學》第三期，就發表過〈以胡適爲中心的洶湧澎湃的文學革命〉的文章，他已預言「魯迅是有著遠大前程的作家」。[6]到了二十年代末期，魯迅作品開始被譯成日文，到了三十年代及四十年代出現了所謂日本中國現代文學研究第一代的許多學者。像青木正兒、正宗白鳥、長與善郎、佐藤春夫、竹內好、山上正義、尾崎秀實、鹿地　、中野重治、增田涉、小田嶽夫、井上紅梅、松枝茂夫、武田泰淳、倉石武四郎、小野忍、波多野太郎、太田辰夫、小川環樹等等，在翻譯與研究上都很有貢獻。在現代作家中，以有關魯迅、老舍、茅盾的翻譯與研究爲數最多，同時也最有系統和深度。[7]

　　早在 1934 年，東京大學的學生組織了日本第一個專門研究中國現代文學研究會。1935 年該會創辦《中國文學月刊》（後改名《中國文學》）。這個研究會的重要成員如竹內好、岡崎俊夫、武田泰淳、松枝茂夫、增田涉及小野忍等都成爲日本第一代研究中國現代文學學者中，最有成就和影響力。而其中又以竹內好的成就與影響力最高。他

---

6 青木正兒〈以胡適爲中心的洶湧澎湃的文學革命〉，見《支那學》1920 年第 3 期；劉柏青〈戰後日本本魯迅研究在國外專輯〉，見《魯迅研究》1984 年第 6 期，頁 58-60。
7 關於魯迅研究在日本的成就，參考劉獻彪、林治廣編《魯迅與中日文化交流》（長沙：湖南人民出版社，1981 年），頁 40-73，頁 341-357，以及劉柏青〈戰後日本魯迅研究概觀〉（見註 6）；關於茅盾研究，見古谷久美編〈日本所出版茅盾研究參考資料目錄〉，《咿啞》第 18、19 號合刊（大阪，1984 年），頁 94-106；關於老舍的研究，見日下恒夫、倉橋幸彥編《日本出版老舍研究文獻目錄》（京都：朋友書店，1984 年）。

所研究魯迅及其他有關問題的專書，在那時代，不但最有深度，而且最有系統。可說已達到了研究中國現代文學的最高水平。[8]竹內好研究中國現代文學作品，尤其是魯迅的作品，除了學術意義本身，他特別強調以魯迅或其他中國作家的作品作爲鏡子，批判日本現代化的道路。研究中國文學作品，可以認識中國，認識中國從鴉片戰爭以來所走過的現代化的道路，進而引起日本人自我反省，發現日本的問題，批判日本現實社會中的種種問題。由於竹內好等人發現魯迅是一位偉大的啓蒙者，主張通過拒斥、抵抗、保留方式，獨立自主的精神向西方學習，而日本人一般缺少獨立自主的精神，把西方的一切都當成權威，奴隸主義地吸收進來，結果實現了一個假的現代化。竹內好這種研究中國現代作家與作品的精神與主張，一直深深影響到今天日本第二代，甚至第三代的中國現代文學學者。明白這點，才能了解爲什麼過去日本學者主要都集中在研究魯迅及其他少數作家的作品。[9]

　　日本研究中國現代文學的第二代學者是在五十及六十年代間崛起的，當時東京大學、東京都立大學、關西地區如京都大學都出現了不少研究中國現代文學的學生。1953 年東京大學學習的學生組織了一個魯迅研究會，同時出版了雜誌《魯迅研究》，東京都立大學的學生，出版了《北斗》雜誌，發表研究中國現代文學的成果。這一批青年研究者同時出現有關東與關西的有竹內實、今村與志雄、尾上兼英、高田淳、新島淳良、丸山升、津田孝、木山英雄、松本昭、佐藤保、竹田晃、青山宏、檜山久雄、伊藤虎丸、松井博光、飯倉照平、尾崎秀樹、

8 竹內好重要著作有《魯迅》（東京：日本評論社，1944 年）；《魯迅》（東京：世界評論社，1948 年，1953 年全書加以補充刪改，改名《魯迅入門》）；《魯迅雜記》（東京：世界評論社，1949 年）。目前東京筑摩書房已出版《竹內好全集》，最後的第十七集已在 1982 年出版。有關他的生平著作，見嚴紹璗《日本的中國學家》，頁636-637。
9 參考劉柏青〈戰後日本魯迅研究概觀〉，見《魯迅研究》1984 年第 6 期，頁 64-44。

吉田富夫、伊藤正文、相浦杲、中川俊、山田敬三、北岡正子、杉本達夫、稻葉昭二、伊藤敬一等等。現在這些第二代的學者年紀都在五十左右，都站在中國文學研究的第一線上（第一代的學者像武田泰淳、竹內好、增田涉、小野忍在七十年代末期相繼逝世了）。

在上述座談會的出席名單中，第一位至第十一位，加上第廿八位，共十二位，如果再加上尾上兼英教授提議我去訪問東京以外的中野美代子、丸尾常喜、竹內實、相浦杲、山田敬三、北岡正子、片山智行及秋吉久紀夫，則形成了研究中國現代文學第二代相當完整的代表陣容。名單中第十二位至廿七位是研究中國現代文學的第三代學者，他們的年齡大都在三十至四十多之間，正是年輕一代的代表。這一代所研究的範圍很廣闊，課題也多樣化，譬如小島久代研究沈從文；蘆田肇研究中日文學關係；佐治俊彥研究 1920 到 1930 年代左翼文學；近藤龍哉搞三十年代的文學，特別是胡風；尾崎文昭研究周作人；江上幸子研究丁玲；下出鐵男研究蕭軍；佐藤普美子研究二十年代的新詩；刈間文俊研究當代文學與電影。

在東京地區研究中國現代文學第二代的學者中，雖然他們多數都在魯迅研究中表現出很優秀的成績，繼承第一代的研究傳統，像丸山升的《魯迅——他的文學與革命》與《魯迅與革命文學》被認為是竹內好以後最重要的成就，受到日本國內外之重視，其他像尾上兼英、伊藤虎丸、飯倉照平、木山英雄等人對魯迅研究都有很高的成就，但像伊藤敬一研究老舍，伊藤虎丸研究郁達夫，松井博光研究茅盾，蘆田孝昭研究巴金、老舍，飯倉照平研究周作人，釜屋修研究趙樹理，他們興趣的課題已增加了，已經把研究領域拓展開了。[10]

---

10 稍微翻閱一下《中國關係論說資料索引》（第 1 號至 20 號，1964-1978 年）.（東京：論說資料保存會，1982 年）中有關中國現代文藝論文目錄，頁 217-224，更可明白這種發展趨勢。

近年來東京地區研究中國現代文學的最大推動力，以丸山升、伊藤虎丸、木山英雄、尾上兼英等所組成的中國三十年代文學研究會（1969 年成立）最有表現。他們研究的成績，最具體的表現在《東洋文化》的三期特輯上。[11]目前東洋文化研究所又有由尾上兼英教授擔任主任的 1930 年代左翼文藝運動研究班。東京地區有其他不少推動研究中國現代文學的組織社團，像新青年讀書會，經常舉辦座談會，並出版《貓頭鷹》，主要發表研究中國現代文學思潮與文學論文。[12]又有邊鼓社，目前以編集出版日本研究中國現代文學文獻目錄為主要任務，至今已出現了《現代・當代中國文學研究文獻目錄》一、二集及《夏衍與丁玲》。[13]此外還有魯迅之會，並出版《魯迅之會會報》[14]，1984 年 3 月老舍研究會在柴垣芳太郎、伊藤敬一等人發起之下成立了。

三、關西地區：日本研究中國現代文學之第二重鎮

離開東京後，我便沿著尾上兼英教授在信中所列的大學路線繼續前進。先去拜訪了橫濱市立大學的鈴木正夫及北海道大學的丸尾常喜[15]，他們兩位與東京派的中國現代文學學者關係密切，可是兩人都出

---

11 這些論文特輯分別刊於下列三期：第一輯，《東洋文化》，1972 年第 52 期，作者有：小野忍、佐治俊彥、蘆田肇、丸山升、木村靜江、前田利昭、城谷武男及北岡正子；第二輯，《東洋文化》，1976 年第 56 期，作者有丸山升、前田利昭、丸尾常喜、佐治俊彥、三寶政美及北岡正子；第三輯，《東洋文化》第 65 期（1985 年 3 月），作者有：尾上兼英、陳正醍、佐治俊彥、小谷一郎、尾崎文昭、伊藤虎丸、宮島敦子、小島久代、下出鐵男及新村徹。

12 譬如《貓頭鷹》1984 第 3 期為巴金研究特輯。

13 這兩本目錄收錄單篇論文與專著，第一集包括 1977-1980 年出版者，第二集 1981-1982 年，如果能繼續出版，將是最完整的有關日本中國現代文學研究之目錄。《夏衍與丁玲》出版於 1982 年，收有阿部幸夫與高 B 穰的論文。

14 我見到最新一期為《魯迅之會會報》，1984 年第 8 期。

15 鈴木正夫與伊藤虎丸及稻葉昭二編《郁達夫資料》（東京大學東洋文化研究所，1969 年），補篇上及下先後在 1973 及 1974 年出版。丸尾常喜東大中文系畢業，大阪市立大學碩士，著有《魯迅》（東京：集英社，1985 年），為《魯迅全集》第二卷《彷

身自關西地區的大阪市立大學。北海道以前有武田泰淳在開墾中國現代文學研究，後來像尾上兼英也曾在那裏任教，因此丸尾常喜也是東京的三十年代文學研究重要的一份子。北海道大學校園曾經出版過一份專門發表研究中國現代文學論文的雜誌──《熱風》。

到了京都大學，該校中文系主任清水茂教授安排我拜訪京都大學人文科學研究所的竹內實教授。他是第二代日本研究中國現代文學專家中年紀稍大的長輩，他的專著如《現代中國的文學》、《魯迅的遠景》和《魯迅周邊》，都是日本國內外深受重視及推崇的研究成果。[16]目前他集合了日本各地的重要學人重新譯注並出版《魯迅全集》，同時又編寫一部自 1840 年至今日的《中國現代文學年表》，這兩項巨大的研究計劃，將在兩年內完成。竹內實在日本研究中國現代文學圈中是一位舉足輕重的重要人物，他在 1949 年畢業於京都大學，曾任中國研究所研究員、東京都立大學教授，1973 年起擔任京都大學人文科學研究所教授，對關西地區急速發展為另一個中國現代文學研究中心，頗具極大的影響作用。

清水茂教授另外再安排我拜訪大阪外語大學。在那裏我會見了相浦杲、中川俊教授和是永駿副教授。相浦杲教授是日本研究中國現代文學第二代學者，他在關西地區具有很大領導力，他著有《現代的中國文學》，曾翻譯王蒙的《蝴蝶》[17]，還有許多研究茅盾、三十年代和當代文學的論文。中川俊所研究的中國作家是丁玲、趙樹理和蕭紅等

徨》之翻譯者。

16 《現代中國的文學》（東京：研究社，1972 年）、《魯迅遠景》（東京：田畑書店，1978 年）、《魯迅周邊》（東京：田畑書店，1981 年）。關於竹內實較詳細生平及著作，見嚴紹璗《日本的中國學家》，頁 640-641。

17 《現代的中國文學》（東京，日本放送出版協會，1972 年）；王蒙《蝴蝶》（日文）（東京：みすお書房，1981 年）。

等。[18]第三代日本研究中國文學成就最大的為是永駿，他的著作豐富，近年來論著茅盾作品很多。[19]關西地區屬於第二代、研究成績卓越的，如尾上兼英所指出，尚有神戶大學的山田敬三副教授（研究魯迅及當代文學）、北岡正子教授（研究丁玲及魯迅等）、片山智行教授（研究魯迅及中國現代文學問題）、秋吉久紀夫教授（著有《華北根據地的文學運動的形成和發展》、《近代中國文學運動的研究》及《江西蘇區文學運動資料集》）。[20]關西地區研究中國現代中國文學的第二代學者固然多，屬於第二代研究者更多。只要翻開該區出版有關研究中國現代文學的雜誌便可知道。關西目前這類期刊，遠勝東京地區。在京都，除了一些學報如《東方學報》（京都大學人文科學研究所出版）及《中國文學報》（京都大學中國文學會出版）這一類學報外，最重要的是京都大學研究中國現代文學的學者們組織的颺風之會所出版的《颺風》[21]，而關西地區的中國現代文學研究會，頗具影響力的是中國文藝研究會（會址設在大阪經濟大學現代中國文學中國語言研究室，領導人為相浦杲教授），目前擁有會員兩百多人，在 1970 年創刊的《野草》，至今已經出版了三十五期（1985 年），每期都以一特輯的形式出版，以下即是前三十期的專輯題目：

　　創刊號　魯迅特集

　　第 2 號　清末小說特集

　　第 3 號　現代中國文學

---

18 中川俊的論文目錄，請參考《中國關係論說資料索引（1964-1978）》（東京：論說資料保存會，1982 年），頁 217-222。

19 是久駿所發表研究茅盾之論文，見古谷久美子編《日本所出版茅盾研究參考資料目錄》，見《啞啞》1984 年第 18 及 19 期，頁 94-106。

20 關於他們的研究著作，參考中國社會科學院文學研究所編《文學研究動態》1982 年 14 及 18 期，頁 7-12，頁 1-9（《日本中國現代文學研究主要文獻索引》1970-1981 年），同時又見《中國關係論說資料索引（1964-1978）》，頁 217-224。

21 《颺風》至 1985 年，共出版了十八期。

第 4 號　中國の古典文學と現代

第 5 號　魯迅特集(2)

第 6 號　五四時代の文學

第 7 號　中國文學と日本の教育

第 8 號　三〇年代文學

第 9 號　魯迅特集(3)

第 10 號　解放區の文藝

第 11 號　日本の現代文學と中國

第 12 號　作家論

第 13 號　魯迅特集(4)

第 14.15 號　三〇年代文學(2)

第 16 號　仙台における魯迅の記錄

第 17 號　日中文學交流の一斷面

第 18 號　近現代中國文學

第 19 號　魯迅特集(5)

第 20 號　近現代中國文學

第 21 號　魯迅特集(6)

四人組批判後の中國文學

第 22 號　近現代中國文學

第 23 號　文學の現在

第 24 號　讀書の日日

第 25 號　文學の現在(2)

第 26 號　特集　資料

第 27 號　創刊十周年紀念號

第 28 號　人と書物を旅する

第 29 號　魯迅特集(8)

第30號　茅盾特集

該刊所發表的論文研究領域很廣闊，從五四運動到今日大陸文學，每個專輯是收集全日本各地區研究中國現代文學當代學者（第二及第三代)的精華。中國文藝研究會另有出版《中國文藝研究會會報》，1985年2月已出版了第五十期，每期約有五十頁，內容包括論文及會訊。在大阪市，已故關西大學教授增田涉的一些學生所組織的咿啞之會，主要領導人是中島利郎，該會以發表研究中國現代文學爲主所出版的學報《咿啞》，目前共出版了二十期（1985年），在學術界占有相當的份量。再者，該會另有出版《咿啞匯報》。神戶大學中文學會在山田敬三副教授的領導下，在1982年2月創刊《未名》雜誌，也是以發表中國現代文學研究論文爲主。同時，1982年也成立了一個臺灣文學研究會，於同年6月，該會出版了《台灣文學研究會會報》創刊號，現在已出版了四期（1984），主要發表臺灣現代文學的介紹和研究論文，一年兩期，這是日本研究臺灣文學唯一的團體，也是唯一的刊物。在大阪，1984年太田進等人組織茅盾研究會，而且出版了《茅盾研究會會報》，該會報在1984年7月及11月出版了第一及第二期。

四、日本各大學的中國現代文學課程內容

在日本，目前大多數的大學都設有現代漢語與中國現代文學之課程。即使在研究院，中國現代文學課程也占了極重要的比例。在東京的大學，像東京大學、早稻田大學、東京都立大學、東洋大學、和光大學、御茶水女子大學，東京女子大學等都有中國現代文學課程，其他地區，特別是關西地區的京都大學、大阪外語大學、神戶大學、關西大學、大阪市立大學、北九州大學、九州大學等各大學的大學部和研究所都設有相當專門的中國現代文學課程。我訪問各大學的時候，都特別請教各教授所開設課程的內容，以下就是一些實際的例子：

東京大學

1. 1930 年代文學研究（丸山升教授，以魯迅爲主）

2. 中國近代、現代文學研究（丸山升教授，以左聯爲主）

3. 魯迅第二卷《彷徨》、《野草》、《朝花夕拾》、《故事新編》（丸山升教授，特別演習）

4. 現代作家研究（伊藤敬一教授，以老舍爲主）

5. 現代作家研究（丸山升教授，以朱自清爲主）

6. 周作人研究（木山英雄教授）

早稻田大學

1. 中國現代文學研究（杉本達夫教授，演習課，以選讀自傳性文章爲主）

2. 老舍與抗戰時期文藝運動資料（杉本達夫教授）

3. 中國小說史（蘆田孝昭教授，以現代小說史爲主）

京都大學

1. 中國現代文學の諸相（竹內實教授，以魯迅爲主）

2. 現代戲劇選讀

3. 中國語作文（以老舍《正紅旗下》爲主）

大阪外語大學

1. 中國現代文學史（是永駿副教授，以文學論爭爲主題）

2. 中國現代文學演習（是永駿副教授，以茅盾作品爲主）

3. 中國文學研究：日中比較文學研究（相浦杲、宿玉堂教授，以研究魯迅、郭沫若、郁達夫與日本文壇之關係爲主題）

4. 中國文學演習：中國當代文學研究（是永駿副教授，選讀中國大陸文學刊物上的作品）

東洋大學

1. 中國現代文學史概說（中下正治教授）

2. 中國現代文學演習（金岡照光教授，選讀老舍作品爲主）

北海道大學

1. 中國文學演習（丸尾常喜副教授，1979-1985 年先後講過：柳
　青《創業史》、曹禺《家》，1920 年代文學，魯迅《阿 Q 正傳》、
　《社戲》、老舍《鼓書藝人》、艾蕪《南行記》及魯迅《徬徨》）

2. 中國文學演習（藤本幸三副教授，先後講過 1930 年代戲劇、
　中國現代鄉土文學、當代中國文學作品選讀）

　　從上列五間大學的課程來看，日本大學中國現代文學的授課內容
很專門，很少通論性的基本課，通常教授都是以自己最專長的研究作
爲教學的主題。像丸尾常喜，曾經以一學年的時間講授魯迅的一篇小
說《社戲》，像丸山升和竹內實兩人分別在東京大學和京都大學開了一
門名稱相同的中國現代文學的種種問題，他們主要講授目前自己最有
權威性的魯迅研究。是永駿專門研究茅盾，在古谷久美子編的《日本
出版茅盾研究參考資料目錄》中，他研究茅盾的論文就有十三篇[22]，
所以他在大阪外語大學教授的中國文學演習，就以分析茅盾作品爲
主。日本各大學的這種授課與自己專門研究密切的關係，致使教學者
的研究不但不因教學中斷，反而推動他們的研究，促使研究論文源源
不斷產生。像早稻田大學的杉本達夫教授由於開的課是講授老舍，近
年來他發表有關老舍的研究論文就特別多。[23]同樣的，大阪外語大學
的是永駿講授的是茅盾，故這些年來發表有關茅盾的論文也特別多。
大阪外語大學的相浦杲教授講授現代中日文學關係，尤其關於魯迅、
郁達夫和郭沫若等人所受日本文學之影響，因此近年來他從比較文學
的角度研究中國現代文學，而發表了一些十分受重視的研究論文，譬

---

22 見《啞啞》1984 年第 18、19 期，頁 94-106。
23 見日下恒夫與倉橋幸彥編《日本出版老舍研究文獻目錄》（京都：朋友書店，1984
　年）。

如〈從比較文學之角度看魯迅散文詩・野草〉及〈魯迅與廚川白村〉[24]，
便是這種制度下的產品。

　　上列五間大學的教學內容雖然代表性不大，但它反映出，近年來
教學者已勇於打破傳統，除了幾位作家如魯迅、老舍、茅盾受到特別
重視外，其他作家與作品，特別是當代作家已被接納進大學講堂，像
大阪外語大學，開一門課是專讀目前出版的中國文藝雜誌中的文學作
品。

五、今日日本中國現代文學研究之新方向

　　近年來由於研究人員結構的變化，促使中國現代文學研究的面貌
也發生了變化。下面是目前所呈現的一些特點：

（一）、從魯迅到臺灣文學

　　日本第一代研究中國文學學者的研究課題都很狹小，探討的領域
全國學人專心一致的集中在少數幾個中國作家身上。日本論說資料保
存會出版的《中國關係論文資料索引》（1964-1978）中「現代文學」
部分，共收錄了通論與作家作品專論論文二百多篇，其中專論魯迅的
就有七十左右，第二多者為茅盾，有十五篇，老舍九篇，郁達夫七篇，
其他作家的專論，最多者都只有三、四篇，如丁玲、趙樹理、周作人、
郭沫若等人。再看中國社會科學院文學研究動態組所編的《日本中國
現代文學研究主要文獻索引》之二（1970-1981），共收錄專論作家與
作品之論文或專著目錄共約二百四十條，其中魯迅約一百條，茅盾有
二十四條，郁達夫十三條，老舍八條。這兩種目錄可反映日本過去的
研究領域之一般情形。從最近這幾年，由於第三代的研究學者人數驟
然增加，而且漸露頭角，像上述關西地區很多專發表中國現代作家之

---

24 第一篇發表於《國際關係論的綜合研究》（大阪，1982 年），頁 1-48：第二篇發表
　　於《野草》1981 年第 29 期，頁 5-51。

研究成果之期刊的出現，便是最明顯之變化，已經出版了三十五期的《野草》，二十期的《咿啞》之內容，是最好的證據。《日本所出版現代·當代中國文學研究》第一集（1977-1980）及第二集（1981-1982）的目錄也很明顯的反映年輕的學者競爭地研究不同作家和不同的問題，雖然舊傳統還延續下來，目前最多人研究的作家與作品，集中在魯迅、茅盾、老舍，尤其近年來研究茅盾與老舍的論文非常多，甚至遠超過研究魯迅的數目，至於文學問題，東京地區最近集中在 1930年代文學，而關西地區開拓了中國當代文學和臺灣文學的研究，第二代的著名學者如相浦杲也領導重視當代作家。

（二）、從「鏡子」到學術

第一代的日本學者研究中國現代文學作家與作品，出發點特別強調竹內好的「鏡子」理論，就是借著研究中國作家作爲一面鏡子，作爲自我反省的參考，批判日本的現代化的道路。從這一認識出發，實在不容易找到有如此偉大的中國作家，因此過去研究的對角主要以有限的幾位作家及其他有關問題爲主。現在年輕一代，多數不習慣從政治角度、革命角度來研究，對他們來說，中國作家魯迅或任何一位作家，是世界上許多在文學創作上有成就的一個，此外別無意義。他們研究這些作家，不外是爲學位，爲學術地位與興趣。所以他們今天多數是純從文學主義，純學術觀點來做研究。由於這樣，年輕一代學者爭先恐後的爭取研究過去被忽略的作家。譬如東京的學者最新的研究成果，發表在 1983 年 3 月出版的《東洋文化》上，研究的作家有沈從文（尾崎文昭、小島久代）、郭沫若（伊藤虎丸），丁玲（宮島敦子）、蕭軍（下出鐵男）及葉紹鈞（新村徹）。[25]

（三）、多種角度，深入問題的研究方法

---

25 見《東洋文化：特集 1930 年代中國文學研究之三》，1985 年第 65 期。

　　眾多的新人，從不同的角度來研究各種文學問題，各個作家與作品，這是擺脫或突破傳統的政治與文學的框框的結果。第二代權威性的學者如丸山升，就強調讓事實說話的方法，如擺脫中國大陸的牽制，以日本人的立場來研究問題。這種實證科學方法，另一方面特別強調重視一手資料，發掘資料，不發無根據的空論。[26]像北岡正子〈摩羅詩力說材料來源考證〉研究，便是一個考證細密的好例子。[27]

（四）、中日現代文學比較研究

　　早在 1974 年，山田敬三就以〈以比較文學的方法研究中國現代文學〉為題[28]，提出以比較文學的方法來研究現代中國和日本文學。這種研究方法，近年來受到很大的重視，研究現代中國作家與日本文學之關係的論文，越來越多，對了解許多中國現代文學問題，有極大的貢獻。檜山久雄《魯迅與漱石》、伊藤虎丸的《魯迅和日本人》和《魯迅和終末論》等專書，是以比較手法來研究現代中日文學的權威性著作。[29]相浦杲教授目前在大阪外語大學講解《日中比較文學研究》一課，正是努力推動這方面研究的具體表現。他的近作〈以比較的角度來分析魯迅散文詩「野草」〉和〈魯迅與廚川白村〉是精細的力作，是最典型的所謂比較研究的論文。伊藤虎丸與松永正義合著的論文〈明治三十年代文學與魯迅〉也是如此有份量的研究。[30]

（五）、中國現代文學研究在日本大學圍牆內外

26　參考劉柏青〈戰後日本魯迅研究概觀〉，見《魯迅研究》1984 年第 6 期，頁 58-77。

27　北岡正子的〈摩羅詩力說材料來源考〉從 1972 年開始在第 7 號《野草》連載，至 30 號（1982 年）尚未完。

28　〈以比較文學的方法研究中國現代文學〉，見《文學論輯》（九州大學，1974 年第 21 期，頁 1-12。

29　檜山久雄《魯迅與漱石》（東京：第三文明社，1977 年）；伊藤虎丸《魯迅和日本人》（東京：朝日新聞，1983 年），《魯迅和終末論：現代現實主義的形成》（東京：龍溪書，1975 年）。

30　原文載《日本文學》1980 第 6 期，中文譯文見《河北大學學報》1982 年第 2 期，頁 82-93。

　　我這次訪問日本，所了解的只限於大學圍牆之內的中國現代文學研究，大學外面因爲學術興趣而研究的獨立學術人員完全沒有機會接觸，我們知道像國際著名的竹內好，日本學術界今認爲最有成就的第一代中國現代文學學者，一直生活在大學研究機構之外。竹內實也是在 1970 年代末才受聘於大學。從目前研究的條件來說，將會有更多優秀的第三代學者在大學之外繼續做研究。過去研究的成果，主要靠大學的「紀要」及學術專刊如東京大學的《東洋文化》、《中哲文學會報》，京都大學的《東方學報》、早稻田大學的《中國文學研究》及中國研究所的《中國研究月報》等等，這些學術刊物，雖然愈來愈多發表研究中國現代文學的論文，但如果作者不是跟有關大學有職務上的聯繫，發表機會不大。自從大學外的中國文學研究團體如中國文藝研究會的刊物《野草》，飆風社的《飆風》，新青年讀書會的《貓頭鷹》刊物的出版，並在日本國內外一直受到重視，大學圍牆內的學者更易將研究成果發表。

　　在戰後，日本中國現代文學研究已從國立大學走到市立或都立大學，甚至私立大學，然後也在大學圍牆外生了根。

（六）、新馬華文文學研究

　　我訪問過東京東洋大學今富正巳教授、橫濱市立大學鈴木正夫副教授、北九州大學的山本哲也教授，以及下關市立大學的小木裕文副教授，他們都寫過不少有關新馬華文文學的研究論文，發表在有關中國現代文學雜誌如《野草》和《中國文藝研究會會報》、《中國語》等刊物上。除了他們，愛知學院大學的櫻井明治曾翻譯過不少新加坡華文及英文文學作品成爲日文[31]，另外筑波大學的陳俊勳和每日新聞的福永平和曾翻譯《新加坡華文小說選 1945-1965》（上）及苗秀的《殘夜

31　櫻井明治的譯作，多數發表在 1975 至 1978 年間出版的《亞洲展望》雜誌上。

行》。[32]

六、結　論

　　第二次世界大戰後，日本多數大學都有教授中國語的課程。幾十年來，培養了不少在中國語言和中國現代文學都有研究基礎的學生。加上中國大陸與日本建交以來，兩國關係日愈密切，日本搞中國現代文學的研究生或學者常有機會到中國學習，不但學會流利的中國話，而且實地考察研究，與中國作家發生密切關係。近年來中國國內舉行像 1982 年在濟南山東大學舉行的老舍學術討論會，1984 年在北京舉行的全國茅盾研究學術討論會，日本學者都有受邀參加。這種聯繫會促使日本中國現代文學研究更蓬勃地發展。

　　大學中國語言課程之普遍設立，是產生中國現代文學研究學者最好基礎，而且目前大學教授中國語，主要是教白話文，自然以白話文學作品為教材，這也是容易引起學生研究興趣之一大因素。怪不得東京大學的丸山升教授說，目前他們的研究生，有一半以中國現代文學為研究對象。其中大學也大致如此。

　　日本各大學及研究機構的中文藏書都給中國現代文學研究者帶來很方便和有利條件。由於日本沒有政治禁書上的問題，中國及臺灣及其他地區各個時期出版的中文研究資料，從書籍到期刊，各大學圖書館都相當齊全，像東京大學東洋文化研究所收藏有關中國現代文學之資料，很足夠作一般的研究用。日本的中文書店，像東京的中華書店、內山書店、東方書店，京都的朋友書店、大阪的橫田書店、福岡的中國書店，對中國大陸出版的書籍報刊，非常齊全，港臺的書籍也不少。據最近幾年常去中國大陸的日本學者及日本的中國留學生說，在日本

32　《新加坡華文小說選，1945-65》出版於 1983 年，《殘夜行》1985 年，兩書均由東京井村文化事業社出版。

最大規模的中國書店出售有關中國現代文學的書刊，常常比在中國的書店更多（作者 2006 年說：目前情況已不是如此），雖然價錢非常高昂。我個人的經驗，東京的東方書店、中華書店和內山書店出售的書，比香港三聯書店或中華書局更完整。

　　目前日本出版有關中國書籍（日文）或出售中文書籍的大書店，都有出版定期刊物，以供專家發表有深度的研究論文或報導、書評性的文章。其中常發表有關中國現代文學者，有岩波書店的《文學》、筑摩書房的《竹內好全集月刊》、學習研究社的《老舍小說全集月報》、東方書店的《東方》月刊等便是把中國現代文學推廣的代表性雜誌。從以上的種種條件看來，日本已成爲中國以外，最適合從事中國現代文學研究的國家。

回到仙台醫專，重新解剖一個中國醫生的死亡：周樹人變成魯迅，棄醫從文的新見解

一、九十年後，我走進魯迅的課室，還聽見槍斃中國人的掌聲

魯迅在 1904 年 9 月 13 日早上 8 點，第一次步入仙台醫學專門學校的第六課室。由於他是當時仙台醫專最早也是唯一的中國留學生，在老師講課之前，教務處特別安排一位書記田總助次郎陪同魯迅進入教室，並且向同學介紹：「這是從中國來的學生！」

大講堂的課室，長條木板座位從左到右共分成三段，魯迅的座位在前面第三排的中間第一個（面向講台），由於日本當時的上課座位是固定的（上每一門課都如此），現在這個座位的桌上貼上紀念＋魯迅的說明文字。

九十年之後，1994 年的 9 月 6 日早上 10 點，我和其他十四位日本與外國研究魯迅的學者一起走進仙台醫專的第六課室。魯迅仙台留學九十周年紀念國際學術文化研究會的工委會主席阿部兼也教授，也模仿當年的情形，向日本學術文化界一一介紹我們。譬如輪到我的時候，他說：「這是來自新加坡的王潤華教授」，然後邀請我上台在古老的黑板上題字留念。我隨手寫了幾個字：「當南洋還在殖民地時代，魯迅已是我們的導師」，下題新加坡王潤華。魯迅在五、六十年代的新加坡與馬來西亞，由於左派思想的流行，被華人文化知識界奉為思想導師，我因此在中學時代即對魯迅特別「崇拜」，這是我研究魯迅的根源。

俄羅斯的漢學家索羅金題的字是「祝中俄文化關係更大發展」，中國的孫中田教授題詞是：「懷念魯迅，向魯迅學習。」牛津大學的劉陶陶教授只簽上自己的姓名。

當眾人步出講堂時，我還是靜靜一個人坐在魯迅當年讀醫科時每天坐的座位上。我突然似乎看見講台白色銀幕上，出現在中國東北土地上，日本戰敗俄國的幻燈片：日軍正要槍斃（一說砍頭）給俄國做偵探的中國人。幻燈片上圍觀的中國人表情麻木，他們與台下的日本同學都拍掌歡呼，這種喝彩聲特別刺耳，才使我清醒過來，發現其他的人都已走出這棟老舊的木板課室。

二、仙台醫學院魯迅雕像充滿疑惑與徬徨的神情

據說目前仙台東北大學（醫學院所屬）很缺建築空間，所以保留住二棟魯迅上過課的房子，完全出於紀念這位中國作家與思想家，因此壓力很大，被拆除的危機隨時會出現。當我走出第六課室，追隨人聲，發現其他人正向當年仙台醫學專門學校遺址上魯迅的人頭塑像走去。魯迅寂寞地在一棵松樹下，向第六課室瞭望，眼睛充滿疑惑，臉色凝重。難道他還在尋找與思考，當年為什麼念了一年半，中途棄醫從文的原因嗎？

魯迅雕像的旁邊就是東北大學紀念資料館，正展覽著魯迅當年在仙台醫學院的上課時間表（包括任課教師與課室），成績單、點名冊，及其他學籍記錄。閱讀了這些文件，我才明白館外魯迅雕像的神情為什麼充滿疑惑：因為他一年級所修讀的七科中，竟有三科的成績被算錯，同學在第一學年結束後，誣告他因藤野先生在修改他的解剖學筆記上做暗號，故意洩露考題，考試才及格。現在看了成績單才知道，魯迅一年級幾乎所有功課都及格，只有藤野及敷波合教的解剖學考不好，只有 59.3 分，可見流言完全出於猜忌與誣蔑，怪不得當時學生會

的幹事檢查魯迅的解剖學講義，找不到藤野教授的記號。

三、監獄旁的魯迅舊居佐藤屋：
與犯人共吃同一鍋煮的飯菜

　　從東北大學醫學院西南邊一個側門出去，走一小段路，便是仙台市片平丁路 52 號，魯迅初到仙台醫專第一間寄宿的樓房，目前稱為「佐藤屋」，當時他租了樓上右邊的一間房子。房東佐藤喜東治還把一樓的房屋租給包辦囚人伙食的人，因為宮城監獄就在旁邊。魯迅在〈藤野先生〉一文中說那裏蚊子多，睡覺時要用被蓋住身體與頭部，只留鼻孔呼吸。不久學校的先生覺得地點不相宜，二來這客店也包監獄犯人的伙食，勸說幾次，魯迅才肯搬到別處去住。不再與犯人共吃同一鍋煮的食物。

　　這次國際研討會的籌備委員，多是魯迅學者，意識到魯迅初到仙台時住在監獄邊緣，與囚犯共吃同一鍋的飯菜，不免使仙台人尷尬難堪，因此就特別招待我們住宿在仙台青葉區的東急國際觀光飯店裏。由於魯迅在仙台期間，曾和日本同學遊覽了松島海邊度假名勝，研討會雖然時間緊湊，費盡苦心地把最後一場論文研討搬去松島海邊的世紀大飯店舉行，這樣我們便能享受魯迅遊覽的松島經驗。為了使我們感受周樹人在仙台醫專如何轉化成救人靈魂的魯迅，除了第一天的上午參觀仙台與魯迅讀書生活有關的地方場所，其餘研討會，都回到東北大學醫學院的賓館艮陵會館內的會堂舉行。每次休息時，我走出會場，遠眺對面現在的醫學院及以前仙台醫學專門學校，便覺得這次研討會意義之深長。

　　魯迅的仙台醫專入學許可是 1904 年 9 月 1 日發出，哪一天抵達仙台，沒確實記錄。我們外國學者抵達仙台是 9 月 5 日，大概就是魯迅抵達的日期，因為開學典禮在 9 月 12 日舉行。

四、重新解剖一個醫生的死因：中國危機感使周樹人變成魯迅

這一次的仙台魯迅國際研討會，共有論文十四篇，我個人覺得其中最有趣的，最大的收穫是重新解剖周樹人在仙台的經驗，尋找出使他變成魯迅的原因。早在 1978 年，仙台東北大學的教職員與當地文化界，出版詳細的《魯訊在仙台的記錄》，但是只是瑣碎的資料收集，沒有作過坦誠與真實的「驗屍報告」。這跟日本當時政府保守的態度有關係吧。自從日本公開承認侵略亞洲各國並道歉以後，學術文化界也就日愈開明，尤其在判斷中日敏感的關係問題上。這一次魯迅仙台留學九十周年國際研討會其中一項目的，根據我個人觀察，就是要作最後的「驗屍報告」，因為某些結論，在幾年前也許對個人服從群體的日本魯迅學者，雖然心裏明白，但還是不敢說出來。

所以宣讀論文之前，我們一起參觀魯迅仙台讀書與生活的地方，公開他的學校記錄與課堂筆記。接著回到醫學院艮陵會館開始論文研討。阿部兼也教授指出，魯迅自己，拿幻燈片事件作為棄醫從文的理由是帶有疑問的，其後面可能隱藏著其他奧秘。他說魯迅在仙台時代，這個城市主要是日軍重要基地，侵略中國土地與俄國作戰的日軍，多從仙台派出，當時人民熱烈響應徵兵制。每次軍隊打勝仗回來，人民和學生都大事慶祝。對中國學生來說，這個「軍隊與學校」的城市使得生活非常沈悶，軍國主義氣息濃厚，因此強化了魯迅對中國危機感的認識。看見日本人上下支持軍隊去侵略中國，隨意誣蔑外國學生考試作弊，促使魯迅對人性反省與批判。

阿部兼也是仙台的老居民，他坦誠指出，當時仙台是一個軍隊城市，侵略中國的軍士，多由這裏出發，而住在監獄邊緣的魯迅，被人誣告考試作弊，懷疑他有能力考試及格的事件，再加上幻燈片上替俄

國做偵探的中國人被槍斃時，班上日本同學大聲呼萬歲，自然加強魯
迅對中國危機感的認識！今天外國人在仙台，四處是青葉，好一個花
園城市，萬萬想不到過去原來是一個軍隊城市！

五、少計算考試成績而不糾正，魯迅對 醫專和教官是怎麼看的？

另一項驚人的發現，由渡邊襄先生提出。他仔細再核算魯迅在仙
台醫專一年級的學年評分表，居然有二個錯誤：生理學應是 65 分（60
＋70÷2＝65），不是 63.3，七科總平均應是 65.8 分（458.6÷7＝65.8），
不是 65.5。另外在學年成績表上，魯迅的倫理學分數是 83，應換算成
乙等，但卻變成丙級。這麼簡單的數學，怎麼竟錯了三處？身為仙台
居民的渡邊襄也不禁要問：「少計了考試成績也不給予糾正，魯迅對醫
專和教官到底是怎麼看的呢？」他的結論是「此事至少對魯迅來說是
件極為不快的事」，而且「這也是使他喪失學習欲望的原因之一」。

魯迅第一年在全班 142 名學生中，竟排名 68 名，全班有 30 人因
總平均成績不及格而不能升級。成績公布後，日本同學派代表檢查他
的解剖學筆記，懷疑藤野在替他修改時做了記號，結果找不到證據。
當時同學還不知道魯迅各科成績，現在我們看見，竟嚇了一跳，解剖
學是七科中唯一不及格的，魯迅只得 59.3 分。可見寫匿名信及檢查筆
記是出於不相信中國人的能力的誣蔑和猜忌。

這些打擊發生在一個軍隊城市裏是很自然的。這些軍隊又是侵略
中國領土的主力，而仙台的普通居民與學生都全心支持這些軍國主義
的士兵。因此魯迅所受的刺激該是很強烈的。他說：「中國是弱國，所
以中國人當然是低能兒，分數在六十分以上，便不是自己的能力了：
也無怪他們疑惑。」

所以第二學年念了一半，就退學了。大會結束前，贈送給與會者

七種魯迅在仙台醫專的學習記錄與證件的複製，作爲紀念品，從申請入學函件到班上的缺課名單（魯迅無故缺課一次）都有，但偏偏沒有他的成績單，大概因爲有三個錯誤，大學當局不好意思讓更多人知道如此丟臉的事吧！

六、藤野「過於熱心」修改解剖學筆記，引起魯迅的反感與消極的影響

過去由於魯迅在〈藤野先生〉中，表示對他一年級解剖老師的尊敬，因爲在軍國主義與種族歧視的環境中，藤野是唯一例外，自動提出要幫忙魯迅修改解剖學筆記，因爲怕他沒能力做筆記，因此遭來同學之猜忌，甚至造謠說藤野在他筆記中做了暗號，故意泄露考題。從這篇文字開始，中日學者便大做文章，把他們二人的關係加以神話化。最後藤野不但是魯迅在醫專的守護神，魯迅現代學術思想之形成之導師，甚至成爲中日關係友好的象徵性人物。

可是至今沒有人詳細檢查過藤野修改過的魯迅解剖學筆記（魯迅說失落了，後來 1951 年才找到，現存北京魯迅博物館）。現任仙台附近的福井縣立大學看護短期大學泉彪之助醫學教授，在 1993 及 1994 兩次詳閱這本筆記，這次在研究會中把他的調查報告《藤野教授與魯迅的醫學筆記》發表了。他不但匯報了真實的內容，而且坦白大膽的發表他的看法。泉彪之助先生說，藤野的修改加筆處，有時幾乎滿滿一頁，他說：「從藤野的修改加筆之中，或許會產生魯迅的醫學筆記錯誤很多的感覺。」其實對一個醫科一年級，日語只學了二年的學生來說，「筆記的內容似乎還是很正確的」，許許多多的地方，都沒有改動的必要。〈藤野先生〉文中所說：「你將這條血管移了一點位置了」。這句話，泉先生說是魯迅表示有所不滿而說的。藤野很多批語，泉先生與他的醫學教授同事討論，都覺得矯枉過正，甚至不正確的。

　　所以泉先生十分驚訝的：「在調查魯迅的筆記以前，我從未認為藤野嚴九郎用紅筆修改的魯迅的筆記一定會對魯迅產生什麼消極的影響，然而，看了藤野所修改的魯迅筆記後，我不禁想到修改加筆之處常常過多，是否偶爾也會引起魯迅的反感呢？」解剖學是醫學的基礎，也是第一年唯一屬於醫學的科目，魯迅竟不及格（59.3 分），偏偏又是藤野的課（其實與敷波合教），對魯迅的信心是一大打擊！泉彪之助責藤野「過於熱心修改」，那是含蓄客氣的話，我總覺得他有大日本主義的心態，要不然怎麼許多像「這裏的錯誤很多」的批語，泉先生及其醫生同事都說「不正確」？

七、以周樹人仙台經驗，解讀魯迅的創作

　　上述的仙台經驗，不但是導致周樹人變成魯迅棄醫從文的原因，而且也構成以後魯迅文學創作中，特別他的小說的重要藝術與思想結構。仙台經驗不斷以千變萬化的形式出現在他的作品中。有一篇論文《歷史位置的抉擇與魯迅的心態》（孫中田）就有這樣的看法。周樹人在幻燈片中所看見麻木的、病態的、蒙昧的看客群眾。愚弱的被日本砍頭示眾的人，日後重覆出現在魯迅的〈藥〉、〈阿Q正傳〉等作品中，如果把周樹人的仙台許多事件，用來解讀魯迅的小說，我們將洞悉其中驚人的聯繫性。譬如由於幻燈事件中愚昧的中國人被砍頭示眾之刺激，在他的小說中麻木的看客與可憐的愚弱國民就不斷在小說中出現。周樹人在習醫時解剖過二十多具屍體，解剖使他知道礦工的肺被炭污染得墨黑，殘缺的嬰兒被花柳病所貽害。日後他在小說中，都在進行解剖中國人與社會，斷定其病症與死因。

從周樹人仙台學醫經驗
解讀魯迅的小說

一、重新解剖周樹人仙台經驗的國際會議

　　1994 年 9 月 6 日至 9 日，日本仙台東北大學的語言與文化學院以小田基與阿部兼也二教授爲首，主辦了魯迅留學仙台 90 周年紀念國際學術與文化研討會。會場設立在東北大學醫學院（前身即仙台醫專）的艮陵會館。[1]這次的國際會議的討探內容，對我個人來說，最有意義與啓發性的，是重新解剖周樹人在仙台的經驗，尋找出魯迅在 1904 年 9 月至 1906 年 3 月在仙台習醫期間，各種環境與生對棄醫從文的影響。[2]

　　日本的魯迅學者，一向重視魯迅在仙台的學習與生活，因爲周樹人在 1906 年走出仙台醫專回返東京以後，就變成日後從事文藝拯救人類心靈的魯迅了。最能代表在這方面的研究，是 1978 出版的《魯迅在仙台的記錄》，那是仙台東北大學教職員與當地文化界，又結合了全日本學者的一部資料報告。可是在整理出這些瑣碎又詳盡的資料後，並沒有人根據它作過真實坦誠的「驗屍報告」。[3]這大概跟以前日本政府

---

1 大會所有宣讀的論文，已印成文集《魯迅仙台留學九十周年紀念國際學術文化研討會論文集》（仙台：東北大學語言文化學院，1994 年）。共有 243 頁，並附續集及續續集二冊。全部論文均有中日或英日文，即原文與翻譯對照。爲省略起見，本文以後引文末只註明《論文集》及頁數。

2 有關這方面最重要者有以下幾篇：阿部兼也〈魯迅和藤野先生－關於現代的學術精神〉，見註 1，頁 1-21，泉彪之助〈藤野教授與魯迅的醫學筆記〉，頁 154-173；渡邊襄〈有關仙台時代魯迅資料研究的研究〉，見註 1《續集》，頁 12-23。

3 魯迅在仙台記錄調查委員會編《魯迅在仙台記錄》（東京：平凡社，1978 年）。另外

保守的政策與日本人不承認錯誤的心態有關係吧。自從前幾年日本政府公開承認侵略亞洲各國並道歉後，日本中國現代文學研究者也跟著日愈開放，尤其在有關於中日敏感的問題上。這一次魯迅留學仙台九十周年紀念國際研討會，其最重要目的，是要根據多年收集的資料與分析，作出最後的「驗屍報告」，因為某些結論，在幾年前也許對個人服從群體的日本魯迅學者，雖然心裏明白，但還是不敢說出來。這一次在會議上，日本學者宣布了許多驚人的結論，講了以前不可能講的真心話。

　　由於會議的重點放在周樹人在仙台習醫的生活與思想，主辦當局別出心裁的設計第一天上午，前往參觀魯迅在仙台留下的遺跡與資料展覽。[4]

二、九十年後我們坐在魯迅的座位上，還聽見槍斃中國人的槍聲

　　魯迅在 1904 年 9 月 13 日（星期二）早上八點第一次步入仙台醫專的教室。由於他是當時仙台醫專最早也是唯一的中國留學生，教務處特別安排一位書記總助次郎陪同魯迅進入教室，並且向同學介紹：「這是從中國來的學生！」[5]

　　大講堂的長條木板座位從左到右，共分成三排，魯迅的座位據說在中間的第三排的最右邊（面向台下）的座位。由於當時學生座位每

魯迅誕生 110 周年仙台紀念節組織委員會編《魯迅與日本》（仙台：委員會自印，1991年），提供了新的資料，尤其是渡邊襄《魯迅與仙台》（頁 20-37），阿部兼也〈棄醫學從文學〉（頁 38-48）及手代木有兒的圖片集〈魯迅的生涯〉（頁 50-123）。

4 本人另有短文記載其事：《回到仙台醫專，重新解剖一個中國醫生的死亡－周樹人變成魯迅，棄醫從文的新見解》，見臺北《聯合報》副刊，1994 年 10 月，又見《魯迅研究月刊》第 153 期（1995 年 1 月 20 日），頁 56-58。又見本書第三章。

5 同註 3，〈魯迅在仙台記錄〉，頁 89-90。

天固定的，現在大學把這個座位貼上紀念魯迅的說明文字。爲了紀念魯迅，目前東北大學特意保留了醫專魯迅時代的二棟課室：目前用作學生醫療室及被稱爲第六教室的尚未改變原貌的建築。

　　九十年後的九月，也是星期二早上，我和其他十四位外國及日本研究魯迅的學者，一起走進魯迅習醫時最常用的第六教室。[6]魯迅留學仙台九十周年紀念國際研討會主席阿部兼也教授，也模仿當年的情形，向日本學術文化界一一介紹我們。譬如輪到我的時候，他說：「這是來自新加坡的王潤華教授。」然後邀請我上台在古老的黑板上題字留念。我隨手寫上：「當南洋還在殖民地時代，魯迅已是我們的導師。」魯迅在五、六十年代的新加坡與馬來西亞，由於中國左派思想之流行，被華人文化知識界奉爲思想導師。這是促使我研究魯迅的起因。

　　當眾人步出講堂時，我還是靜靜一個人坐在魯迅當年讀醫科的每天坐的位子上。不禁想起當年周樹人就是在上細菌學的課時，日本政府爲了配合在中國東北進行著的日俄戰爭的宣傳，灌輸軍國主義思想，經常在上課時放映日本戰勝俄國的幻燈片。有一次幻燈片上出現在中國東北土地上，日俄戰爭時，日軍正要將一個給俄國做偵探的中國人砍頭示眾，圍觀的中國人表情麻木，每次日本同學都拍掌歡呼，高唱萬歲。魯迅後來在 1922 年寫的《吶喊‧自序》說，受了這強烈的刺激，他決定棄醫從文：

> 覺得醫學並非一件緊要事，凡是愚弱的國民，即使體格如何健全，如何茁壯，也只能做毫無意義的示眾的材料和看客，病死多少是不必以為不幸的。所以我們的第一要著，是在改變他們的精神，而善於改變精神的是，我那時以為當然要推文藝。[7]

6 他們是孫中田、吳俊（中國）、李炳漢、申一澈（韓），劉陶陶（英）、高恩德（匈牙利）、索羅金（俄）、泉彪之助、阿部兼也、九尾常喜，及渡邊襄（日本）等人。
7 《吶喊‧自序》，見《魯迅全集》（北京：人民文學出版社，1981 年），第 1 冊，頁

　　長期以來，尤其中國學者，都深信不疑，以這原因作爲周樹人棄醫從文，變成作家魯迅的唯一重要原因。[8]目前日本學者，經過詳細收集與分析魯迅在仙台與東京留學（1902-1909）的經驗資料後，基本上否認「幻燈事件」在魯迅棄醫從文的思想轉變中的重要意義。這次研討會第一篇論文，阿部兼也的〈魯迅和藤野先生 — 關於近代的學術精神〉就提出質疑：

> 然而，對這一理由人們多少是可以有疑問的。試想手無寸鐵的中國民眾面對狂暴的日軍的野蠻行徑，除了忍氣吞聲，又能作些什麼呢？再則，所謂精神高於肉體的說法，似乎是一種能夠使人接受的理由，細細想來，輕視肉體的結果並不必然帶來對精神的重視……。現在的問題是：魯迅何以會提出這些本身常有疑問的理由呢？在這背後，是否隱藏著什麼奧秘呢？[9]

　　這次魯迅留學仙台九十周年研討會的一大貢獻，就是把魯迅棄醫從文背後隱藏著的奧秘解開，因爲在走向廿一世紀的整合世界時，區域性的組合，已大大超越了民族國家的範圍。世界各地的人類社會，在車同軌，書同文（用相同的電腦程序），地球村的局面已形成，共同文化已出現，所以日本學者在打破許多禁忌後，開始重新詮釋許多學術問題。

三、偏見與歧視：考試作弊與算錯成績

　　當我還沈迷在幻想中，日本同學對槍斃中國人的歡呼聲把我驚醒過來，發現其他的人已走出這棟老舊的木板教室，前往不遠處觀看一

416-417。

8 譬如魯迅博物館魯迅研究室主編的《魯迅年譜》（北京：人民文學出版社，1981 年），第 1 卷，還是很強調這點，頁 167。

9 同註 1，《論文集》頁 13。

尊魯迅的塑像，地點正是當年仙台醫學專門學校的遺址中心點。在「仙台醫學專門學校跡」紀念碑旁的魯迅雕像，寂寞的立在一棵松樹下，向第六教室瞭望，滿臉困惑。他似乎還在思考當年中途退學的原因。

魯迅雕像的旁邊，就是東北大學紀念資料館，裏面展覽著魯迅在醫專的上課時間表、成績單、點名冊及其他學籍記錄。細讀了這些文件，聽了後來渡邊襄宣讀的論文〈有關仙台時代魯迅資料研究的研究〉，才明白魯迅迷惑不解的神情。渡邊襄小心檢查現存當年周樹人的成績記錄表，一年級的「學年評點表」中，居然有二個錯誤：生理學應是 65 分（$60+70÷2=65$），不是 63.3 分。七科成績總平均應是 65.8 分（$458.6÷7=65.8$），不是 65.5 分。另外在「第一年學年試驗成績表」上倫理學等級為丙，這是錯誤的，應是乙等，因為在「評點表」上倫理學得 83 分。[10]

這麼簡單的數學，怎麼竟犯了三個錯誤？身為仙台市居民及魯迅仙台留學記錄調查委員會的重要委員渡邊襄不禁感嘆：

> 但我認為，此事至少對魯迅來說是件極為不快的事。儘管在試題泄漏一事上遭到了同學們的偏見和中傷，但及格完全是依靠魯迅自身實力的。少計了考試成績也不給予糾正，魯迅對醫專和教官到底怎麼看的呢？[11]

渡邊襄的結論是：「這也是使他喪失學習欲望的原因之一吧？」[12]

當研討會結束時，主辦當局贈送每一位與會者七種複製當年仙台醫專有關魯迅的學籍原件資料記錄，包括申請入學函件及缺席記錄，可是偏偏沒有成績記錄。大概因為有三項錯誤，大學當局不好意思讓

---

10 渡邊襄的分析意見，見註 1《續集》，頁 18；各種成績單影印圖片可見於同註 3，〈魯迅在仙台記錄〉，圖片資料三，頁 104 及 137。

11 同註 1《續集》，頁 18。

12 同前註。

很多人知道如此丟臉的事吧！

魯迅第一年在全班一百四十二名同學中，排名六十八，全班有三十人因總平均成績不及格而留班。正如魯迅在〈藤野先生〉一文中所說，成績公布後，日本同學派代表檢查魯迅的解剖學的筆記，接著寄來一封匿名信，誣告藤野教授在替他修改筆記時做了暗號。可是日本同學找不到證據。當時同學也還不知道魯迅各科所得的成績呢，現在我們看見，竟嚇了一跳，藤野所教的解剖學是七科中唯一不及格的，魯迅只得 59.3 分。可見檢查筆記與匿名信純是因為當時大日本主義者不相信中國人的能力的污蔑與猜忌。魯迅在〈藤野先生〉中感嘆道：

> 中國是弱國，所以中國人當然是低能兒，分數在六十分以上，
> 便不是自己的能力了，也無怪他們疑惑。[13]

這些強烈刺激周樹人成為魯迅的事件，發生在仙台，是很自然的事。阿部兼也的論文〈魯迅與藤野〉中，特別強調當時仙台是一個軍國主義思想很強烈的城市，他稱它為「軍隊與學校的城市」，整個城裏，官吏、教員、軍隊占絕大多數的人口，而學校與政府部門，與軍隊沒有分別，所以上課時，也經常放映鼓吹侵略戰爭的幻燈片，全民熱烈響應徵兵制，市民與學生常為日軍的侵略而舉行祝賀會。魯迅離開中國到日本，目的是追求自由與新思想，但是卻在仙台落入軍國主義統治的沈悶的城市裏。死記硬背的學習生活，加上受歧視的環境與軍國主義思想橫行，所以阿部說出仙台的軍國主義社會環境「強化他對中國的危機感的認識」。在中國，人民與清朝政府有不共戴天之仇，而在日本，上下團結一致，而且還到外國去侵略搶奪。在國內則輕蔑中國人的能力。這種種社會背景，通過誣告試題洩漏，檢查筆記與幻燈事件，刺激周樹人對人性之反省與批判。[14]

---

13 同註 7，第 2 冊，頁 306。
14 同註 1，《論文集》，頁 13-20。

據說魯迅在仙台第二學年開始解剖實習時，解剖了二十多具屍體，他發現礦工的肺如墨一般黑，那是被工作環境的黑炭所污染，而胎中嬰孩殘缺不全，是受了父母花柳病毒之害。由此他更明白如何解剖病態的人與社會之癥結。[15]

四、藤野「過於熱心」修改解剖學筆記，引起魯迅的反感與消極的影響

過去由於魯迅在《吶喊‧自序》（1922）及〈藤野先生〉（1926）中，表示對他一年級解剖老師的尊敬，因為在軍國主義與種族歧視的環境中，藤野是唯一例外，自動提出要幫忙魯迅修改解剖學筆記。由於擔心他沒能力做筆記，因此遭來同學之猜忌，甚至造謠說藤野在他筆記中做了暗號，故意泄露考題。從這二篇文章開始，中日學者便大做文章，把他們二人的關係加以神話化。最後藤野不但是魯迅在醫專的守護神，魯迅現代學術思想形成之導師，甚至成為中日關係友好的象徵性人物。[16]

可是至今沒有人詳細檢查過藤野修改過的魯迅解剖學筆記。魯迅在〈藤野先生〉中說它失落了，他不會想到在 1951 年在紹興親戚家被尋獲，現存於北京魯迅博物館。現任仙台附近的福井縣立大學看護短期大學泉彪之助醫學教授，在 1993 及 1994 兩次詳閱這本筆記，這次在研討會中把他的調查報告〈藤野教授與魯迅的醫學筆記〉[17]發表了。他不但匯報了真實的內容，而且坦白大膽的發表他的看法。泉彪之助先生說，藤野的修改加筆處，有時幾乎滿滿一頁，他說：「從藤野的修

---

15 許壽裳〈亡友魯迅印象記〉，《作家談魯迅》（香港：文學出版社，1966 年），頁 16。

16 幾乎絕大多數中國與日本出版魯迅的傳記資料，都給人這樣的印象，見註 8，頁 122-177，及劉獻彪與林治廣編《魯迅與中日文化交流》（長沙：湖南人民出版社，1981 年），《魯迅在仙台記錄》等書有關部分。

17 同註 1，《論文集》，頁 154-173。

改加筆之中，或許會產生魯迅的醫學筆記錯誤很多的感覺。」其實對一個醫科一年級，日語只學了二年的學生來說，「筆記的內容似乎還是很正確的」，許許多多地方，都沒有改動的必要。〈藤野先生〉文中所說「你將這條血管移了一點位置了」這句話，泉先生說是魯迅表示有所不滿而說的。藤野很多批語，泉先生與他的醫學教授同事討論，都覺得矯枉過正，甚至不正確的。[18]

所以泉先生十分驚訝的：「在調查魯迅的筆記以前，我從未認為藤野嚴九郎用紅筆修改的魯迅的筆記一定會對魯迅產生什麼消極的影響，然而，看了藤野所修改的魯迅筆記後，我不禁想到修改加筆之處常常過多，是否偶爾也會引起魯迅的反感呢？」（《論文集》，頁168）解剖學是醫學的基礎，也是第一年唯一屬於醫學的科目，魯迅竟不及格（59.3分），偏偏又是藤野的課（其實與敷波合教），對魯迅的信心是一大打擊！泉彪之助責藤野「過於熱心修改」，那是含蓄客氣的話，我總覺得他有大日本主義的心態，要不然怎麼許多像「這裏的錯誤很多」的批語，泉先生及其醫生同事都說「不正確」？

五、以周樹人仙台經驗，解讀魯迅的創作

上述的仙台經驗，不但是導致周樹人變成魯迅棄醫從文的原因，而且也構成以後魯迅文學創作中，特別他的小說的重要藝術與思想結構。仙台經驗不斷以千變萬化的形式出現在他的作品中。孫中田的論文〈歷史位置的抉擇與魯迅的心態〉[19]就有這樣的看法與啟示。周樹人在幻燈片中所看見麻木的、病態的、蒙昧的看客群眾，愚弱的被日本砍頭示眾的人，日後重覆出現在魯迅的〈藥〉、〈阿Q正傳〉等作品

---

18 同註1，《論文集》，頁168-169。泉彪之助分析的筆記，重要部分的相片印在《魯迅與日本》中，手代木有兒編的「魯迅生涯圖錄」中，頁56-67。
19 見註1，《論文集》，頁52-69。

中。[20] 如果把周樹人的仙台許多事件，用來解讀魯迅的小說，我們將洞悉其中驚人的聯繫性。譬如由於幻燈事件中愚昧的中國人被砍頭示眾之刺激，在他的小說中麻木的看客與可憐的愚弱國民就不斷在小說中出現。周樹人在習醫時解剖過二十多具屍體，解剖使他知道礦工的肺被炭污染得墨黑，殘缺的嬰兒被花柳病所貽害。日後他在小說中，都在進行解剖中國人與社會，斷定其病症與死因。[21]

　　過去前往仙台訪問的中外魯迅學者，都被這個號稱森林之都、青葉之城的自然秀麗所迷惑，即使現在仙台還是一個青翠美麗又現代化的理想城市，沒有做過深入的研究，連日本人也不能了解魯迅在當年仙台經驗之複雜性，絕不是單一的幻燈事件所能涵蓋，更難於解釋其奧秘。

　　所以重新了解了使學醫的周樹人變成從事文藝創作的魯迅的原因，我們再運用仙台這一連串事件來解讀其小說，也許能找到新的意義。

六、從紹興、仙台到魯鎮：從地方性到普遍的意義之創造

　　在魯迅心中，仙台是「一個鄉間」，是「一個市鎮，並不大」。[22]許多地方使人想起滿清軍隊統治下的紹興，或是日後他所創作小說中的魯鎮。仙台是軍國主義統治之小城鎮，學習生活使他感到與舊中國如紹興舊學堂沒兩樣，因爲「只求記憶，不須思索，修習未久，腦力頓鈍」。他擔心「四年後，恐如木偶人」。才到仙台一個月，他已很不喜

20 除了這次研討會孫中田的論文，在這之前，王德威〈從頭談起〉見《小說中國》（臺北：麥田出版社，1990 年），頁 15-29，就曾從幻燈事件闡述魯迅小說中的砍頭意象的意義；又見 Leo Lee（李歐梵）*Voices From the Iron House: A Study of Lu Xun*（Bloomington: Indiana University Press, 1987），pp.17-18。

21 我在〈探索病態社會與黑暗之魂靈之旅：魯迅小說中遊記結構研究〉中，對魯迅小說的這種努力有所探討，見王潤華《魯迅小說新論》（臺北：東大圖書公司，1992 年），頁 67-88；或大陸版，上海：學林出版社，1993 年，頁 46-60。

22 前者見《吶喊・自序》，後者見《藤野先生》，同註 7，第 1 冊，頁 416 及第 2 冊，頁 302。

歡那裏的生活環境，「爾來索居仙台，又復匝月，形不吊影，彌覺無聊」[23]，原因就是因爲我上面所闡述的仙台是一個軍國主義思想化的地方。雖然物以稀爲貴，日本對他還客氣，但由於受軍國主義裏之污染，日本同學自視優越，像歐洲十九世紀的雅利安人，自視「高貴人種」，都是種族主義者：

> 惟日本同學來訪者頗不寡，此阿利安人亦懶與酬對……敢決言其思想行為不居我震旦青年之上……。[24]

魯迅抵達仙台，先在學校旁片平丁五十四號的田中旅店住了幾天，即搬到隔壁的片平丁五十二號的「佐藤屋」公寓住宿。這棟二層木房子目前還在，座落在當時宮城監獄旁邊，魯迅的生活與囚犯相似，因爲一樓的一部分房屋是經營監獄犯人的伙食的：

> 我先是住在監獄旁邊一個客店裡的，初冬已經頗冷，蚊子卻還多，後來用被蓋了全身，用衣服包了頭臉，只留兩個鼻孔出氣，……但一位先生卻以為這客店也包辦囚人的飯食，我住在那裡不相宜。[25]

再加上槍斃中國人事件，侵略中國的日本軍隊的勝利，仇視與歧視來自弱國的中國人，誣告考試作弊等原因，使我從仙台回來，深深覺悟到周樹人在這地方變成魯迅，因爲他不但解剖了人體，也剖析了社會，因而引起他對人性與社會的反思與批判。仙台環境之惡劣，群眾之盲目與無情，便是日後魯迅小說中的舊中國與人類惡劣社會的縮影。怪不得我們讀魯迅小說，既是有地方性，也有世界人類的普遍意義。它是由紹興與仙台合而爲一創造出來的世界。

如果沒有仙台的經驗之參與，單憑紹興的舊生活，魯迅小說中的

23　1904 年致蔣抑卮信，見註 7，卷 11，頁 32-322。
24　同註 23。
25　同註 7，《藤野先生》，第 2 冊，頁 303。

紹興，大概與許多同代作家一樣。其意義只停留在批判舊中國意義上，
會缺少世界性，全人類性的意義。魯迅在日本仍然對中國日思夜想，
剛到仙台一個月，他就「曼思故國」：

> 樹人到仙台後，離中國主人翁頗遙，所恨尚有怪事奇聞由新聞
> 紙以解我目。曼思故國，來日方長，載悲黑奴前車如是，彌益
> 感喟……。[26]

魯迅在仙台時，同學注意到他經常在午飯時間，到學校附近牛奶
點心店「晚翠軒」邊吃午餐邊看報，極留意中國東北進行中的日俄國
戰爭及清使館的政治活動。[27]當魯迅回到中國以後，仙台的事件還時
時影響著他的思想情感：

> 此後回到中國來，我看見那些閒看槍斃犯人的人們，他們何嘗
> 不酒醉似的喝采，── 嗚呼，無法可想，但在那時那地，我的
> 意見卻變化了。[28]

在仙台時，種族主義思想促使日本同學懷疑他考試作弊，寫匿名
信罵他，第一句是「你改悔罷」。據魯迅自己解釋，這是《聖經・新約》
裏的句子，當時日俄正為爭霸中國土地而戰，托爾斯泰（Leo Tolstol,
1828-1910）寫信譴責俄國與日本皇帝，開首便是這一句。可是魯迅回
中國後在 1918 年寫第一篇白話小說〈狂人日記〉時，又用上了，這次
是用來罵聖人的人：

> 你們可以改了，從真心改起！要曉得將來容不得吃人的人，活
> 在世上。

這裏「吃人的人」不止是中國的舊封建，「世上」也不限於中國的

26　同註 23，頁 321。
27　同註 3，〈魯迅在仙台記錄〉，頁 198-199。
28　同註 25，頁 306。

土地。[29]

七、從藤野解剖事件到魯迅小說創作中的鬼魂論

魯迅在仙台醫專的第二年修讀的解剖學，已開始實習解剖屍體。雖然，第二年只念了一個學期，據說他已解剖過二十多具屍體。解剖實習才上了一個星期，他的老師藤野感到有點意外，高興地對他說：

> 我因為聽說中國人是很敬重鬼的，所以很擔心，怕你不肯解剖屍體。現在總算放心了，沒有這回事。[30]

仙台醫專有沒有鬼的談話，在魯迅日後許多作品中，包括小說、散文、雜文，一直不斷還回響著。譬如〈祝福〉中祥林嫂問小說中的「我」：「一個人死了之後，究竟有沒有魂靈的？」[31]丸尾常喜為了魯迅作品中「鬼」的意義，寫了一本專書《魯迅「人」「鬼」之葛藤》，做了徹底的探討。靈魂依附人體活在世上，人一旦死後到了陰間，靈魂便變成鬼。丸尾的結論說，鬼象徵著中國人的國民性或民族的劣根性。所以五四時代打倒傳統被稱為打鬼，阿Q含有阿鬼之意，槍斃阿Q就是槍斃民族劣根性。[32]

魯迅一再強調寫小說和其他作品，是要畫出「國民的魂靈來」，雖然他知道這魂靈不太容易捉住：「我雖然竭力想摸索人們的魂靈，但時時總自憾有些隔膜。」[33]他的小說，我曾經從它主要遊記結構來論析，並認為探索中國社會之病態與中國國民之魂靈，是其最大的貢獻。[34]

由於魯迅讀過醫科，他甚至擁有解剖人體來斷定其症結與死因之

29 同註7，第1冊，頁431。
30 同註25，頁305。
31 同註7，第2冊，頁7。
32 丸尾常喜《魯迅「人」「鬼」之葛藤》（東京：岩波書店，1993年）。
33 《俄文譯本〈阿Q正傳〉序文》，同註7，第7冊，頁81。
34 同註21。

實際經驗，這種醫學經驗，大大影響了他的文藝理論的文字。譬如他說寫作目的是要「將舊社會的病根暴露出來，催人留心，設法加以療法」。[35]另一個文章他又說：「我的取材，多採取病態社會的不幸的人們中，意思是在揭出病苦，引起療救的注意。」[36]「病根」、「療治」、「病態」、「療救」不但屬於醫學術語也是一個醫生治病的方法與過程。關於這一點，下面再詳論。

　　日本有些學者目前肯定藤野與魯迅的「解剖事件」是象徵魯迅從傳統走向現代學術一大變化。從此他不但不相信鬼或靈魂，而且以打鬼作爲終身的職責。

八、從「幻燈事件」中演變出來的示衆材料與看客

　　周樹人在仙台醫專的「幻燈事件」，前後在三篇文章中提起，〈藤野先生〉中說是槍斃，其餘二篇《吶喊·自序》及《俄文譯本·阿Q正傳序》說是砍首。這個在仙台醫專幻燈上看見的中國愚弱國民被殺頭的事件，有些學者已注意到其重要性：日後成爲魯迅作品中的一個重要母題。[37]魯迅在《吶喊·自序》中所見的身體強壯，神情麻木的中國人被日軍砍頭示衆，在《吶喊》與《彷徨》中，經常成爲小說中的重要人物。那些作爲砍首示衆的愚弱國民，包括〈藥〉中的夏瑜，他雖然是一個革命志士，但社會上的人，包括告發他的自己的叔叔夏三爺，都是愚昧、麻木、自私、無情的人。他死後還被愚弱的國民華老栓拿去治療兒子華小栓的癆病。〈阿Q正傳〉中的阿Q固然是勤樸的勞動者，他愚昧、麻木、不覺醒，他的奴性和排外，想造反又遲疑和怯懦，終於被趙太爺誣告爲搶劫犯，慘死在革命政府的槍彈下，革命

35　《自選集·自序》，見註7，第4冊，頁455。
36　《我怎麼做起小說來》，同註7，第4冊，頁512。
37　同註20。

本該解放阿Q，阿Q本是革命之主力，卻被革命槍殺，主要就是「愚弱」，喜歡陶醉在精神勝利之中。〈示眾〉的背景在北京，中國的文化之都，北洋軍閥統治下的首都，那位被一位面黃肌瘦的巡警用繩索牽去殺頭的男子沒有姓名，他身體高大，所犯罪狀也不清楚，就莫名其妙被送去砍首。他沒姓名，因為他代表了一般中國人。

《吶喊》和《彷徨》的小說中有很多人物的死亡。[38]除了夏瑜被砍頭，阿Q被槍決，在首善之區的西城被砍首的高個子男人外，祥林嫂倒斃街頭，孔乙己挨打後傷殘致死，陳士成科舉考試失敗後發狂投湖自盡，魏連殳帶著憤恨和冷嘲吐血而終，子君懷著無限的哀怨離開人間。小栓癆病，被人血饅頭醫死了，寶兒因病夭折，順姑病亡，阿毛被狼吃掉。表面上這些人是因為無情的人殘酷迫害，疾病侵蝕或野獸襲擊，實際上他們都是被人與人之間冷酷天情與隔膜的社會所殺，是另一種砍頭槍斃的人。他們原來都是體格強壯的人，可惜都是愚弱的國民。

至於體格健全的看客，魯迅的小說中，則幾乎每篇都有。在〈示眾〉，作者似乎在指出，在北洋軍閥統治下的首都北京，所有市民都是看客，不管男女老少，一有殺頭示眾的事件，便圍了好幾圈，車伕、坐客、學生、抱著孩子的婦女，禿頭的男人，都喜看殺頭的熱鬧。〈藥〉裏那些鑑賞殺頭場面的庸眾「頸項都伸長，彷彿許多鴨，被無形的手捏住了的，向上提著」。〈阿Q正傳〉中阿Q不但是被殺頭示眾者，他也是冷漠麻木的看客，喜愛與其他閒人看殺革命黨人，而且幸災樂禍。阿Q被槍斃後，未莊的輿論都說阿Q壞，而城裏人卻不滿足，「以為槍斃並無殺頭這般好看……遊了那麼久的街，竟沒有唱一句戲」。〈孔乙己〉中咸亨酒店的掌櫃、小伙計、酒客，他們對孔乙己的不幸，百般

38　參本人所著〈五四小說人物的「狂」和「死」與反對傳統主題〉，見註21，頁27-50。

嘲笑、侮辱、欺凌，以他的傷殘爲樂事，這是另一種看客。〈祝福〉中魯家的短工、柳媽以及其他鄰人，他們自私、冷漠、把祥林嫂的傷疤傳爲笑料，〈明天〉中咸亨酒店的常客如紅鼻子老拱，藍皮阿五、王九媽都是麻木不仁，落井下石的看客。還有〈長明燈〉裏的三角臉、方頭、灰五嬸等人，也是來自幻燈的看客原型人物，他們都是麻木、自私、愚昧的愚弱國民。

　　由於幻燈事件對周樹人轉化成魯迅的重要性過分強調，而且幻燈片中殺頭與看客形成一種神話原型，以後千變萬化的出現在魯迅的小說其他作品中，因此引起一些學者如李歐梵與王德威等人的懷疑，後者說它可能出於杜撰，「本身是一件文學虛構」，並斷言「恐怕要成爲文學史上的一椿無頭公案」。[39]其實日本學者已經證實這是真實的事件。魯迅自己說過，當時是在上細菌學課上觀看幻燈片。1965 年，日本學者果然在仙台東北大學醫學院所屬的仙台醫專舊建築中一個細菌教室裏，發現十五枚幻燈片，不過沒有魯迅所說的殺頭那一枚，這一組幻燈片原有二十枚，其中編號第二、四、五、十二及十六已遺失，大概殺頭那張就在裏頭。根據 1905 年 1 月 6 日仙台的《河北新報》的廣告，被發現的幻燈片爲東京鶴淵幻燈鋪所印製，還印製好幾集有關日俄戰爭的幻燈片，根據當時報紙及刊物，魯迅所說砍頭的鏡頭，確是常常出現。[40]另外魯迅當年同班的同學也說曾觀看過魯迅所說的殺人鏡頭。[41]

九、從醫學上的解剖屍體到小說中的剖析
中國人的靈魂：尋找病根，加以治療

39　同註 20。
40　渡邊襄《魯迅與仙台》，見註 3，頁 31-35。圖片見頁 95，圖 77。
41　《魯迅仙台的記錄》，同註 3，頁 109-110，頁 143-148，頁 157 及 192-193。

我在前面說過，由於魯迅讀醫科時，有解剖人體的經驗，據說他前後解剖了二十多具屍體，發現礦工的死亡後，肺像墨一樣黑，爲炭灰所污染，而胎死腹中的胎兒，四肢殘缺不全，爲父母花柳病之毒所害。這種醫學經驗，大大影響了他的小說創作理論及其文學觀。

在《吶喊・自序》中，他承認自己前往日本仙台工醫專學醫，是要「救治像我父親似的被誤的病人的疾苦」。當他在「幻燈事件」後了解到「凡是愚弱的國民，不管體格如何壯健，只能當示眾的材料和看客，病死多少是不必以爲不幸的」。他日後談到創作小說的動機與文學功能，總是以醫生看病與治療的角度來立論。在〈我怎麼做起小說來〉，他又說：「我仍抱著十多年前的啟蒙主義」，以爲必須是「爲人生」，而且「要改良這人生……所以我的取材，多採取病態社會的不幸的人們中」，意思是在揭出痛苦，引起療救的注意。在《自選集・自序》他說：「將舊社會的病根暴露出來，催人留心，設法加以療治的希望。」在俄文譯本《阿Q正傳・序》中，他「竭力想摸索人們的魂靈」，「要畫出這樣沈默的國民的魂靈來」，「能夠寫出一個現代的我們國人的魂靈來」。[42]由此可見他的文學觀是建立在醫學的功能論上面。

我曾分析過魯迅那些具有遊記結構的小說。這些小說不管是「故鄉之旅」、「城鎮之旅」還是「街道之旅」，其旅程都是具有高度象徵性：都是探索病態社會與黑暗魂靈之旅。小說中的「我」，所回去的不管是魯鎮、平橋村還是S城，都是舊中國的一般農村的縮影，回去故鄉或其他城鎮，代表魯迅要重新認識中國農村，整個舊社會與中國人的病根。在〈故鄉〉、〈祝福〉的旅程裏，作者讓我們看見農村破落、農民愚昧、墮落的景象，也就解剖了舊社會的病態與國民的魂靈。〈在酒樓上〉和〈孤獨者〉的旅途中所遇的呂緯甫與魏連殳，二位曾一度熱心

---

42 魯迅回顧創作種種經驗與問題之文章，均收入《魯迅論創作》（上海：上海文藝出版社，1983年）。以上所引各篇，見第1輯，頁3-50。

革命的知識分子，先後向舊勢力投降。作者把中國知識分子的內心黑暗挖掘出來，讓我們看看，讓我們明白，當時的革命也救不了中國。如阿Q嚮往造反，卻被地主趙太爺誣告為搶劫犯，慘死在革命黨的槍斃下。〈藥〉所呈現的，不徹底的辛亥革命，對於封建的中國也是一帖失效的藥，就如華老栓買來革命者的血，希望救治兒子的癆病而無效。[43]

　　解讀魯迅小說時，一般學者不管有沒有覺察到魯迅的醫學救人式的小說理論，他們都清楚的發覺魯迅是在解剖舊社會或愚弱的國民，例如，當我隨手翻開《魯迅創作藝術談》這本論文集，就可隨手摘錄到以下的句子：

　　一、從對呂緯甫頹唐精神的嚴峻的剖析中，使人們看到自身的
　　　　弱點。

　　二、他的小說……著重揭發他們身上的弱點，並剖析造成這些
　　　　弱點的社會歷史根源。

　　三、魯迅的筆，宛如一把鋒銳犀利的靈魂解剖刀……。

　　四、對知識分子的靈魂深處，則著重於進行細緻精確的剖析，
　　　　把人物的心靈的複雜細微活動過程，很有層次地發掘出
　　　　來，解剖給人看。[44]

　　所以周樹人在1904年到仙台學醫，練習解剖人體，尋求死因，希望以後回到中國救治體弱病死的中國人。1906年，當他相信這些「麻木」的中國人病死多少，不必以為不幸時，他棄醫從文，離開仙台去了東京。從此周樹人雖不從醫，他還是沒有放棄解剖刀，更沒有停止解剖人，唯一不同是他以筆代刀來解剖中國人。這就是為什麼每讀魯迅的小說，都會感覺到他是在解剖人。

---

43 同註21。

44 南開大學中文系魯迅研究室編《魯迅創作藝術談》（天津：天津人民出版社，1982
　　年），頁17、112、144、151。作者個別為田本相、劉正強及劉家鳴。

十、解剖麻木的中國人：魯迅小說的母題與民族寓言

迅每次回顧創作之路時，都從習醫開始，尤其喜歡以解剖屍體尋找病根與在課上看見幻燈片裏的中國愚弱國民作爲出發點，因爲這不但說明他的「改造民族靈魂」的文學觀，而且說明他的小說作品中的母題：強壯體格但精神麻木的作爲示眾與看客的中國人之悲哀。[45]美國後現代主義理論大師詹明信（Fredric Jameson）讀了魯迅的小說，也說他雖然棄醫從文，他還是保留作爲診斷學家（diagnostician）與治病醫生（physician）的工作使命。詹明信也認識到魯迅小說的結構是以第三世界文學作品中常見的民族寓言（national allegory）來呈現。儘管小說是敘述個人的遭遇與命運，他與這個民族國家的政治文化息息相關。[46]

中國現代文學第一代的作家包括魯迅在內，深受嚴復在 1896 年所譯赫胥黎（Thomas Huxley, 1825-1895）的《天演論》（*Evolution and Ethics*, 1894）[47]中物競天擇說的影響。適者生存，強者勝、弱者敗的進化論思想，促使他們思考愚弱的中華民族被淘汰的危險，因此把他們從生活中感受到的民族危機感提高到最高度。「日本維新是大半發端於西方醫學」的認識促使周樹人去日本仙台醫專讀醫科，在那裏他學會如何診斷病因，可是當他了解到「改變精神」比身體健康重要，便棄醫從文，從事醫治靈魂的文學工作。因此以周樹人的仙台學醫經驗來解讀魯迅的小說及其文學觀，便能理解他解剖與醫治人類靈魂的理論與作品。

---

45 錢理群等《中國現代文學三十年》（上海：上海文藝出版社，1987 年），頁 1-8。

46 Fredric Jameson, "World Literature in the Era of Multinational Capitalism", in Clayton Koelb and Virgil Lokke（eds），*The Current in Criticism*（West Lafayette: Purdue University Press, 1987），pp.139-158.

47 嚴幾道（嚴復）述、赫胥黎著《天演論》（上海：富文書局，1901 年）。

從反殖民到殖民者：魯迅與新馬後殖民文學

一、從魯迅榮獲百年小說冠軍談起：世界性的魯迅神話

　　今年（1999）6 月，在二十世紀只剩下最後二百天的時候，《亞洲周刊》編輯部與十四位來自全球各地的華人學者作家，聯合評選出《二十世紀中文小說一百強》。魯迅的《吶喊》奪得自清末百年來，在全球華文作家中最重要的一百部小說的冠軍。魯迅的第二部小說集《彷徨》也登上第十二名的位置。生於 1881 年，卒於 1936 年，逝世六十三年後的魯迅，評選人都毫無爭議的推崇魯迅，給他的小說投下高票，一再肯定魯迅的重要性。[1]

　　魯迅為何是世紀冠軍？當我們正要跨進二十一世紀時，這是值得令人思考的世界華文文學的共同性問題。百年來的華文文學經典作品，正如《二十世紀中文小說一百強》排行榜的作品所顯示，以三、四十年代寫實的作品為主導力量。所以魯迅、沈從文、老舍、錢鍾書、茅盾、巴金、蕭紅七人的代表作高居前十名榜首。百年來的小說，儘管隨文學潮流、美學經驗變化無窮，從中國大陸、香港、臺灣到東南亞及歐美各地區，不論作者住在第一世界還是第三世界，獨立自主還是殖民地的國家地區，處處還是展現，清末逐漸形成譴責小說的社會批評與憂患意識，魯迅及其同代人所推展的現代文學作品的人文啟蒙

---

1 《百年的〈吶喊〉,〈傳奇〉的世紀》及其他報導，《亞洲週刊》，1999 年 6 月 14 日 -6 月 20 日，頁 32-45。

精神，知識分子感時憂國的情懷與歷史使命感、國族的寓意主題。[2]

　　魯迅是中國採用西式文體寫小說的第一人，幾乎可以說中國現代小說在魯迅手中開始，在魯迅手種成熟。魯迅最早受到自由主義派的作家學者如胡適、陳西瀅的肯定。在 1929 年他開始向左派靠攏之前，左派批評家對他大力攻擊。可是在他最後的六年裏，成為左派文藝界的文化偶像。1936 年逝世後，在毛澤東及中國共產黨機器的吹捧下，產生了魯迅神話。毛澤東在 1940 年寫的〈新民主主義論〉，用盡了一切偉大的詞彙，塑造了他的偉大形象，於是魯迅神話便開始從中國大陸流傳到世界各地有中華文化的地方：[3]

> 在「五四」以後，中國產生了完全嶄新的文化生力軍，這就是中國共產黨人所領導的共產主義的文化思想，即共產主義的宇宙和社會革命論。……而魯迅，就是這個文化新軍的最偉大和最英勇的旗手。魯迅是中國文化革命的主將，他不但是偉大的文學家，而且是偉大的思想家和偉大的革命家。魯迅的骨頭是最硬的，他沒有絲毫的奴顏和媚骨，這是殖民地半殖民地人民最可寶貴的性格。魯迅是在文化戰線上，代表全民族的大多數，向著敵人衝鋒陷陣的最正確、最勇敢、最堅決、最忠實、最熱忱的空前的民族英雄。魯迅的方向，就是中華民族新文化的方向。[4]

　　毛澤東不但總結左右派文化界所肯定的魯迅，還加以神化，因此魯迅的偉大之處很多：（一）魯迅是共產主義的文化思想的偉大和最英

2　參考章海陵〈魯迅為何是世紀冠軍〉及〈沈重時代中的緊迫感〉，見《亞洲週刊》，同前註，頁 35；頁 38-39。

3　見夏志清《中國現代小說史》（臺北：傳記文學出版社，1979 年），頁 63-64；原著見 C. T. Hsia, *A History of Modern Chinese Fiction* (New Heaven, conn.: Yale University Press)，頁 28-29。

4　毛澤東《毛澤東選集》（北京：人民文學出版社，1952 年），第 2 卷，頁 668-669。

勇的旗手；（二）魯迅是中國文化革命的主將；（三）魯迅是偉大的文
學家；（三）魯迅是偉大的思想家和偉大的革命家；（五）魯迅是最具
有反殖民主義的性格與勇氣。

　　毛澤東和中國共產黨機器所製造的魯迅神話，在走進廿一世紀的
今天，其效用已很過時，甚至產生厭倦與反感，但魯迅的神化，至今
還是歷久不衰，一百強中的魯迅，說明全球華人集體閱讀與寫作經驗，
文化美學意識，還是受著魯迅神話的支配，因為魯迅神話已形成中國
文化霸權或優勢文化的一個重要部分。

　　本文嘗試以新加坡與馬來亞（Malaya）（1957 年獨立後改稱馬來
西亞 Malaysia），在第二次世界大戰前後的魯迅經驗，來解讀魯迅神話
在新馬。由於新馬是英國殖民，曾受日本占領及統治三年零八個月，
在戰後，又遭受以華人為主的馬來語共產黨與英國殖民政府爭奪主權
的戰爭，新馬當年的華人移民，因為要反殖民主義，反帝國主義侵略，
力圖以民族主義為基礎來抵抗殖民文化，結果中國文化所建立的威
力，最後對落地生根的華人來說，也變成一種殖民的霸權文化。因此
新馬後殖民文學的文化霸權，成為解讀這問題極重要的一把鎖匙。

二、領導左翼聯盟之後：魯迅打著 左派與革命的旗幟登陸新馬

　　魯迅在二十年代的新馬文壇，雖然已是知名作家，但他的知名度
與地位並沒有特別重要，新馬逐漸抬頭的左派作家，反而嫌他思想不
夠前衛。[5]因為從 1923 前後到 1928 年，無產階級與革命文學日益成長，
至 1928 年太陽社創辦的《太陽》月刊，創造社的《創造月刊》，陸續
創刊，共同推動無產階級革命文學。這時候，郭沫若就比魯迅有號召

---

5 參考章翰（韓山元）《魯迅與馬華新文學》（新加坡：風華出版社，1977 年），頁 4-5。

力，因爲他們宣告第一個十年的文學革命已結束，現在已進入第二個十年的革命文學。後期的創造社與太陽社攻擊魯迅、茅盾、郁達夫，向五四時期已成名的作家開刀。[6]他們否定五四新文學傳統之論，也引起了新馬左傾作家的迴響。譬如在 1930 年，《星洲日報》副刊上就有一位署名陵的作者對魯迅不夠前進而失望：

> 我覺得十餘年來，中國的文壇上，還只見幾個很熟悉的人，把持著首席。魯迅、郁達夫一類的老作家，還沒有失去了青年們信仰的重心。這簡直是十年來中國的文藝，絕對沒有能向前一步的鐵證。本來，像他們那樣過重鄉土風味的作家，接承十九世紀左拉自然主義餘緒的肉感派的東西，那裡能捲起文藝狂風……。[7]

另一位悠悠的作者也附和指責魯迅落後：

> 事實上很是明顯，魯迅不是普羅文藝的作家，他與普羅文藝是站在敵對地位的。是的，魯迅過去的作品很有一點底價值，但過去畢竟成了過去，過去的文藝只有適合過去的社會，當然不適合於現在的社會了。現在所需要的是普羅文藝，魯迅既不是普羅文藝的作家，我們只當他是博物院的陳列品。[8]

正如章翰（韓山元）所說：「把魯迅當作一位文藝導師與左翼文藝的領導人的人，在 1930 年以前，畢竟是少之又少。」[9]新馬對中國文壇的反應，迅速敏感。1927 至 1930 年間，新馬的無產階級革命文學

---

6 見錢理群、溫儒敏、吳福輝《中國現代文學三十年（修訂本）》（北京：北京大學出版社，1998 年），頁 191-196。

7 陵〈文藝的方向〉，《星洲日報·野苑》（副刊），1930 年 3 月 19 日，又見方修編《馬華新文學大系》（新加坡：世界書局，1971-1972 年），第 1 冊，頁 69-70。

8 悠悠〈關於文藝的方向〉，《星洲日報·野苑》，1930 年 5 月 14 日，又見方修編《馬華新文學大系》，同註 7，頁 71-74。

9 同前註 5，頁 4-5。

已取得主流的趨勢，其影響是來自創造社與太陽社的無產階級革命文學理論。上面提到的作者就是當時極力推動這運動的重要分子，由於無產階級及革命等字眼，不爲英國殖民政府所容忍，因此採用「新興文學」[10]，而他們言論完全是《太陽》社和創造社的批評的迴響，錢杏村就認爲魯迅的阿Q時代已死去，沒有現代意味。[11]另一位《星洲日報》副刊上發表的滔滔的文章，說得更直接，他們要的文學是《文化評判》刊登的作品：

> 《阿Q正傳》可是表現著辛亥革命時期代表無抵抗的人生。《沉淪》、《塔》等類作品顯示出五四以後的浪漫主義的色彩。在《文化批評》等刊物上發表的或和它類似的作品，是五四以後的，或者較確切點說，是「轉變」以後的東西……。[12]

苗秀，一位在戰前已是很活躍的文學青年說：

> 中國新文學的每個階段的文藝思潮，中國文壇曆年來提出的種種口號，都對馬 華文藝發揮著巨大的指導作用，都由馬華文藝寫作人毫無保留地全部接受下來。例如1928年後中國創造社及太陽社所提倡的「普羅文學運動」，首先就獲得許傑主編的吉隆坡益群報文藝副刊《枯島》響應，接著鄭文通主編的南洋商報版位發刊的《曼陀羅》，新加坡叻報副刊《椰林》等刊物也紛紛響應，在馬華文壇掀起一陣相當激烈的新興文學熱潮，一時間普羅文學作品的寫作，蔚爲風氣。……[13]

在1929年9月前後，中國共產黨指示創造社、太陽社停止攻擊魯

---

10 魯迅也用這名詞，如〈現代新興文學的諸問題·小引〉，《魯迅全集》（北京：人民文學出版社，1981年），第10卷，頁292。
11 同前註6，頁194。
12 同前註7，頁80-81。
13 苗秀〈導論〉，見《新馬華文文學大系》，（新加坡：教育出版社，1971-1975年），第1集（理論），頁7。

迅，讓他們同魯迅以及其他革命的同路人聯合起來，成立統一的革命
文學組織，對抗國民黨的文化攻勢，特別對革命文學、無產階級文學
的扼殺。這樣歷時二年的論爭便停止。1930年3月2日在上海成立中
國左翼作家聯盟，沈端先、馮乃超、錢杏村、田漢、鄭伯奇、洪靈菲
七人爲常務委員。在大會上，魯迅發表〈對於左翼作家聯盟的意見〉
的重要說話。魯迅在後來幾年的領導地位[14]，很快便在新馬產生新的
形象：他不只是新文學運動第一個十年的重要作家，更重要的是，他
是反資產階級、左派的、屬於無產階級的革命文學的作家。

　　魯迅在新馬1930年以後的聲望，主要不是依靠對他的文學的閱讀
所產生的文學影響，而是歸功於移居新馬的受左派影響的中國作家與
文化人所替他做的非文學性宣傳。中國作家在1927年北伐失敗，國民
黨清黨期間，許多知識分子南渡新馬。1937年中國抗戰爆發到1942
年新馬淪陷日軍手中，又造成不少作家與文化人前來避難或宣傳抗
日。第三個時期是1945年日本投降之後，中國國內發生國共內亂的時
候。[15]如果只以在南來之前，就已成名的中國作家，這三個時期的南
下作家就有不少：

> 洪靈菲、老舍、艾蕪、吳天（葉尼）、許傑（1927-1937）、郁達
> 夫、胡愈之、高雲覽、沈茲九、楊騷、王任叔（巴人）、金山、
> 王紀元、汪金丁、陳殘雲、王瑩、馬寧（1937-1941）、杜運燮、
> 岳野、夏衍（1945-1948）。[16]

但是如果把「中國作家」一詞包含不只是著名的作家，還包括文

---

14 同前註6，頁194。關於魯迅與左聯的真正關係，參考夏濟安的論文：Hsia Tsi-an,
　"Lu Hsun and the Dissolution of the League of Leftist Writers", *The Gate of
　Darkness*（Seattle: University of Washington Press, 1968），pp.101-145。

15 參考林萬菁《中國作家在新加坡及其影響（1927-1948）》（新加坡：萬裏書局，1994
　年修訂本），頁1-22。

16 關於這些作家在新加坡及其影響，參考前註15林萬菁的著作。

化人、或南來以後才成名，甚至成爲本地作家，則多不勝數了，所以
趙戎及其他學者也把丘家珍、陳如舊、白寒、丘康（張天白）、林參天、
絮絮、米軍、李汝琳、王哥空、李潤湖、上官豸（韋暈）都看作中國
南來作家。[17]

　　在這些南下的中國作家中，尤其一些左派文藝青年如張天白（丘
康），往往成爲把魯迅神話移植新馬的大功臣。[18]他甚至高喊「魯迅先
生是中國文壇文學之父」的口號。[19]這些來自中國的作家及文化人宣
揚魯迅的文章，有些收錄在《馬華新文學大系》的第一、二（理論批
評）及十集（出版史料）。[20]

三、紀念魯迅逝世活動：魯迅神話在新馬的誕生

　　魯迅在 1936 年 10 月 19 日在上海逝世。《南洋商報》當天收到從
上海拍來的電報，第二天便在第二版發布一則新聞，標題是〈魯迅病
重逝世，享壽五十六歲，因寫作過度所致〉。新聞內容也很簡短平實：

　　（上海電）以《阿 Q 正傳》而名馳中外之中國名作家魯迅（周
　　樹人），已於昨晨在上海醫院病逝，享壽五十六歲，他曾患肺病
　　多月，迨至本月十七日因寫作過度，病況加劇一蹶不起也。[21]

---

17 趙戎《現階段的馬華文學運動》，見同註 13，頁 89-104；苗秀《馬華文學史話》（新
　　加坡：青年書局，1963 年），頁 408-109；方修〈中國文學對馬華文學的影響〉，《新
　　馬文學史論集》（香港：三聯書店，1986 年），頁 38-43。

18 章翰（韓山元）的論文〈張天白論魯迅〉認爲張天白（常用馬達、丘康、太陽等筆
　　名）在三十年代，爲文崇揚魯迅最多，見同前註 5，頁 50-56。張天白論魯迅的文
　　章，分別收集在方修主編《張天白作品選》（新加坡：上海書局，1979 年），有二
　　篇附錄在《魯迅與馬華新文學》，同前註 5；張天白其他文章可見《新馬新文學大
　　系》，第一及二集。

19 丘康《七七抗戰後的馬華文壇》，同前註 5，頁 11；又見《馬華新文學大系》，第 1
　　集，頁 505。

20 同前註 7。

21 章翰《魯迅逝世在馬華文藝界的反應》，同前註 5，頁 17-35。魯迅病逝寓所，不是

　　《星洲日報》也在 10 月 20 日在第一版上報導魯迅的逝世，標題是〈我國名作家魯迅在滬逝世，因在上星期著述過勞，以痼疾加劇遂告不治〉。因內容是上海拍來的電報，內容平實簡要：

> （上海）名作家周樹人（別署魯迅）已於昨拾九日上午在滬寓逝世。遺下一母一妻及一子，周氏乃因在上星期內著述過勞，致、痼疾加劇辛告不治。[22]

　　我想新馬文化界對來自上海的電訊，一定非常不滿意，因此新馬本地報紙在三天左右，快速的作出了強烈的反應，各報不斷發表推崇魯迅的文章，而且都推出《魯迅紀念專號》，被認為是新馬文化界追悼一位作家最隆重、最莊嚴的一次，也是空前絕後的一次。1932 年 10 月 19 日舉行的魯迅逝世一周年紀念，居然有二十五個團體參加。章翰在〈魯迅逝世在馬華文藝界的反應〉及〈馬華文化界兩次盛大的魯迅紀念活動〉二文中詳細分析了這些追悼魯迅逝世的文章。[23]當時新馬文化人對魯迅的推崇，特別強調魯迅的戰鬥精神，民族英雄形象，年青人的導師、抗日救亡的英雄。從下面常出現的頌詞，可了解當時左派文化人所要塑造的魯迅英雄形象及其目的：

1. 一員英勇的戰士，一位優良的導師。（劉郎）
2. 這位為著祖國爭取自由，為著世界爭取和平的巨人，……他曾衝破四周的黑暗勢力；他為中國文化開闢了光明的道路；他領導了現階段的抗日救亡的文化陣線……在抗敵救亡的文化陣線裡指揮作戰……。（曙明）
3. 魯迅先生是一個偉大的戰士……。（陳培青）
4. 偉大的人群的導師。（辛辛）

醫院，這是誤傳。
22 同前註，頁 20。
23 同前註 5，頁 11-35；頁 44-49。

5. 新時代戰士的奮鬥精神……肩擔著人生正確的任務。—— 以魯迅先生為榜樣。(紫鳳)

6. 魯迅先生可以說是真正的民族文藝家，普羅文藝英雄了。(二克)

7. 魯迅不但是中國新文學之父，而且是一個使我們可敬畏的「嚴父」。(陳祖山)

8. 我們要紀念我們英勇的導師。(俠魂)

從戰士、巨人、導師、嚴父，甚至「新文學之父」，都是政治化以後盲目的吹捧，其目的不外是製造一個萬人崇拜的神像。

1927 年，因為中國大陸國民黨清黨，新馬左派文化人走奔南洋，而新馬的國民黨也清黨。這些新馬左翼分子在中國共產黨派來的代表的協助下，成立了以新加坡為大本營的南洋共產黨。1930 年南洋共產黨解散，成立以新馬為基地的馬來亞共產黨。到了 1936 年，馬共活躍起來，到處煽動工潮，更滲透或控制主要報紙媒體、文化機構，已開始敢向英國政府挑戰。[24]共產黨在新馬殖民社會裏，為了塑造一個代表左翼人士的崇拜偶像，他們採用中國的模式，拿出一個文學家來作為膜拜的對象。這樣這個英雄才能被英國殖民主義政府接受。所以魯迅是一個很理想的偶像，他變成一把旗幟、一個徽章、一個神話、一種宗教儀式，成為左派或共產黨的宣傳工具。

魯迅在 1936 逝世時，正是馬來亞共產黨開始顯示與擴大其群眾力量的時候，而新馬年青人，多數只有小學或初中教育程度，所以魯迅神話便在少數南來中國文化人的移植下，流傳在新馬華人心中。

四、戰後的魯迅：反帝國主義反殖民主義的戰鬥精神

---

24 崔貴強〈國共內戰衝擊下的華人社會〉及〈戰後初期馬共的國家認同（1945-1948）〉，見《新馬華人國家認同的轉向（1945-1959）》（新加坡：南洋學會，1990 年），頁 98-152；頁 206-222。

1945 年日本軍隊投降，英國軍隊又重新占領新馬，恢複其殖民統治權。在 1941 至 1945 年日軍侵略新馬前後曾一度與英軍攜手聯合抗日的馬共，從 1946 年開始，公開提出打倒英殖民政府，建立一個「馬來亞民主共和國」。不過英軍政府（British Military Administration）初期，採取言論、出版與結社自由的政策，因此造成戰後馬共言論報章蓬勃發展。[25] 日軍占領時期完全消失的魯迅，又重新出現，而且爲了推展新的政治社會運動，左派言論特別強調與發揮魯迅徹底的反帝國主義、反殖民主義的精神。所以當時左派名報人張楚琨的言論很具代表性：

> 學習魯迅並不僅是學習魯迅先生的行文措詞造句，主要的是學習魯迅先生那種潑辣的英勇的戰鬥精神。[26]

幾乎所有在戰後推崇魯迅的文章，都重複表揚魯迅的戰鬥精神。譬如高揚（流冰）也說：「我們現在需要的正是魯迅先生一樣的戰鬥精神。」[27] 因爲在戰後，馬來亞共產黨除了以魯迅來左右群眾的思想行爲，更進一步用他來煽動群眾，以實際行動來與英國殖民主義與資本主義戰鬥。最明顯的轉變，便是在 1941 年之前及 1945 年戰後的魯迅紀念活動，不再留停在報章雜誌的文字上，而把魯迅帶上街頭。在 1947 年 10 月，新加坡紀念魯迅十一周年逝世的紀念活動，除了出版紀念特刊，更重要的是舉行擁有巨大群眾的紀念會及文藝晚會。主辦單位更不限於文藝及文化團體，連海員聯合會、職工總會、婦女聯合會參與大搞特搞這類原來只是紀念文學家魯迅逝世紀念會，而且他已逝世十幾年了。來自中國的左派作家胡愈之、汪金丁都受邀說話，這也說明魯迅神話是由這些僑居的中國親共文人所移植到新馬的。請看這篇報

---

25 崔貴強〈戰後初期馬共的國家認同（1945-1948）〉，同前註，頁 210-212。
26 張楚琨〈讀了鬱達夫的幾個問題‧附言〉，見《馬華新文學大系》，第 2 集，頁 449-451。
27 高揚（流冰）〈我們對你卻仍覺失望〉，《馬華新文學大系》，第 2 集，頁 460-463。

導：

> 一九四七年十月十九日，星洲各界代表在小坡余街的海員聯合
> 會舉行了隆重而熱烈的魯迅逝世十一周年紀念大會。出席的人
> 有幾百名，大會主席是當時著名作家金丁。在大會上講話的有
> 著名政論家胡愈之、文化工作者張楚琨與吳昆華、職工總會代
> 表謝儀、婦女聯合會代表伍亞雪及戰劇界人士楊嘉、教育界人
> 士薛永黍等。胡愈之的講話強調：「魯迅不僅是中國翻身的導
> 師，而在整個亞洲亦然，他永遠代表被壓迫人民說話，對民族
> 問題（的主張）是一切平等，教人不要做奴隸。」職工總會的
> 代表指出：魯迅也教育了勞苦工人，他呼籲大家以實際的行動
> 紀念魯迅。婦聯代表強調必須面對馬來亞的現實。（根據一九
> 四七年十月二十日《星洲日報》的報導）[28]

這一天晚上七時，在大世界遊藝場舉行的「紀念魯迅文藝晚會」，表演的節目有十五個之多，歌、舞、話劇都有。二十一日同樣的時間與地點，又有同樣的晚會。這是馬華文化藝術界搞的第一次紀念魯迅的盛大演出。

像這類動員廣大群眾的魯迅紀念會，在 1937 年就辦過一次，共有二十五個文化/學校/工人團體參加。[29]這些活動成功的把魯迅崇拜轉變成以新馬為重心的戰鬥精神，要利用魯迅的神話來實現本地的左派，甚至共產黨的政治目標：推翻英殖民地，建立馬來共和國服務。

---

28 馬華文化界兩次盛大的魯迅紀念活動〉，同前註 5，頁 47-49。

29 同前註，頁 44-47。章翰曾借我一個小本子《偉大的文學家·思想家》，沒作者，只印上表演藝術出版社，1969 年 10 月 19 日出版，共 20 頁。這是提供給各種左派藝術團體、學校、工會中的學習小組學習的手冊。在城市、鄉村或森林中的馬共遊擊隊，都以這方式學習魯迅思想。我在馬來亞讀中學時，也曾參加學習小組讀這類全是歌頌魯迅偉大的小冊子。

五、魯迅從反殖民英雄變成殖民霸權文化

今天世界上有四分之三的人口曾受過殖民主義統治，其生活、思想、文化都受到改造與壓扁。這種殖民主義的影響，深入文學作品，便產生所謂後殖民文學。英國軍官萊佛士（Stamford Raffles）在 1819年 1 月 25 日在新加坡河口登陸後，新馬便淪為英國殖民地。馬來亞在1958 年獨立，新加坡拖延到 1965 年才擺脫殖民統治。新馬就像其他曾受英國統治的國家如印度、巴基斯坦，從殖民時期一直到今天，雖然帝國統治已遠去，經濟、政治、文化上的殖民主義，仍然繼續存在，話語被控制著，歷史、文化與民族思想已被淡化，當他們審思本土文化時，往往還不自覺的被殖民主義思想套住。「後殖民」一詞被用來涵蓋一切受帝國霸權文化侵蝕的文化。新馬的文學便是典型的後殖民文學。[30]

當我們討論後殖民文學時，注意力都落在以前被異族入侵的被侵略的殖民地（the invaded colonies），如印度，較少思考同族、同文化、同語言的移民者殖民地（settler colonies），像美國、澳大利亞、紐西蘭的白人便是另一種殖民地。美國、澳大利亞、紐西蘭的白人作家也在英國霸權文化與本土文化衝突中建構其本土性（indigeneity），創造既有獨立性又有自己特殊性的另一種文學傳統。[31]在這些殖民地中，

---

30 Bill Ashcroft,et al, *The Empire Writes Back: Theory and Practice in Post-Colonical Literatures*（London: Routledge, 1989），pp.1-11，中譯本見劉自荃譯《逆寫帝國：後殖民文學的理論與實踐》（臺北：駱駝出版社，1998 年），頁 1-7。

31 31 同前註，英文本，頁 133-136；中文本，頁 144-156。

32 同前註，英文本，頁 6-7；中文本，頁 7-8。

33 同前註，英文本，頁 133-139；中文本，頁 144-157。我曾討論新加坡作家受了兩種不同文化霸權影響下產生的二種不同的後殖民文學文本，見王潤華〈魚尾獅與橡膠樹：新加坡後殖民文學解讀〉，1998 年在美國加州大學（UCSB）舉行世華文學的研討會論文，共 20 頁。

英國的經典著作被大力推崇，結果被當成文學理念、品味、價值的最高標準。這些從英國文學得出的文學概念被殖民者當作放之四海而皆準的模式與典範，統治著殖民地的文化產品。這種文化霸權（cultural hegemony）通過它所設立的經典作家及其作品的典範，從殖民時期到今天，繼續影響著本土文學。魯迅便是這樣的一種霸權文化。[32]

　　新馬的華文文學，作為一種後殖民文學，它具有入侵殖民地與移民殖民地的兩種後殖民文學的特性。在新馬，雖然政治、社會結構都是英國殖民文化的強迫性留下的遺產或孽種，但是在文學上，同樣是

---

34 張天白論魯迅的文章，目前收錄於《張天白作品選》、《魯迅與馬華新文藝》及《馬華新文學大系》等書中。

35 見《馬華新文學大系》，第 1 集，頁 505-506。

36 歐清池《方修及其作品研究》（新加坡國立大學博士論文，1997 年），頁 649。書後有方修著作編輯書目。

37 參考方修《避席集》（新加坡：文藝出版社，1960 年）中〈亦談雜文〉、〈魯迅和青年〉、〈魯迅為什麼被稱為聖人？〉，頁 37-44；頁 67-71；頁 77-81。

38 同前註 5，頁 6 及 11。

39 章翰《文藝學習與文藝評論》（新加坡：萬裏文化企業公司，1973 年）。

40 同前註 5，頁 1-2。

41 同前註，頁 1。

42 我曾從不同角度討論過這問題，有關馬華文學之獨立，見王潤華〈從中國文學傳統到本土文學傳統〉論文，收入《從新馬文學到世界華文文學》（新加坡：潮洲八邑會館，1994 年），頁 3-33；有關報紙副刊曾是中國作家之殖民地與本土新馬華文作家的獨立鬥爭戰場，見〈從戰後新馬華文報紙副刊看華文文學之發展〉，《世界中文報紙副刊學綜論》（臺北：文建會，1997 年），頁 494-505。

43 同前註 30，英文本，頁 6-7；中文本，頁 7-8。

44 趙戎《論馬華作家與作品》（新加坡：青年書局，1967 年），頁 3、9 及 17。

45 方修《新馬文學史論集》，頁 41。

46 同前註，頁 355。

47 方北方《馬華文學及其他》（香港：三聯書店，1987 年），頁 5。

48 高潮〈魯迅與馬華新文學〉，《憶農廬雜文》（香港：中流出版社，1973 年），頁 67-69。

49 同前註，頁 69。

50 同前註 30，英文本，頁 38-115；中文本，頁 41-125。

32 同前註，英文本，頁 6-7；中文本，頁 7-8。

華人，卻由於受到英國文化霸權與中國文化霸權之不同模式與典範的
統治與控制，卻產生二種截然不同的後殖民文學與文化。一種像侵略
殖民地如印度的以英文書寫的後殖民文學，另一種像澳大利亞、紐西
蘭的移民殖民地的以華文書寫的後殖民文學。[33]

　　魯迅在新馬，由於被過度推崇，最後也被尊為放之四海皆準的中
國文學的最高典範，一直影響著新馬的文學產品。從上述的論析中，
我們認識到左派文化人，通過文學、文化、政治、社會、群眾運動，
魯迅已被塑造成左派文化人、年青人與群眾的導師、反封建、反殖民、
反帝國、資本主義的偉大英雄，而負責發揚魯迅的偉大性的人，都是
來自中國的左派文人，像胡愈之、汪金丁、吳天、許傑、巴人、杜運
燮，及其他著名作家，都大力建構魯迅的神化形象。但還有更多的文
化人，名氣不大，他們更全心更力去發揮魯迅的影響力。我前面提過
的張天白就是最好的例子。他在三十年代南下新馬，歷任中學教師與
報副刊編輯。戰後回返中國。在第二次世界大戰之前，他除了自己推
崇魯迅備至，寫出很多魯迅風的雜文，更以行動來捍衛與宣傳魯迅精
神[34]，他放肆的吹捧魯迅為「偉大的民族英雄」與「魯迅先生是中國
文壇文學之父」。[35]

　　從戰前到戰後，隔一、二十年，新馬都曾出現捍衛與宣傳魯迅偉
大形象的作家或文化人。張天白代表三、四十年代的發言人，到了五、
六十年代，方修（1921-）便是最虔誠勇猛的魯迅的推崇者。他論述新

---

33 同前註，英文本，頁 133-139；中文本，頁 144-157。我曾討論新加坡作家受了兩
　　種不同文化霸權影響下產生的二種不同的後殖民文學文本，見王潤華〈魚尾獅與橡
　　膠樹：新加坡後殖民文學解讀〉，1998 年在美國加州大學（UCSB）舉行世華文學
　　的研討會論文，共 20 頁。

34 張天白論魯迅的文章，目前收錄於《張天白作品選》、《魯迅與馬華新文藝》及《馬
　　華新文學大系》等書中。

35 見《馬華新文學大系》，第 1 集，頁 505-506。

馬華文文學的著作很多[36]，其論斷問題，多從魯迅的思想出發，但他在 1955 至 1956 年間寫的魯迅式的雜感文集《避席集》，最能表現他對魯迅精神的推崇與魯迅神話的捍衛。他除了論述文學問題總要依據魯迅的言論，如闡述雜文的定義，他也因爲別人懷疑或不能接受稱頌魯迅爲「青年導師」或「新中國的聖人」而想盡辦法爲魯迅辯護，最後不惜引用毛澤東《新民主主義論》的吹捧魯迅的話作爲論證魯迅就是「具有最高的道德品質的人」。[37]這種宗教性的崇高信仰，正說明魯迅爲什麼在跨入二十一世紀前的二百天，魯迅還當選一百強之首。

因爲魯迅是「具有最高的道德品質」的「聖人」，所以他能產生一種道德宗教式的精神力量，每個人要按照他的教導辦事，照魯迅的話來分析問題，加強宗教的論證。章翰（韓山元）說：

> 把魯迅當作導師，在寫作時不時引用魯迅的話以加強自己的論據，或以魯迅的話作為分析問題的指針。馬華文藝作者在寫作時引用魯迅的話的現象也相當普遍，這不是為了趨時，而是表示大家要按魯迅先生的教導辦事。[38]

韓山元出生於馬來亞，在魯迅的文化霸權之影響下長大，而且成爲一個作家，我認爲他代表新馬最後一個最虔誠的魯迅信徒，或是最後一代之中最崇拜魯迅的信徒。如果方修代表五、六十年代新馬推崇與發揚魯迅精神的代言人，韓山元則代表七十年代，因爲他的兩本代表作《魯迅與馬華新文藝》與《文藝學習與文藝評論》[39]，最能說明魯迅霸權文化之力量：魯迅是所有新馬各門各類文藝工作者（從文學

---

36 歐清池《方修及其作品研究》（新加坡國立大學博士論文，1997 年），頁 649。書後有方修著作編輯書目。
37 參考方修《避席集》（新加坡：文藝出版社，1960 年）中〈亦談雜文〉、〈魯迅和青年〉、〈魯迅爲什麼被稱爲聖人？〉，頁 37-44；頁 67-71；頁 77-81。
38 同前註 5，頁 6 及 11。
39 章翰《文藝學習與文藝評論》（新加坡：萬裏文化企業公司，1973 年）。

到視覺及表演藝術）、知識分子、工農兵學習的「光輝典範」，更是各種鬥爭（如反殖民、反封建、反資本帝國主義、爭取民主自由）的「銳利思想武器」，因此「向魯迅學習」，「不僅是文藝工作者的口號，而且也是整個民眾運動的口號」。[40]韓山元下面這些話是他本人心靈歷程中的肺腑之言：

> 魯迅是對馬華文藝影響最大、最深、最廣的中國現代文學家。作為一位偉大的革命家、思想家，魯迅對於馬華文藝的影響，不僅是文藝創作，而且也遍及文藝路線、文藝工作者的世界觀的改造等各個方面。不僅是馬華文學工作者深受魯迅的影響，就是馬華的美術、戲劇、音樂工作者，長期以來也深受魯迅的影響。不僅是在文學藝術領域，就是在星馬社會運動的各條戰線，魯迅的影響也是巨大和深遠的。……魯迅一直是本地文藝工作者、知識份子學習的光輝典範。我們找不到第二個中國作家，在馬來亞享有像魯迅那樣崇高的威信。魯迅的著作，充滿了反帝反殖反封建精神，……對於進行反殖反封建的馬來亞人民是極大的鼓舞和啟發，是馬來亞人民爭取民主與自由的銳利思想武器。[41]

韓山元（章翰）的《文藝學習與文藝評論》，共收二十篇，從第一篇〈認真學習語言〉開始，中間有〈改造自己，改造世界〉、〈向魯迅學寫作〉，到最後一篇，全是他自己所說「按魯迅先生的教導辦事」。無論是學語言、爲人做事、思想，或探討如何搞表演藝術活動，都需向魯迅學習。從韓山元的這個例子，令人心服口服的說明殖民的霸權文化，即使在殖民主義遠去後，其文化霸權所發揮的影響力，還是強大無比。韓山元本地出生，其家族早已落地生根，但中國的優勢文化，

---

40 同前註 5，頁 1-2。
41 同前註，頁 1。

還是抵制住本土文化之成長。[42]

六、魯迅的經典傳統：文學品味與價值的試金石

我在上面說過，在移民殖民地如澳洲、紐西蘭，英國及歐洲的經典作家及作品，依然成為文學品味與價值的試金石，繼續有威力的支配著大部分後殖民世界的文學文化生產。這種文學或文化霸權所以能維持，主要是殖民文學觀念的建立，只有符合英國或歐洲中心的評價標準（Eurocentric standards of judgement）的作家與作品，才能被承認其重要性，要不然就不被接受。[43]魯迅作為一個經典作家，就被人建立起這樣的一種文學霸權。魯迅本來被人從中國殖植過來，是要學他反殖民、反舊文化，徹底革命，可是最終為了拿出民族主義與中國中心思想來與歐洲文化中心抗衡，卻把魯迅變成另一種殖民文化，尤其在文學思想、形式、題材與風格上。

新馬戰後的著名作家兼評論家趙戎（1920-1998），雖然新加坡出生，他的文學觀完全受中國新文學的經典所支配，他也不是最前線的魯迅神話的發揚與捍衛者，但他在中國中心優勢文化影響下，也一樣的處處以魯迅為導師，無時無刻不忘記引用魯迅為典範，引用他的話來加強自己的論據或作為引證。他的《論馬華作家與作品》就很清楚看到魯迅及中國新文學前期的經典如何支配著他。在《苗秀論》（1953）中，在論述〈苗秀底藝術和藝術風格〉一節，趙戎馬上說：

> 比如魯迅、茅盾、老舍、巴金……等等，他們底藝術風格是各

---

42 我曾從不同角度討論過這問題，有關馬華文學之獨立，見王潤華〈從中國文學傳統到本土文學傳統〉論文，收入《從新馬文學到世界華文文學》（新加坡：潮州八邑會館，1994年），頁3-33；有關報紙副刊曾是中國作家之殖民地與本土新馬華文作家的獨立鬥爭戰場，見〈從戰後新馬華文報紙副刊看華文文學之發展〉，《世界中文報紙副刊學綜論》（臺北：文建會，1997年），頁494-505。

43 同前註30，英文本，頁6-7；中文本，頁7-8。

不相同的……。[44]

在討論〈苗秀底人生觀和創作態度〉，他一開始，就引用魯迅為例：

> 魯迅、茅盾們的小說，……他們所以偉大，其作品所以不朽，都決定於作者的人生觀……。

趙戎論析苗秀的中篇小說《小城之戀》時，把小說中幹抗日鋤奸的文化青年歸類為會寫「魯迅風」雜文的文化青年，因為他在革命中愛上一女子，因此否定苗秀的描寫，認為這是大缺點：

> 而且，一個會寫「魯迅風」雜文的文化青年，當他底工作緊張的時候，總不致把愛當作第一義的吧！作者底的意思是寫戀愛悲劇，但可以不必這般寫的……。

我在上述已提起方修及其《避席集》，雖是向魯迅學習的心得之作，這本書使方修成為五、六十年代魯迅精神的發揚與推崇的首要發言人。在他大量的論述新華文學的著作中，魯迅是非論及不可的，在《中國文學對馬華文學的影響》（1970）一文中，魯迅及其他作家是「學習或模仿的對象」：

> 學習中國個別作家的風格 —— 中國著名的作家，如魯迅、郭沫若、巴金、艾青、臧克家、田間等人，他們的作品風格都成為馬華作家學習或模仿的對象。[45]

在《馬華文學的主流 —— 現實主義的發展》（1975），方修認識只有魯迅的作品是舊現實主義中最高一級的徹底的評判的現實主義，只有魯迅的作品達到這個高度。[46]馬來西亞的資深作家方北方（1919-），即使在 1980 年代論述馬華文學時，如在《馬華文學及其他》論文集中，處處都以魯迅的現實主義創作手法、魯迅的人格精神，魯迅的作品，

---

44 趙戎《論馬華作家與作品》（新加坡：青年書局，1967 年），頁 3、9 及 17。
45 方修《新馬文學史論集》，頁 41。
46 同前註，頁 355。

為最高的典範與模式。[47]

七、受困於模仿與學習的後殖民文本

　　當五四新文學為中心的文學觀成為殖民文化的主導思潮，只有被來自中國中心的文學觀所認同的生活經驗或文學技巧形式，才能被人接受，因此不少新馬寫作人，從戰前到戰後，一直到今天，受困於模仿與學習某些五四新文學的經典作品。來自中心的真確性（authenticity）拒絕本土作家去尋找新題材、新形成，因此不少人被迫去寫遠離新馬殖民地的生活經驗。譬如當魯迅的雜文被推崇，成為一種主導性寫作潮流，寫抒情感傷的散文，被看成一種墮落，即使在新馬，也要罵林語堂的幽默與汪精衛，下面這一段有關魯迅雜文的影響力便告訴我們中國中心文學觀的霸權文化控制了文學生產：

> 雜文，這種魯迅所一手創造的文藝匕首，已被我們的一般作者所普遍掌握；早期的雜文作者如一工、孫藝文、古月、林仙嶠、景黎升等，他們的作品都或多或少地接受了魯迅雜文的影響；而稍後出現的丘康、陳南、流冰、田堅、吳達、之丘、山兄、蕭克等人的雜文，更是深入地繼承了魯迅雜文底精神，而獲得了高度成就的。不但是純粹的雜文，即一般較有現實內容，較有思想骨力而又生動活潑的政論散文，也是多少采取了魯迅雜文底批判精神和評判方式的。在《馬華新文學大系》的《理論批評二集》和《劇運特輯》中，有許多短小精悍的理論批評文章基本上都可以說是魯迅式底雜文，因為魯迅雜文底內容本來就是無限廣闊，而在形式上又是多樣化的。在《馬華新文學大系》的《散文集》中，則更有不少雜文的基本內容是和魯迅雜

---

47 方北方《馬華文學及其他》（香港：三聯書店，1987 年），頁 5。

文一脈相承的。那些被魯迅所批判過，否定過的「阿Q性」學者、文人、幫閑藝術家等等，往往在一般雜文作者的筆下得到了廣泛反映。例如：古月的《關於徐志摩的死》一文，是批判新月派文人的；丘康的《關於批判幽默作風的說明》，是駁斥林語堂之流的墮落文藝觀的；丘康的《說話和做人》及陳南的《黨派關系》，是對汪精衛輩的開火；田堅的《用不著太息》，是揭發「阿Q性」在新時代中的遺毒的；而丘康的《論中國傾向作家的領導》，則是批判田漢等行幫份子的。諸如此類，都可以和魯迅作品互相印證。至於專論魯迅，或引用魯迅的話的文章，則以丘康、陳南、吳達、饒楚瑜、辜斧夫等人的作品為多。[48]

作者還很驕傲的為魯迅的霸權指出：

總之，在馬華新文學史上，只有真正接受魯迅底教導，真正追隨魯迅的文藝工作者，才能堅持走堅實底文藝道路，負起新時代所賦予的歷史任務。[49]

上述戰前的新馬作家受困於模仿與學習魯迅的情形，到了戰後，很明顯的，尤其土生的一代新馬作家開始把左派的、霸權文化代表的魯迅文學觀進行調整與修改，使它能表達和承載新的新馬殖民地的生活經驗。正如下述的雲裡風、黃孟文、曾也魯（吐虹）的作品所顯示，企圖在拒絕和抵制下破除權威性（Abrogation），在修改與調整的挪用（appropriation）中，破除神化的魯迅的規範性與正確性。他們重新為中文與文本定位。[50]

最近古遠清發表〈魯迅精神在五十年代的馬華文壇〉，是他讀了《雲

---

48 高潮〈魯迅與馬華新文學〉，《憶農廬雜文》（香港：中流出版社，1973年），頁67-69。
49 同前註，頁69。
50 同前註30，英文本，頁38-115；中文本，頁41-125。

裡風文集》中十篇散文的評論。[51]他發現幾乎每一篇,「都能感受到魯迅精神的閃光」。他還說:「不能說沒有模仿著魯迅散文詩《野草》的痕跡,但他不願用因襲代替創作,總是用自己的生活實踐去獲取新的感悟。」雲裡風的《狂奔》情節與人物設置使人聯想起魯迅的《過客》、《文明人與瘋子》的文明人應借鑒過魯迅《聰明人和傻子和奴才》中的聰明人,《未央草》靈感來自魯迅的《影的告別》[52],《夢與現實》以「我夢見我在」開始,很像魯迅《死火》以「我夢見自己」開始,不過根據古遠清的分析,雖然夢境、韌性的戰鬥精神,對黑暗社會的意、詩情和哲理相似,他還是可以感到一些作者改造與移置的痕跡:「雲裡風註意改造,移植魯迅的作品,這一藝術經驗值得我們重視。」當然,作為一位中國學者,古遠清很高興看見中國文化的霸權在五十年代還繼續發展:「可看出魯迅精神在五十年代馬華文壇如何發揚光大。」[53]

　　其實從 1950 年到今天,魯迅的作品所建立的經典典範還是具有生命力,新馬的作家,多多少少都曾經向他學習過。吐虹的〈「美是大」阿 Q 正傳〉,作於 1957 年[54],模仿《阿 Q 正傳》,諷刺曾擔任南洋大學校長的林語堂(小說中叫淩雨唐)。孟毅(黃孟文)的〈再見惠蘭的時候〉作於 1968 年,它跟魯迅的《故鄉》有許多相似的地方。[55]林萬菁在 1985 年寫的〈阿 Q 後傳〉,又是一篇讀了《阿 Q 正傳》的再創作。[56]

　　在移民殖民地如澳洲、紐西蘭,白人移民作家首要使命便是要建

---

51 古遠清〈魯迅精神在五十年代的馬華文壇〉,《新華文學》第 46 期(新加坡,1999年 6 月),頁 98-102。

52 同前註,頁 98。

53 同前註,頁 102。

54 收集在作者第一本短篇小說集,吐虹《第一次飛》(新加坡:海燕文化社,1958 年),頁 29-48。

55 收集在作者第一本短篇小說集,吐虹《第一次飛》(新加坡:海燕文化社,1958 年),頁 29-48。

56 林萬菁〈阿 Q 後傳〉,《香港文學》第 6 期(1985 年 6 月),頁 38-39。

構本土性。他們與侵略殖民地的印度作家不一樣。後者在英國殖民統治離去後，主要使命是重新尋找或重建本土上原有的文化，白人作家則要去創造這種本土性。他們爲了創造雙重的傳統：進口與本土（the imported and the indigeuous）的傳統，這些白人作家需要不斷採取破除權威與挪用（appropriation）的寫作策略。[57]新馬華文作家他們在許多地方其處境與澳洲的白人作家相似，他們需要建立雙重的文學傳統。[58]

在上述作家之中，孟毅最成功的修正從中國殖植過來的中文與文本，因爲它已承載住中國的文化經驗，必須經過調整與修正，破除其規範性與正確性，才能表達與承載新馬殖民地新的生活經驗與思想感情。〈再見惠蘭的時候〉在瓦解中國的經典（或魯迅經典）與重建新馬經典，成爲新馬後殖民文學演變的典範模式。

這篇以馬來亞經驗所嘗試創造的一種新文本，根據麗鹿（王嶽山）的論文《〈再見惠蘭的時候〉與魯迅〈故鄉〉》[59]，具有主題共通性（悲傷兒時鄉下玩伴的貧困遭遇）、情節的模式（回到離別很久的故鄉，小朋友落魄，故鄉落後貧窮）、故事人物相似（我、母親、鄉土與我、母親、惠蘭對比）及四種表現手法（第一人稱敘述法、倒敘手法、對比手法與反諷技巧）。孟毅雖然受到魯迅的《故鄉》的啓示與影響，作者把舊中國荒蕪落後的魯迅式的農村全部瓦解，放棄他的中國情節，重建英國殖民地的馬來亞一個橡膠園農村及其移民，從題材、語言到感情都是馬來亞橡膠園，礦場地區的特殊經驗。小說中所呈現的因爲英

---

57 同前註 30，英文本，頁 38-115；中文本，頁 41-125。

58 周策縱與我曾在 1988 年的第二屆華文文學大同世界國際會議上，發表雙重傳統（native and Chinese traditions）及多元中心論，參考王潤華編《東南亞華文文學》（新加坡：哥德學院與新加坡作協，1989 年），頁 359-662；王潤華《從新華文到世界華文文學》中第 3 卷《世界華文文學的大同世界：新方向新傳統考察》，同前註 22，頁 243-276。

59 這篇論文原是我在南洋大學中文系所授《比較文學》班上的學術報告，見《南洋商報》副刊《學林》，1981 年 1 月 15 日及 16 日。

軍與馬共爭奪馬來亞統治權所引發的游擊戰而引發當地居民複雜的生活與思想情況，特別對當年英軍宣布的緊急狀態下集中營（新村）的無奈，都通過新馬殖民地的產品表現出來。邢些鋅板屋、移殖區、甲巴拉、邦達布、水客、田雞、香蕉、讀紅毛書本身就承載著新馬人的新文化與感情。這邊緣性產生的後殖民文本，終於把本土性的新華華文文學傳建構起來。

八、「個個是魯迅」與「死抱了魯迅不放」到學術研究

　　魯迅如何走進新馬後殖民文學中，及其接受與影響，還有其意義，是一個錯綜複雜的問題。魯迅以其經典作品引起新馬華人的注意後，又以左翼文人的領袖形象被移居新馬的文化人用來宣揚與推展左派文學思潮。除了左派文人，共產黨、抗日救國的愛國華僑都盡了最大的努力去塑造魯迅的神話。有的為了左派思想，有的為了抗拒，有的為了愛中國。魯迅最後竟變成代表中國文化或中國，沒有人可以拒絕魯迅，因為魯迅代表了中國在新馬的勢力。1939 年郁達夫在新馬的時候，已完全看見魯迅將變成神，新馬人人膜拜的神。從文學觀點看，他擔心「個個是魯迅」，人人「死抱了魯迅不放」。他說這話主要是「對死抱了魯迅不放，只在抄襲他的作風的一般人說的話」。可是郁達夫這幾句話，引起左派文人的全面圍攻，郁達夫甚至以《晨星》主編特權，停止爭論文章發表。攻擊他的人如耶魯（黃望青，曾駐日本大使）、張楚琨在當年不只左傾，也是共黨的發言人。反對魯迅就等於反對「戰鬥」，反對抗戰，反對反殖民主義，最後等於反對中國文化。[60]高揚就激昂的說死抱住魯迅、抄襲他的作風都無所謂，「因為最低限度，學習一個戰士，在目前對於抗戰是有益」。[61]

---

60 這些文章收集於《馬華新文學大系》第 2 集，同前註 7，頁 444-471。
61 同前註，頁 461。

　　把魯迅冷靜認真的當作文學經典著作來研究，目前方興未艾，也需要洋洋幾萬言才能論述其要。它的開始也很早。鄭子瑜早在 1949年就寫過《〈秋夜〉精讀指導》，1952 年的專著《魯迅詩話》及年青時的手稿，最近才出版的《阿 Q 正傳鄭箋》[62]，後兩部專著已有陳子善及林非等人的專論。[63]鄭子瑜代表新馬以修辭的方法來研究魯迅。目前的林萬菁便是集大成者，他著有《論魯迅修辭：從技巧到規律》，另外也發表許多論文如《試釋魯迅「絕望之為虛妄，正與希望相同」》、《〈阿 Q 正傳〉三種英譯的比較》。[64]王潤華則開拓從文學藝術與比較文學的角度與方法去研究魯迅的小說，主要專著有《魯迅小說新論》，及其他專篇論文如〈從周樹人仙台學醫經驗解讀魯迅的小說〉、〈回到仙台醫專，重新解剖一個中國醫生的死亡〉等論文。[65]

　　從目前的局勢看，魯迅已從街頭走向大專學府，作為冷靜學術思考的對象，我自己就指導很多研究魯迅的學術論文，如《魯迅對中國古典小說的評價》、《魯迅小說人物的「狂」與「死」及其社會意義》、《魯迅小說散文中「世紀末」文藝思想與風格研究》、《魯迅舊體詩研究》等。[66]

---

62 《〈秋夜〉精讀指導》收集於《鄭子瑜選集》（新加坡：世界書局，1960 年），頁 65-75；《魯迅詩話》（香港：大公書局，1852 年）。

63 見宗廷虎編《鄭子瑜的學術研究和學術工作》（上海：復旦大學出版社，1993 年），頁 61-66；頁 67-71。

64 林萬菁《論魯迅修辭：從技巧到規律》（新加坡：萬裏書局，1986 年）；其餘二篇論文都是由新加坡國立大學中文系所出版，前後為 1983 年，26 頁；1985 年，29頁。

65 王潤華《魯迅小說新論》（臺北：東大圖書公司，1992 年；上海：學林出版社，1993年）；〈從周樹人仙台學醫經驗解讀魯迅的小說〉（新加坡國立大學單篇論文，1996年），22 頁；〈回到仙台醫專，重新解剖一個中國醫生的死亡〉，《魯迅研究月刊》1995 年第 1 期，頁 56-58。

66 前三本為新加坡國立大學中文系榮譽班論文，1988 年、1990 年及 1995 年，後一本碩士論文，1996 年。

林文慶與魯迅/馬華作家與郁達夫衝突的多元解讀：誰是中心誰是邊緣？

一、解構中國中心與南洋邊緣的衝突

在 1926 年，尋求西方科技與華族文化結合的新馬華人林文慶（1869-1957）與追求現代性、反舊傳統的中國作家魯迅（1881-1936）在中國的土地上發生衝突。原因是林文慶擔任廈門大學校長時，聘請魯迅擔任國學研究所的教授，魯迅有所不滿，只做了 4 個月零 12 天就辭職了。多數學者認為，那是魯迅反林文慶尊孔的事件，代表新與舊的衝突。[1]

過了 13 年後，自我放逐南洋，擁抱新馬華人邊緣文化的郁達夫，在 1939 與擁抱中國文學傳統的新馬中國僑居作家與本土華文作家也發生衝突，多數學者說，那是中國傳統/中心與本土化的矛盾，郁達夫不瞭解本土情緒高漲，反對本土化，另一方面又反對魯迅所代表的中國中心傳統。[2]

---

1 關於中國早期的論述見薛綏之（編）《魯迅生平史料彙編》第四輯（天津：天津人民出版社，1983），尤其俞荻、俞念遠、陳夢韶、川島的文章。我曾指導一篇碩士論文，把這場"爭論"從所有發表過的文章中，給予分析，見莫顯英《重新解讀魯迅與林文慶在夏大的衝突》（新加坡：新加坡國立大學中文系，2001。關於事件有關的資料，可見該論文完整的參考書目。

2 鬱達夫與當時作者討論的論文收集于方修編《馬華新文學大系》，理論批評第二集，（新加坡：星洲世界書局，1971）。楊松年〈從鬱達夫〈幾個問題〉引起的論爭看南洋知識分子的心態〉《亞洲文化》23 起（1999 年 6 月），pp.103-111；鄒慧珊、李秀萍、黃文青〈魯迅與鬱達夫在新馬的論爭—華文後殖民文學情境的解讀〉，2002 在王潤華《中國現代文學專題》（新加坡國立大學中文系）的報告。共 13 頁。

以前我們稱他們之間發生「衝突」,「對」與「不對」來解讀,那是單元的思考,以中國爲文化思考中心或本土中心單元的解釋模式的話語。在今天多元文化,多元思考的後現代後結構時代,我們應該把衝突解構,改稱爲「對話」,也需要重新思考與解讀。從這二宗中國與馬華文化/文學的爭論中,可釋放出許多有關中國與馬華文化/文學有關中心與邊緣的新意義。

二、父親的意外死亡刺激林文慶與魯迅學醫救國救人

林文慶與魯迅都是學醫。林文慶在英殖民地的新加坡出生與長大,出身自來自檳城的一個峇峇(Baba)、英文教育的家庭,其父親因修刮鬍子割傷而中毒死亡,這意外刺激他立志學醫救人。林文慶在1892 年前往英格蘭愛丁堡大學讀醫科。1892 年獲得醫學學士與碩士學位。他的志願是回返殖民地爲新馬被殖民者從事醫藥服務。[3]

魯迅深感中國帝國的衰落無能,人民的病弱愚昧,他在父親糊裏糊塗被庸醫胡亂治病醫死了後,深痛醫學的落後,中國人思想的愚昧,1904 年進入日本仙台醫學專門學校學醫,希望古老落後的中國能像現代日本,從西方醫學走向現代化,解救中國人的病弱的生命。[4]

三、民族危機感,促使兩位邊緣人棄醫從文,替中國打脈

林文慶在 1887 至 1893 年在英國生活,原本很滿足也很驕傲做大英帝國的臣民。但在目睹英國大英帝國的威權霸力,對弱小民族與落後土地的侵略與剝削,而發現自己中國人在倫敦受盡白人的污辱,自

---

3 見李元瑾,《林文慶的思想:中西文化的匯流與矛盾》(新加坡:亞洲學會,2000);李元瑾,《東西文化的撞擊與新華知識分子的三種回應》(新加坡:新加坡國立大學中文系/八方文化,2001)。
4 王潤華〈回到仙台醫專,重新解剖一個中國醫生的死亡〉《魯迅研究月刊》1995 年第一期, pp.56-58.

己又不懂中國語文與文中國文化，他的羞愧與憤怒，于是喚醒了對母族文化的精感與民族意識。他于是拼命學習中文與古典文化，使人想起魯迅在東京也向章太炎學過學，讀《說文解字》。在 1895，林文慶開始發表論文討論中國的儒家思想與中國革新。所以魯迅與林文慶都是在自我放逐、生活在異鄉，作爲一位邊緣人時，中國及華族的危機感觸發了他們民族自尊，決定以文學／文化來啓蒙中國人，改變中國的社會與國家命運。[5]

魯迅在仙台的時代，這個城市是日軍重要基地，侵略中國和俄國的日本軍隊，多從仙台出發，此地濃厚軍國主義的氣息，因此强化了魯迅對中國危機的認識。看見日本人上下支持軍隊去侵略中國，親身經驗日本同學隨意誣衊中國學生考試作弊，懷疑中國人的能力，促使魯迅對人性反省與批判，也喚醒了他的民族主義，特別思考被壓迫的民族.他離開仙台，到了東京聽章太炎講文字學，漢文字的奧秘，加上他的國學根底，引爆了他的對中國文化情感。[6]

無論出于自身願意還是强逼，林文慶與魯迅都曾自我放逐異鄉，置身邊緣。在身體上與思想上流亡異鄉的作家，他們生存在中間地帶（median state），永遠處在漂移狀態中，他們即拒絕認同新環境，又沒有完全與舊的切斷開，尷尬的困擾在半參與半游移狀態中。他們一方面懷舊傷感，另一方面又善於應變或成爲被放逐的人。游移于局內人與局外人之間，他們焦慮不安、孤獨、四處探索，無所置身。這種流亡與邊緣的作家，就像漂泊不定的旅人或客人，愛感受新奇。當邊緣作家看世界，他以過去的與目前互相參考比較，因此他不但不把問題孤立起來看，他有雙重的透視力（double perspective）。每種出現在新國家的景物，都會引起故國同樣景物的思考。因此任何思想與經驗

5 同前註 1，李元瑾，《東西文化的撞擊與新華知識分子的三種回應》，pp.43-53.
6 同前註 3，pp. 57-58.

都會用另一套來平衡思考，使到新的舊的都用另一種全新，難以意料的眼光來審視。[7]

　　林文慶與魯迅都經過這種邊緣人的生活與思考。林文慶在新加坡與英國，都是被殖民者，華族被剝削、不公平的待遇，感受尤深。魯迅出國前在滿清皇朝下，他是個被壓迫的邊緣人，到了日本，流亡的感覺就更深。他們這多元的、邊緣思考使到他們不約而同的最終都放弃醫學，以文學/文化來啓蒙愚昧的國民，但還是像醫生那樣療救被壓迫者的病苦，找出「舊社會的病根」，「加以療治」。[8]

四、中國人與海外華人：誰是中國文化中心誰是邊緣？

　　這兩位分別處于半殖民地的中國與英殖民地的馬來亞權政中心之外的邊緣地帶的知識分子，同是被權力與中心文化霸權放逐的人，同是身爲邊緣思考的人，他們又怎麼會衝突呢？

　　魯迅在 1909 年的夏天回返中國，他仍然處于中國威權、社會與文化的中心之外，即使滿清政權崩潰，民國成立（1911）以後，甚至 1926 年他成爲名作家學者，被林文慶聘請到夏門大學出任國學院教授時，他還是中國社會與主流文化的邊緣人。魯迅一輩子都活在邊緣的位置，造成他一輩子都在反抗社會的黑暗，國民性的黑暗。邊緣是最好的反抗霸權話語的空間，邊遠的位置給人各種大膽、極端的視野，從而去發現創造、幻想另一種新世界。[9]當魯迅在廈門見到林文慶時，自己只是國學院的一名教授，後者是雇主/校長，而且大力提倡儒家思

---

7 Edward Said, "Intellectual Exile: Expatriated and Marginals", *Representation of the Intellectual* (London: Vintage,1994) ,pp.35-48.

8 王潤華 《魯迅小說新論》（上海：學林出版社，1993），pp58.

9 Bell Hooks, "Marginality as Site of Resistance" in　Russell Ferguson and others ,eds., *Out There: Marginalization and Contemporary Culture* （Cambridge, Mass: MIT Press, 1990）,pp.341-342.

想，在夏大講演時常用英文演說，于是在魯迅的眼中，林文慶反而容易被誤讀成與中國傳統文化中心、社會權力中心結合的圈內人，不再是邊緣人。[10]

另外因爲林文慶自小接受英國教育，深受維多利亞時代英國文化的氣魄與眼光所影響，有膽識、有領導改革的才華，年輕時就被英國接受，肯定爲優秀的英國海外子民，對民族主義思想日愈强大、本土化的中國人來說，林文慶的背景甚至被誤看成是殖民者的代言人。

對林文慶來說，他前往中國廈門出任夏大校長時，更是在邊緣之邊緣。爲了把話說清楚，他常要求說英文。在新加坡原本就是邊緣人，天天反抗英殖民統治者對底層華人的壓迫，評擊殖民政府的剝削，爲華人社會的弊病而深感憂心。對殖民地統治者，他更是邊緣人，因此他努力推行中華語言與儒家思想的復興運動。他的熱心改革新馬社群，贏得英國殖民者的稱贊，享受到殖民者的權益。那是殖民者想要消除他的邊緣位置，與殖民者認同的策略。

林文慶的中華民族主義，促使他曾先後響應中國維新運動，支持保皇黨，大力協助孫中山的革命，還成爲孫總統機要秘書、衛生部長等職位。這些都是反抗殖民者霸權與傳統落後中國的中心的行動，也是向中華民族認同的追求。具有海外華人民族主義複雜的政治、思想、愛國主義的林文慶，爲了實際改革，實現民主、科學、文化的中國，表面上他終于成爲中國權力/社會中心，成爲圈內人。[11]

其實林文慶應該很明白自己的位置，作爲一個海外華人，在新五四新文化運動以後，中國追求現代性的知識分子堅持徹底打倒舊文

---

10 王賡武，〈魯迅、林文慶和儒家思想〉《中國與海外華人》（臺北：臺灣商務印書館，1994），pp. 193.

11 李元瑾，《林文慶的思想：中西文化的匯流與矛盾》；李元瑾，《東西文化的撞擊與新華知識分子的三種回應》,pp. 43-52, 237-296.

化，如林毓生所說的[12]，反偶像崇拜的反傳統主義（iconoclastic anti-tradition）的霸權話語中，因此林文慶肯定是邊緣人，持有霸權話語的是反傳統的知識分子。但據有西方科技與文明的經驗的林醫生，爲了建構現代科技與文化結合的中國，他還是勇往直前。

　　以出任夏大校長的林文慶來說，具有海外華人民族主義複雜的政治、思想、愛國主義的林文慶，爲了實際改革，實現民主、科學、文化結合的中國，他需要進出中國權力/社會中心。Bell Hooks 在〈邊緣作爲反抗的場域〉（Marginality as Site of Resistance）叙述早年黑人的在種族隔離政策下的生活，可作爲最好的比喻。黑人住在鐵道之外，肯德基（Kentucky）城市的邊緣地帶，白天他們可以進城做勞動工作，晚上必須回去鐵道外的窮人區。[13]說明白，林文慶只是如此的一個人而已。所以王賡武教授說，當時魯迅或中國學者對林文慶的批評，顯示他們沒有脫離中國文人學士歷來的成見，對海外華人，受西方教育，要參與改造中國的人沒有好感。[14]

　　海外華人林文慶的民族主義，携帶著作西方教育與文明科技，國際性的視野，擁抱本土傳統文化，尤其儒家傳統文化，結果他的邊緣被看成了中心，實際上也會變成中心。魯迅土生土長，追求現代性，以五四反傳統的革命精神出發，追求現代性，他的革命容納不了傳統。遇見“尊孔的”，講英文的上流社會的校長，自己更感邊緣化，更把對方看成中心。因此被「尊孔」妨礙了對話。魯迅在夏大的講演〈少讀中國書，做好事之徒〉，其中「做好事之徒」，魯迅便以創設夏大，大學中提倡的西方文化（圖書館有英文雜志）爲例，大大稱贊夏大的

---

12 林毓生，《中國意識的危機》（貴州：貴州人民出版社，1988），pp.235-236.
13 同前註 9，pp. 341.
14 同前註 10，pp. 186-187.

新文化一般，[15]林文慶聽說後也高興。不過在後來單元的政治文化論述中，學者總是把他們看作中心/傳統與現代/邊緣對立的衝突。[16]

五、郁達夫的南洋邊緣話語：去中國中心/本土主義

郁達夫于 1938 年 12 月 28 日抵達新加坡，受《星洲日報》之聘，擔任副刊編輯。1939 年 1 月 21 日，他在《星洲日報》與檳城的《星檳日報》同時發表〈幾個問題〉的文章。這是他在檳成與文藝青年對話後的所想到的問題。這篇論文引起最大的爭議，是針對南洋文藝界把國內的課題全盤搬過來的現象的意見。他用魯迅爲例：[17]

> 上海在最近，很有一些人在提出魯迅風的雜文題，在現在是不是還可以適用？對最這問題，我以爲不必這樣的用全副精神來對付，因爲這不過是文體與作風的問題。假如參加討論的幾位先生個個都是魯迅，那試問這問題，會不會發生？再試問參加討論者中間，連一個魯迅都不會再生，則討論了，也終于何益處？法國有一位批評家說，問者人也……若要舍己耘人，拼命去矯揉造作，那樣何苦？

後來郁達夫又寫了〈我對你們却沒有失望〉與〈我對你們還是不失望〉二文[18]，強調說「這是對死抱了魯迅不放，只是抄襲他的作風的一般人說的話」。郁達夫與僑居新馬的中國作家如張楚琨以及本土長大的新馬作家的其中一個衝突點，是反對盲目跟著中國文壇走，抄襲中國作家的文風，人人學魯迅的戰鬥散文便是一例。郁達夫這個看法

---

15 同前註 10，pp.181-183.
16 莫顯英對兩種不同的看法都有分析，見《重新解讀魯迅與林文慶在夏大的衝突》，pp. 11-68.
17 方修（編）《馬華新文學大系》，理論批評第二集，pp. 444-448
18 同上註 18，pp.452-453;457-458.

激怒了許多在新馬的中國作家與本土華文作家。[19]魯迅在 1930 年後，正如我在〈從反殖民到殖民：魯迅與新馬後殖民文學〉所指出[20]，在左派文化人的政治話語下，魯迅神話也開始移植到新馬，最後他代表了中國的五四以來的現代與革命文化思想。自然受到代表中國中心思想作家的張楚琨與代表本土主義作家的耶魯等人的圍攻。

　　來到當時文化低落的南洋，郁達夫應該擁抱中國中心的優越感，一切思考從一元中國中心的出發，他却意外的不認同中國的主流，反對當地的文學觀、寫作的題材與風格太受當時中國的文壇的潮流支配。他另一方面也對當時本土意識過分強烈的華文作家有所保留，他說：「提到有關南洋色彩的問題只在這色彩的濃厚，如果一味的強調地方色彩，而使作品主題，退居到第二位去的寫作手法，不是上乘的作風」[21]。這說明郁達夫具有邊緣人的雙重透視力。從留學日本到回到中國，他的小說散文很明顯的表現出郁達夫一直在自我流放。在中國他是圈外人（outsider）、零餘者、頹廢文人、自我放逐者。[22]到了南洋，他的心態就更加如此。他遠離社會權力結構的中心、厭惡霸權華語與集體意識。所以又一次證明，中國人不一定個個都喜歡中國的傳統╱中心話語。往往海外的華人或外國人比中國的學者更捍衛傳統。所以Edward Sils 在其《中心與邊緣》（Center and Periphery）書中說，所謂的中心，其與空間與地理位置無關。它代表價值觀、信仰、與權力。[23]

六、中心也是邊緣，邊緣也是中心

---

19 這些文章有些收集於《馬華新文學大系》（同上註），pp.444-471.

20 王潤華《華文後殖民文學》（臺北：文史哲出版社，2001），pp. 51-76.

21 同前註 17，pp. 452.

22 可參考曾焯文，《達夫心經》（香港：香江出版社，1999）。

23 Edward Sils, *Center and Periphery: Essays in Macrosociology* （Chicago: University of Chicago Press,1975），p. 3.

其實所謂知識分子或作家或文化/文學的邊緣，其情境往往是隱喻性的。屬于一個國家社會的人，在同一個社會的人，可以成爲局外人（outsider）或局內人（insider），往往屬于地理/精神上的。其實所有一流前衛的知識分子或作家，永遠都在流亡/邊緣，不管身在國內或國外，因爲知識分子原本就位居社會邊緣，遠離政治權力，置身于正統文化/文學之外，這樣知識分子/作家便可以誠實的捍衛與批評社會，擁有令人嘆爲觀止的觀察力，遠在他人發現之前，他已覺察出潮流與問題。古往今來，流亡者都有跨文化與跨國族的視野。[24]

任何國籍的人都會成爲具有儒家修養的人，只要他研讀儒家的經典著作。中國雖是中國文化的發源地，不一定是永遠的唯一中華文化中心，就如佛教源自印度，佛教已流傳成多中心，而這些中心已發長成新的佛教傳統。今天儒家文化不只是中國的，也是世界的。研讀儒家的經典著作，可將它發揚光大。如儒學的傳統在韓國、日本、越南、東南亞。杜維明在〈文化中國：邊緣中心論〉（Cultural China:The Periphery as the Center）、〈文化中國與儒家傳統〉、〈文化中國精神資源的開發〉諸文章中，提出"文化中國"的概念，因爲中國不只是一個政治結構、社會組織，也是一個文化理念。今日產生重大影響力的有關中國文化的關心、發展、研究、論述，主要在海外，而這些人包括在外國出生的華人或研究中國文化的非華人，這個文化中國的中心超越中國，而由中國、香港、臺灣與散居世界各地的以華人爲主的人所構成。其實正如《長青樹：今日改變中的華人》（The Living Tree: The Changing Meaning of Being Chinese）中其它文章所觀察，華人的意義不斷在改變中，中國以外邊緣地帶華人建構了文化中國中心。[25]

---

24 同前註 7，p.39.

25 Tu Wei-ming, "Cultural China: The Periphery as the Center" in Tu Wei-ming, ed., *The Living Tree: The Changing Meaning of Being Chinese Today*", op. cit. ,pp.1-34; 杜維明

文化是有生命的，中國文化/中華文化不斷在創新發展，不斷在衍生，從中國國土蔓延到世界各地生長起來。英國文學移植到北美洲及世界各地，在各國各族移民的社區發展的英文文學，大大超越英國本土的英文文學，建立了新的傳統。華文文學也是如此，它多元共生，多傳統多中心。

1989 年在新加坡舉行的東南亞華文文學國際會議上，周策縱教授特地收邀前來作總評。在聽取了二十七篇論文的報告和討論後，他指出，中國本土以外的華文文學的發展，已經産生「雙重傳統」（Double Tradition）的特性，同時目前我們必須建立起「多元文學中心」（Multiple Literary Centers）的觀念，這樣才能認識中國本土以外的華文文學的重要性。我認爲世界各國的華文文學的作者與學者，都應該對這兩個觀念有所認識。[26]

任何有成就的文學都有它的歷史淵源，現代文學也必然有它的文學傳統。在中國本土上，自先秦以來，就有一個完整的大文學傳統。東南亞的華文文學，自然不能拋弃從先秦發展下來的那個中國文學傳統，沒有這一個文學傳統的根，東南亞，甚至世界其它地區的華文文學，都不能成長。然而單靠這個根，是結不了果實的，因爲海外華人多是生活在別的國家裏，自有他們的土地、人民、風俗、習慣、文化和歷史。這些作家，當他們把各地區的生活經驗及其它文學傳統吸收進去時，本身自然會形成一種「本土的文學傳統」（Native Literary Tradition）。新加坡和東南亞地區的華文文學，以我的觀察，都已融合了「中國文學傳統」和「本土文學傳統」而發展著。我們目前如果讀

〈文化中國與儒家傳統〉，《1995 吳德耀文化講座》（新加坡：國大藝術中心，1996），pp.31；杜維明〈文化中國精神資源的開發〉，《鄭文龍（編）《杜維明學術文化隨筆》（北京：中國青年出版社，1999），頁 63-73。

26 周策縱〈總評〉《東南亞華文文學》，王潤華等編（新加坡：作家協會與歌德學院，1989），頁 359-362。

一本新加坡的小說集或詩集，雖然是以華文創作，但字裏行間的世界觀、取材、甚至文字之使用，對內行人來說，跟大陸的作品比較，是有差別的，因爲它容納了“本土文學傳統”的元素。

當一個地區的文學建立了本土文學傳統之後，這種文學便不能稱之爲中國文學，更不能把它看作中國文學之支流。因此，周策縱教授認爲我們應建立起多元文學中心的觀念。華文文學，本來只有一個中心，那就是中國。可是華人偏居海外，而且建立起自己的文化與文學，自然會形成另一個華文文學中心；目前我們已承認有新加坡華文文學中心、馬來西亞華文文學中心的存在。這已是一個既成的事實。因此，我們今天需要從多元文學中心的觀念來看詩集華文文學，需承認世界上有不少的華文文學中心。我們不能再把新加坡華文文學看作「邊緣文學」或中國文學的「支流文學」，而是一種新的華文文學傳統。我在《從新華文學到世界華文文學》與《華文後殖民文學》二書中，反復從個個角度與課題來討論多元文學中心的形成，又以新馬華文文學爲例，說明本土文學傳統在語言、主題、個方面如何形成。[27]

所以林文慶與魯迅、郁達夫與中國僑居/新馬本土作家的例子，正可以說明誰是中心，誰是邊緣的脚色是難于區分，中心與邊緣的意義可以互換的，當文學在逐漸走向多元文化、全球化的時候，中心與邊緣的界限就更模糊了，更沒有意義了，最後邊緣也是中心。

---

27 王潤華《從新華華文文學到世界華文文學》(新加坡：潮州八邑會館，1994。我最今的論文未收入這二本論文集的有〈後殖民離散族群的華文文學：包涵又超越種族、地域、語言和宗教的文學空間〉，15頁。新世紀華文文學發展國際學術研討會論文，1991年5月19日，臺灣元智大學；〈邊緣思考與邊緣文學〉12頁，香港教育學院第二界亞太區中文教學研討工作坊：新的文化視野下的中國文學研究論文，2002年3月13-15日。

沈從文論魯迅：
中國現代小說的新傳統

一、肯定魯迅肯定自己：書寫被物質
文明毀滅的鄉村小說的傳統

沈從文在二十年代末以後，開始大力描寫以湘西沅水流域爲背景的小說。他自己很欣賞沅水流域所激發出來的傑作，在〈《沈從文小說選集》‧題記〉（1957），他回憶道：

一九二八年到學校教小說習作以後，由于爲同學作習題舉例，更需要試用各種不同表現方法，處理不同問題，因之在一九二八年到一九四七年約二十年間，我寫了一大堆東西。其中除小部分在表現問題，結構組織和文字風格上，稍微有些新意，也只是近于學習中應有的收穫，說不上什麼真正的成就。至于文字中一部分充滿泥土氣息，一部分又文白雜揉，故事在寫實中依舊浸透一種抒情幻想成分，內容見出雜而不純，實由于試驗習題所形成。筆下涉及社會面雖比較廣闊，最親切熟悉的，或許還是我的家鄉和一條延長千里的沅水，及各個支流縣分鄉村人事。這地方的人民愛惡哀樂、生活感情的式樣，都各有鮮明特徵。我的生命在這個環境中長成，因之和這一切分不開。（《文集》，11：70）[1]

1　《沈從文文集》（廣州：花城出版社，香港三聯，1982-1985），共 12 冊。本文簡稱《文集》，如注明 11：70，表示第 11 卷，頁 70。

這是他作品中，他「最滿意的文章」，因為表現問題、結構、和文字都有「新意」。這不但是他的也是中國現代文學的新收穫，所以沈從文以湘西富有傳奇神秘色彩的生活、語言、地方色彩創造出突破性的新小說。他在〈我的寫作與水的關係〉（1937）說：

> 到十五歲以後，我的生活同一條辰河無從分開……我雖離開了
> 那條河流，我所寫的故事，却多數是水邊的故事。故事中我所
> 最滿意的文章，常用船上水上作為背景。我故事中人物的性
> 格，全為我在水邊船上所見到的人物性格。我文字中一點憂鬱
> 氣氛，便因為被過去十五年前南方的陰雨天氣影響而來。我文
> 字風格，假若還有些值得注意處，那只是因為我記得水上人的
> 言語太多了。（《文集》，11：325）

到了三十年代至四十年代中期，沈從文從區域文化的角將來窺探和再現鄉村中國的生活方式及鄉下人的靈魂的小說已有成就，他開始有信心的從他自己所追求與試驗的小說觀點來考察當時比他早成名的小說家之小說。這些評論，其實是為自己努力創作的小說爭取承認，建設其新小說傳統而寫的。這些批評自然也泄露他自己的小說的奧秘。所以詩人批評家艾略特的話，可以很恰當的用來說明沈從文這些評論文章的特點。

> 我最好的文學批評……便是討論那些影響過我的詩人及詩劇
> 家的論文。這是我創作室的副產品，或是發揚一下構成我創作
> 詩歌的一些思想概念。現在回想起來，我明白我所以寫得好，
> 因為在我沒計劃寫，或沒機會寫之前，這些影響過我的詩人之
> 作品，我早就讀得滾瓜爛熟了……你必須把它跟我寫的詩歌聯
> 繫起來考察，才能看出它的權威性與局限性。[2]

---

2 T.S. Eliot, "The Frontiers of Criticism", *On Poetry and Poets* （New York: The Monday Press, 1961），p,117。

我始終相信，詩人的文評……目的是要替他所寫的那種詩辯護，或是爲他的詩建設理論基礎。尤其當他還年輕，正積極的爲他所要實踐的那種詩歌而戰鬥的時候，他是從自己的作品來看過去的詩歌：因此對那些他學習過的已逝世的詩人，他就表示感激和贊賞，對那些與他詩學背道而馳的就過分的冷漠。這種詩人批評家要執行的不是一個主持公道的法官的任務，而是一個替人辯護的律師。[3]

沈從文在許多當代小說作品中找到了與自己相似之處，譬如在〈論施蟄存與羅黑芷〉一文中他說：「這兩人皆爲以被都市文明侵入後小城小鎮的毀滅爲創作基礎」（《文集》，11：107），下面二段文字，如果不知道作者，會被誤以爲是在分析沈從文小說的特點，其實是他對廢名小說的一種認同：

> 作者的作品，是充滿了一切農村寂靜的美。差不多每篇都可以看到一個我們所熟悉的農民，在一個我們生長的鄉村，如我們同樣生活過來那樣活到那片土地上。不但那農村少女動人清朗的笑聲，那聰明的姿態，小小的一條河，一株孤零零長在菜園一角的葵樹，我們可以從作品中接近，就是那略帶牛糞氣味與略帶稻草味的鄉村空氣，也是仿佛把書拿來就可以嗅出的。（《文集》，11：96-97）

> 作者……所采取的背景也仍然是那類小小鄉村方面。譬如小溪河、破廟、老人、小孩，這些那些……作者地方性強，且顯明表現在作品人物語言上。按照自己的習慣，使文字離去一切文法束縛與藻飾，使文字變成言語……（《文集》，11：98）

沈從文還特地指出他與廢名相同之處是：「同樣努力爲仿佛我們世界以外那一個被人疏忽遺忘的世界，加以詳細的注解，使人有對于另

---

3 T.S. Eliot, "The Music of Poetry", 同上注，pp. 17-18。

一世界憧憬以外的認識。」(《文集》，11：1000)；農村所保持的和平靜穆，在天災人禍貧窮變亂中，慢慢地也全毀了，「一則因爲對農村觀察相同，一則因背景地方風俗習慣也相同。」(〈論馮文炳〉《文集》，11：100)。 沈從文特別喜愛廢名的小說，因爲「由最純粹農村散文詩形式出現」(《文集》，11：100)，在〈夫婦‧序言〉中，他甚至坦白承認受了廢名抒情詩小說之影響(《文集》，8：393)。

　　沈從文稱他自己所寫的這種小說的傳統，可追溯到魯訊的小說。從魯迅〈故鄉〉、〈社戲〉，魯迅影響了王魯彥、許欽文、羅黑芷、黎錦明、施蟄存，從而建立了鄉土文學的傳統：

> 以被都市物質文明毀滅的中國中部城鎮鄉村人物作模範，用略帶嘲弄的悲憫的畫筆，塗上鮮明準確的顏色，調子美麗悅目，而顯出的人物姿態又不免有時使人發笑，是魯迅先生的作品獨造處。分得了這一部分長處，是王魯彥，許欽文同黎錦明。王魯彥把恢諧嘲弄拿去；許欽文則在其作品中，顯現了無數魯迅所描寫過的人物行動言語的輪廓；黎錦明，在他的粗中不失其爲細緻的筆下，又把魯迅的諷刺與魯彥平分了。另外一點，就是因年齡、體質這些理由，使魯迅筆下憂鬱的氣氛，在魯彥作品雖略略見到，却沒有文章風格異趣的羅黑芷那麼同魯迅相似。另外，于江南風物，農村靜穆和平，作抒情的幻想，寫了如〈故鄉〉、〈社戲〉諸篇表現的親切，許欽文等沒有做到，施蟄存君，却也用與魯迅風格各異的文章，補充了魯迅的說明。

　　(《文集》，11：107-108)

　　沈從文自己承認，他的鄉土小說是因受了魯迅同類的小說的啓發才開始創作。在〈沈從文小說選集‧題記〉一文說，除了中國古典文學，外國作家如契可夫(Anton Chekhov, 1860-1904)和莫泊桑(Guy de Maupassant, 1850-1893)的短篇，「加之由魯迅小說起始以鄉村回憶做題材的小說正受廣大讀者歡迎，我的學習用筆，因之獲得不少勇氣和信心。」(《文集》，11：69) 不但如此，在 1947 年寫的〈學魯迅〉中，他還尊魯迅爲中國鄉土文學之始祖，而肯定這種鄉土文學成爲二十多年來小說的主流：

> 於鄉土文學的發軔，作爲領路者，使新作家群的筆，從教條觀念拘束中脫出，貼近土地，挹取滋養，新文學的發展，進入一個新的領域，而描寫土地人民成爲近二十年文學主流。(《文集》，11：233)

在 1931 年寫的〈論中國創作小說〉(《文集》，11：163-186) 中沈從文用較多的篇幅評論魯迅在現代小說史的位置。他不但肯定其開創了鄉土小說的貢獻，而且把小說的題材與技巧，帶進成熟的境界。沈從文認爲，第一時期的小說，寫得極其膚淺，即是「嚇人的單純」，而「人生文學」沒有「多少意義」，因爲「所要說到的問題太大，而所能說到的却太小了。」當時的作者只注意自己作品的實用目的，忘却了讀者，魯迅「從教條觀念拘束中脫出，貼近土地，挹取滋養。」魯迅小說展覽「一幅幅鄉村的風景畫在眼前」，使各人皆從自己回想中去印證；中國農村在長期混戰、土匪騷擾，新的物質侵入中逐漸毀滅了。沈從文也特別喜愛魯迅作品中的頹廢、苦悶、幻想、憂鬱、感傷和冷嘲。請讀下列兩段評論：

> 魯迅的作品，混和的有一點頹廢，一點冷嘲，一點幻想的美，同時又能應用較完全的文字，處置所有作品到一個較好的篇章裏去，因此魯迅的《吶喊》，成爲讀者所歡喜的一本書了。(《文集》，11：166)
>
> 還有一個情形，就是在當時「人生文學」能拘束作者的方向，却無從概括讀者的興味，作者許可有一個高尚尊嚴的企圖，而讀者却需要一個恢諧美麗的故事。一些作者都只注意自己"作

品"乃忘却了"讀者"。魯迅一來，寫了〈故鄉〉、〈社戲〉，
給年青人展覽一幅幅鄉村的風景畫在眼前，使各人皆從自己回
想中去印證。又從〈阿Q正傳〉上，顯出一個大家熟習的中國
人的姿態，用一種諧趣的稍稍誇張的刻畫，寫成了這個作品。
作者在這個工作上恰恰給了一些讀者一種精神的糧食，魯迅因
此成功了。作者注意到那故事諧謔的筆法，不甚與創作相宜，
這作品雖得到無數的稱贊，第二個集子〈仿徨〉，却沒有那種
寫作的方法了。在《吶喊》上的〈故鄉〉與《仿徨》上的〈示
衆〉一類作品，說明作者創作所達到的純粹，是帶著一點憂鬱，
用作風景畫那種態度，長處在以準確鮮明的色，畫出都市與農
村的動靜。作者的年齡，使之成爲沉靜，作者的生活各種因緣，
却又使之焦躁不寧，作品中憎與愛相互混和，所非常厭惡的世
事，乃同時顯出非常愛著的固執，因此作品中感傷的氣氛，并
不比郁達夫爲少。所不同的，郁達夫是以個人的失望而呼喊，
魯迅的悲哀，是看清楚了一切，辱罵一切，嘲笑一切，却同時
仍然爲一切所困窘，陷到無從自拔的悶裏去了的。(《文集》, 11:
166-167)

　　從上面所舉的一些例證，正可說明沈從文幾乎僅用自己作品獨特
的創意來進行解釋和判斷魯迅及其他人的作品。他的批評的視境很
小，只論鄉土作家的作品，也正因如此；他獨具慧眼，透視了魯迅及
其他人的小說。過去由於沈從文作品被郭沫若等人斥爲「反動文藝」，
沈從文被歪曲和誤解爲魯迅的敵人，因此他對魯迅小說評價沒有受到
學者應有的重視。[4]今天如果我們根據沈從文的評論去評析魯迅的小
說，我們更能深入的瞭解魯迅的小說特點與成就，其小說在歷史的定

---

4 譬如袁良駿的《魯迅研究史》上卷（西安；陝西人民出版社,1986），并沒提到沈從
　文對魯迅小說的看法。

位，將更準確。所以沈從文對魯迅小說的評論，參考價值之高，是許多後代學者所難於超越的。可惜至今尚未被學人采納，用來評析魯迅的小說，更未注意到沈從文的一個有關小說史的定位的論點：從魯迅到沈從文，他們建立了一個中國小說的新傳統。[5]

從沈從文對魯迅及其他小說家的評論，更可以清楚的看出，他努力建立一種小說的新傳統。這個傳統由魯迅開始，他們都是擺脫許多二三十年代寫作教條觀念的拘束，貼近土地去描寫被物質文明毀滅的鄉村小鎮。這種作品的語言文字表現風格特點是，充滿抒情的語言、冷靜、感傷、憂鬱，還混合著頹廢、冷嘲和幻想美。[6]

二、用鄉村中國的眼光看現代文明：都市小說的開始

雖然沈從文的小說給人的印象，主要是描寫湘西的鄉村中國，其實他的城市小說幾乎占了全部作品的一半。在《沈從文文集》中的小說，有76篇以城市為主題，87篇以鄉村為主題。[7]在他描寫鄉村社會的小說中，對都市文明的批判也有所表現，像〈雨後〉（1928）、〈蕭蕭〉、〈夫婦〉（1929）、〈菜園〉（1929）、〈三三〉（1931）、〈貴生〉（1937）等小說，就是很好的例子。沈從文的這些鄉村小說，不只表現區域文化，他更以鄉村中國的文學視野，一方面監視著在城市商業文明的包圍、侵襲下，農材緩慢發生的一切，同時又在原始野性的活力中，顯現都市人的沉落靈魂。[8]例如，在〈三三〉（《文集，4：120-148》那篇

---

5 一般論鄉土文學的文章，并沒有接納沈從文，把他放在魯迅創導的鄉土小說中。

6 我有專文探討沈從文對魯迅小說之批評，見王潤華〈沈從文論魯迅：中國現代小說的新傳統〉，見《沈從文小說理論與作品新論》（臺北：文史哲出版社，1998，pp.71-86）。

7 關於這個問題，我曾指導過一篇學位論文研究其城鄉主題，見梁其功《沈從文作品中城鄉主題的比較研究》（新加坡國立大學中文系碩士論文，1994）。

8 吳福輝〈鄉村中國的文化形態：論京派小說〉見《帶著枷鎖的笑》（杭州：浙江文藝出版社，1991），頁113-135。

小說中呈現的是鄉村中國的自然人發現都市人的病態及荒謬性。三三和她的寡母住在苗區山彎堡子裏過著世外桃源的生活。有一天城裏來了一個白面書生，他原來是希望到鄉下養病，享受農村田野的新鮮空氣，吃些新鮮鷄蛋蔬菜，滋補身體，然後把病治好。三三的媽媽希望把女兒嫁給這位青年，可是城市人突然得狂病死了。整個村落的人開始對城市及從城市來的人感到驚恐，他們認識到城市人與病人是同等意義的。在〈三三〉小說中，通過象徵性的語言，解剖了鄉村中國與城市中國的第一次相遇後，鄉村人對城市的夢幻開始破滅，而大自然的靈藥也救治不了城市人的死亡，因爲他患的已是第三期的癆病。

　　在另一篇充滿抒情幻想的抒情詩小說〈夫婦〉(《文集》,8：384-393）中，城市人在現代文明的污染與壓力下，生命變得空虛，因此患上神經衰弱症。最後他回歸大自然去尋找自然的生命力來治療自己的病。可是原本潛藏著生命力的鄉村世界却正在都市文明的侵染下逐漸失去那原始的人性美與生命力。保護鄉村的團衛就是都市文明的化身：它亂用權力，虛僞，公報私仇。〈菜園〉(《文集》，2：261-271）中的"縣府"，胡亂處决玉少琛及其妻子，代表現代文明只是一場慘無人道的政治鬥爭，在白色恐怖中，許多無辜的老百姓慘遭殺害。這是另一種現代文明帶來的災難。

　　所以沈從文在他的被稱爲最具魅力，充滿泥土氣息的小說中，仍然沒有忘記都市文化無孔不入的侵人其間，而引起自然生活秩序的錯亂，美麗的自然大地的受破壞。沈從文在一九三一年寫〈記胡也頻〉裏，對當時上海新感覺　派都市文學作家如劉吶鷗、穆時英、葉靈鳳很有好感。他說：「上海方面還　有幾個‘都市文學’的作家，也仿佛儼然能造成一種空氣」(《文集》，9：80），沈從文以都市主題爲中心的小說，如〈紳士的太太〉(1929)、〈虎雛〉(1931)、〈八駿圖〉(1935)

等小說中[9]他又以鄉下人的目光來觀察都市人生來看都市人生荒謬性與社會病態現象。沈從文的鄉村中國的視野是具有道德與價值的一把尺，一把稱：

> 我是一個鄉下人，走到任何一處照例都帶了一把尺，一把稱，和普通社會總是不合。一切來到我命運中的事事物物，我有我自己的尺寸和分量，采證實生命的價值與意義。（〈水雲〉《文集》，10：266）

所以他對都市人的觀察，依據的是「鄉下人」的標準。他把人類病態精神看作都市文明— 外部環境對人性的扭曲，那就是他拒絕的「社會」。這種扭 曲的人性與自然相衝突，在〈虎雛〉小說中，小兵虎雛被放置在城市中，接受 現代文明的教育與文化，從野蠻湘西鄉村來的他，做出直覺的抗爭，最後他 因在城裏打死一個城市人而消失。他打死一個城市人，表示他打死了城市文明，他的消失是暗喻鄉下人逃回到自然的鄉村去尋找失落的生命與意義。

這些小說都是通過鄉村中國的眼光在看中國城市，來觀察現代文明；真正屬於大多數人的中國是農村中國，而它正在逐漸消失。沈從文小說中的人物，都感到只有回歸到鄉村中國，才能找回失落的精神和品質。他們始終無法與都市文化認同。

沈從文這種鄉村中國的詩學，從鄉村中國來考察城市中國的小說，可說代表了中國五四時期以後的城市小說與詩歌的寫作視野與思維方式。從魯迅、王魯彥到施蟄存的鄉土作家，他們作品的主題是呈現現代物質文明如何慢慢毀滅中國的鄉鎮。即使到了上海現代派作家，像劉吶鷗、穆時英、杜衡、葉靈鳳和戴望舒。他們雖然長期生活在中國現代的上海，對現代都市有些認同，但對都市文明的困惑還是

---

9 各篇小說依次見《文集》，4：88-118；4：149-175；6：166-194。

很多，因爲他們多是從帶有鄉土味的鄉村或小城鎮走出城市的人家；結果還是站在現代大都市的邊緣來窺探都市人的觀念行爲模式。[10]

　　根據楊義的分析，三十年代上海現代派的都市文學作品對現代人的認識，也就是現代人的病症，可分爲三大類。第一種是「陌生人」。由於受了大都會物質文明和商業文明的極大誘惑，從城鄉湧進大都會的中國人，脫離了地緣、血緣，與倫理道德的維繫，他們一步一步掉進無底的深淵。所以從「片面人」又變成了「片面人」，最後變成「變態人」。[11]不屬於任何文學派別的老舍的城市小說，被稱爲「城市庶民文學的高峰」，而且是少數出身都市（北京）貧民階層的作家，但是老舍的代表作《駱駝祥子》，是關于一個出生農村的年輕人樣子，城市文明使他從鄉間帶朵的強壯的身體腐爛，成爲現代都市社會胎裏的產兒。他的墮落也是一步步的，從仁和車廠到大雜院與白房子（妓院），代表他逐漸掉進黑暗腐敗的都市文明的最底層。他也是從「陌生人」、「片面人」而最後被扭曲人性成爲「變態人」。[12]

　　沈從文描寫鄉下人與都市人在鄉鎮和大都市相遇的小說，在今天看來，它實際上構成以後歷久不衰的都市文學的視野與出發點。這種都市文學的詩學，恐怕要在今天臺灣八十年以來的作品中，才開始起了變化。[13]

三、揉詩、游記、散文與抒情幻想成一體的小說

　　吳福輝曾指出，沈從文最教人迷醉的作品，是以湘西沅水流域爲

---

10 楊義〈三十年代上海現代派的都市文化意識〉《二十世紀中國小說與文化》（臺北：業強出版社，1993），頁 217-230。

11 同上。

12 我對這問題在《老舍小說新論》（臺北：東大圖書公司，1995）有關篇章中有所討論。

13 王潤華〈從沈從文的"都市文明"到林耀德的"終端機文化"〉，《當代臺灣都市文學研究會》論文，1994 年 12 月 26-27 日臺北舉行。

背景，描繪富有傳奇神秘色彩的苗族人民生活的小說。在這些小說作品裏，他試驗把抒情詩、散文、游記筆調揉進小說裏，結果創造了突破性的新小說。[14]在上面討論魯迅、廢名、施蟄存等人反映現代物質文明侵襲與毀滅鄉村小說時，我們已注意到沈從文對他們的寫實小說中的抒情、幻想、憂鬱的氣氛非常重視。他在其他論中國現代作家的文章裏，特別注意以抒情詩、散文、游記筆調寫的作品。

　　沈從文自己認爲他曾努力在散文與小說中揉游記、散文和小說爲一體，這是〈新廢郵存底〉（1947）中的一段話：

> 用屠格涅夫寫《獵人日記》方法，揉游記散文和小說故事而爲一，使人事凸浮的西南特有明朗天時地理背景中。一切還帶點"原料"意味，值得特別注意。十三年前我寫《湘行散記》時，即有這種企圖……這麼寫無疑將成爲現代中國小說一格，且在這格式中還可望有些珠玉發現。（《文集》，12：67-68）

　　他主張打破小說、詩歌、散文之觀念，因此也勸別人去嘗試開拓這種新文體：

> 原因之一是將文學限於一種定型格式中，使一般人以爲必如此如彼，才叫作小說，叫作散文，叫作詩歌。習慣觀念縛住了自己一枝筆，無從使用……這工作成就，更無疑將於蘆焚、艾蕪、沙汀等作家，揉小說故事散文游記而爲一的試驗以外，自成一個新的型式。如能好好發展下去，將充滿傳奇性而又富有現實性……這種新的創作，不僅在"小說"上宜有新的珠玉產生，在女作家方面，也可望作到現有成績紀緣的突破……（《文集》，12：63）

　　除了揉詩、游記、散文成一體，沈從文也嘗試把抒情幻想放進寫

---

14 同前注（7）。

實的、充滿泥土氣息的小說中。他在〈《沈從文小說選集》·題記〉中
說：

> 1928 年到 1947 年約二十年間，我寫了一大堆東西……至於文
> 字中一部分充滿泥土氣息，一部分又文白雜揉，故事在寫實中
> 依舊浸透一種抒情幻想成分，內容見出雜而不純，實由於試驗
> 習題所形成……（《文集》，11：70）

在〈短篇小說〉一文中，他一再強調「詩的抒情」在任何藝術中
都應該放在第一位，因爲它能帶來特殊的敏感性能：

> 短篇小說的寫作，從過去傳統有所學習，從文字學文字，個人
> 以爲應當把詩放在第一位，小說放在末一位。一切藝術都容許
> 作者注入一種詩的抒情，短篇小說也不例外。由於對詩的認
> 識，將使一個小說作者對于文字性能具有特殊敏感。（《文集》，
> 12：126）

因此他特別推崇施蟄存「多幻想成分」，「具抒情詩美的交織」的
小說。（《文集》，11：100）

沈從文在〈《沈從文小說選集》·題記〉中，自我肯定他的小說異
於同時代之作家：

> 我的作品稍稍異於同時代作家處，在一開始寫作時，取材的側
> 重在寫我的家鄉……想試拭作綜合處理，看是不是能產生點散
> 文詩的效果。（《文集》，11：80）

〈夫婦〉根據其〈後記〉（《文集》，8：393），那是沈從文自認是
用「抒情詩的筆調」寫的小脫。我也曾分析過〈漁〉，這是大量注入抒
情幻想，成功發揮揉詩、散文、小說成一體的代表作。在這篇小說中，
一個複雜的主題結構，野蠻族人的好殺習俗，復仇、愛情、人類美麗
黑暗的心靈，靜靜的在朦朧的月下的河流、古廟、木魚念經聲中，揮

舞寶刀聲中、枯萎的花裏展現出來。[15]

四、結　論

　　沈從文是中國現代作家中少有的前衛主義作家，沈從文響往原始主義，[16]喜愛用超現實的新觀點來理解生命，同時又敢于嘗試以全新的語言文字來進行創作及理解生命的各種形式。他永遠「企圖從試探中完成一個作品」[17]。沈從文嘲笑憑著高尚目標或理想概念去寫作的作家，他要小說包含著社會人生現象與夢幻現象，他說小說不單是描寫眼見的狀態，更要寫一切官能感覺。沈從文要小說家超越現實，進入夢像，進入一般作家不能到達的地方，描寫眼睛看不到的狀態，探索人類的靈魂或意識底層。他的目的是要發現人，重新對人給予詮釋，甚至把已經破破碎碎的生命與靈魂粘合起來。他要努力創作的，是揉詩、游記、散文與抒情幻想成一體的小說、描寫被現代文明逐漸毀滅的鄉村小說、用鄉村中國的眼光打量城市的小說。沈從文就是這樣一位具有巨大野心的藝術家，從他的創作理論與小說作品，能幫助我們瞭解他努力建立的中國現代小說的新傳統。

---

15 我有專文論析這篇小說，見本書〈一條河流上擴大的抒情幻想：探索人類靈魂意識深處的小說《漁》的解讀〉，同注（6），pp.145-160。
16 參考 Jeffrey Kinkley, *The Odyssey of Shen Congwen* (Stanford: Stanford University Press, 1987), pp. 112-113。
17 凌宇〈沈從文談自己的創作〉《中國現代文學研究叢刊》，1980 年第 4 期，p.317。

解構與建構「故事新編小說」：
補寫文學史的空白

—— 序朱崇科

《張力的狂歡：論魯迅及其來者之故事新編小說中的主體介入》

一、我的學術嗅覺與感覺告訴我，朱崇科
是具有開放的思考與視野的學者

　　朱崇科這個研究題目，我最早在他申請報讀博士班的表格上看見。那是 2000 年，當時我負責新加坡國立大學的碩/博士生入學申請事務，由于我也研究魯迅，自然特別注意。後來系裏審查資格通過後，考慮給予優厚的研究獎學金之前，我還通過電話，跟遠在中國廣州的朱崇科討論這項研究計劃，作爲大學規定執行的面試。從書面數據與對話，我的學術嗅覺與感覺告訴我，朱崇科不是時下很多只是追求高學位爲最後目的的學生，是一位有潛力、有野心的學者，具有開放的思考與視野，將會成爲重新加入國際學術界的中國新一代的學人。因此朱崇科便榮獲新加坡國立大學研究獎學金，順利的在新加坡寫完這篇博士論文。開始的時候我雖然是指導老師，但最後的兩年我去了臺灣，他幾乎是獨立自主的從頭走到底，作爲一個有獨立思考的人，這是朱崇科不幸中的大幸。

　　我說我的學術嗅覺與感覺告訴我，「朱崇科是一位有潛力、有野心的學者，具有開放的思考與視野的學者，將會成爲重新加入國際學術界的中國新一代的學人」。四年後的現在，事實證實我的眼光沒錯。

他到了新加坡後，由于新加坡的學術文化單薄，他搞現代文學，新加坡國立大學中文系這方面的學者當時主要我一個人，他似乎很失望。我告訴他，我們的漢學研究（Chinese Studies）的學術架構與中國不同，不以人數取勝，我們系裏古今文史哲的人才齊全、海外華人文化、從儒家、宗教、文學，到華語研究都有。因此這種另類的學術機構，可以提供我們從事知識整合、跨越學科的思考。他應該從中原爲中心的思考，轉向多元思考，拆掉狹窄的學科的圍墻。可學的地方可不少，這種優越的環境，是肉眼看不見的，數目字呈現不出來的。

我別強調，希望他研究中國現代文學的同時，把世界華文文學/文化納入他的研究領域，還有強大的英文系的英文文學，尤其後殖民文學。這塊新知識的發掘，以後會受用無窮。尤其在中國的學術界，還沒有知識與實地生活/學術經驗具備的人。

果然朱崇科在新加坡這幾年，他最下苦功的地方，不只是中國現代文學，他更興奮與勤勞的研究新馬華文文學。我在研究所「中國新文學專題研究」的討論課裏與同學研討郁達夫的自我放逐南洋的解讀，朱崇科很快就完成了〈丈量旁觀與融入的距離：郁達夫放逐南洋轉變探因〉，馬上就拿去發表。他不像其它同學寫一篇報告交給老師就滿足了。他不久前出版的《本土性的糾葛》論文集的成果，相信幾年前在他離開中國到新加坡前，絕對沒有想像過的研究課題。

二、建構中國文學史上的新文類「故事新編小說」：補寫小說史空白的一頁

這本論文力圖從體裁詩學的新視角進行觀照，利用巴赫金狂歡化理論重讀魯迅的故事新編小說，同時更難得的，又討論此一小說次文類的其它代表性個案，包括、施蟄存、劉以鬯、李碧華、西西/也斯、陶然等人的作品。對接受朱崇科的這套論說的學者而言，以後文學史

便會出現「故事新編小說」這一次文類。這項研究替中國小說史，填補上原來空白的一頁。

為了利用非常複雜的狂歡化理論重讀魯迅的《故事新編》，為了說服巴赫金的狂歡化理論適用性及其分析的合理性，朱崇科化了三分之一的篇幅，不厭其煩的反復論說，請看下面：

> 巴赫金的狂歡化理論對應了魯迅《故事新編》中意義的眾聲喧嘩的多重世界，而且令人驚訝的是，他的有關小說的精妙理論也指出了《故事新編》文體互參以及小說自身的開放性等特質。當然，巴赫金的理論畢竟有其獨特的產生語境和適用範圍，他的關于狂歡化的起源 —— 歐洲狂歡節的特點和表達方式（比如過分誇張和強調飲食、身體等物質特徵）顯然和 20 世紀的中國語境有著較大的差異。
>
> 所以本文首先梳理了歷史語境中巴赫金非常繁複、駁雜精深的狂歡化理論，凸現其自身的適用範圍和內在邏輯，當然在以之分析魯迅等人的故事新編時，選擇了自己吻合的部分進行靈活運用：或者直接關聯，或者關涉其狂歡化精神。
>
> 還需要指出的是，故事新編小說文體的創新和成立同樣也需要狂歡化理論的燭照和獨特視野的認知。甚至有些時候，我們即使能夠認識到魯迅《故事新編》的狂歡色彩，却未見得深入體察此類小說的合法性和命名的正當性。

朱崇科的這種論證的態度與精神，分析的方法，代表他是中國研究現代文學的學術界新一代的學人。

三、從人文的思考到非人文的解構：
這是解構，不是毀壞

朱崇科這本論文的重要性，不但因為研究中提供的具有創見的結論，如分析巴赫金非常複雜的狂歡化理論；從主體介入，探討事新編小說的狂歡品格，故事新編小說的個性；找尋可以評判此次文類小說及分析其作品，本文的研究主題的構想，具體問題的觀察與分析，將在中國現代文學研究具有啓示與歷史性的指標意義，甚至提供了一個再出發的契機。因此有需要理解朱崇科用巴赫金狂歡化理論重讀魯迅的故事新編小說，及此一小說次文類的其它代表性個案後面學術思想。

阿布罕斯（M.H. Abrams）在〈英文文學研究的變化：1930-1995〉（"The Transformation of English Studies:1930-1995" 文見 Thomas Bender and Carl Schorske（eds），*American Academic Culture in Transforamtion: Fifty Years, Four Disciplines*（Princeton: Princeton University Press,1998）中分析了過去五十年來英文文學（包括美國文學）研究的變化.這篇文章雖然寫于 1995，目前已過了十年，還可以用來說明目前的情況。在二十世紀的三十年代之前，文學研究基本上以歷史語言學（philology）的方法爲主流，就如清朝末年至民國初年的訓詁考證，通過語言、歷史、社會事件、作者生平來詮釋文學。從 30 到 60 年代，那是新批評（New Criticism）的全盛時期。他們主張直接內在的以作品本身爲分析對象，以文學論文學，通過細讀（close reading）和分析作品本身的文字與藝術結構，讓普遍、永恒不變的評審標準來評價。由此可見，他們已把文學作品當作自然物來看待，而研究方法，與物理科學家的方法相似。作者生平、創作本意置之不問，文學作品已成爲客觀獨立體。

不過阿不罕斯特別指出，在新批評鼎盛期，它被稱爲壟斷批評界，主要是指大學部的文學課程的設計與評釋方法，在專門的高深研究中，學者的方法還是多元的，如從生平、心理、社會、歷史各個角度來解讀文學。其實在 30 年代後期，跨學科（cross disciplinary）的美國研究（American Studies）、中國研究（Chinese Studies）已發展起來，強調文學、思想、生活不同領域的知識互相整合.這種跨學科的研究，又把文學帶入一個全新的境界（我在我的《越界跨國文學解讀》書中有所論述）。

在六十年代帶末期，解構運動爆發，從女性文學理論、國族、後殖民理論來研究文學突然非常盛行。解構主義運動最大的革命是解除過去長期以西方的思考模式（Western paradigm）來解釋文學的規範，這些西方思考模式產生的文學的解釋模式，基本上是以西方文明爲典範而發展出來的，對其它文化所碰到的課題涵蓋與詮釋性不夠，不過無論它如何去解釋文學，都是人文的思考模式（humanistic paradigm）。解構主義理論則相反，把文本從人間（human world）放置到非人類的場所（non-human site），尤其語言的游戲性與話語（discourse）這是一項極端的改變，因爲他們把人製造的、詮釋的文學作品，以及重現的生活世界，全部通過對語言與話語的力量與結構加予分析。

後結構給文學研究帶來新的力能（energy），使我們相信重新探討原來以爲大家早已認同的文學課題是值得的。新的視野使到舊的、熟悉的問題變成新鮮、引人深感興趣，發現新的價值。這就是朱崇科用巴赫金狂歡化理論重讀魯迅的故事新編的小說，及其它此類文類的其它代表小說，使我們瞭解到以前沒有存在的意義。以解構手法進行的優秀的研究，往往其顛覆的行爲是有理的、有需要的，因爲其目的只是挑戰、質疑、發現問題 、或拆除正統的思考方法。

所以朱崇科這本論文中的研究，這是解構，不是毀壞，它要把有問題的課題重新安置（resituate）或重新立案（reinscribe）。

A Journey to the Heart of Darkness: The Mode of Travel Literature in Lu Xun's Fiction

Literature as a Mode of Travel

When I was a visiting scholar at the University of California at Berkely last year, I discovered an interesting book entitled *The Literature as a Mode of Travel* in the Doe Library. Consisting of five essays, an introduction and a postscript, the book was designed to illustrate ways in which travelers and travel books have extended knowledge, enlarged ideas, and contributed to imaginative literature.Iam particularly intrigued by the relationships between travel literature and fiction.[1] When it is related to Chinese literature, many opportunities lie open for research in this field.

Professional travellers and good writers alike are great explorers. They love to penetrate deep into remote lands, societies and forests to yield up their secrets. They possess the spirit of curiosity and discovery. They will use their practiced and professional eye to observe the customs

---

1 Warner Rice and W.T. Jewkes （eds.）, *The Literature as a Mode of Travel* （New York: New York Public Library, 1963）. I found the following three articles are most interesting: Warner Rice, "Introduction: the Literature and Travel Books," 7-12; W.T. Jewkes, "The Literature of Travel and the Mode of Romance in the Renaissance," pp. 31-52; F. Rogers, "The Road to Reality: Burlesque Travel Literature and Mark Twain's *Roughing It*," 85-100.

and culture of the people. Regardless of the nature or lifestyle witnessed, both professional travelers and writers will utilize their observations to depict defects in their own societies, culture of the people. All writers are, in fact, travelers and explorers. Not only do they tour the many societies and countries, but they also explore the hearts of men in order to discover and understand the ugliness of the human soul.

Professional travellers, good writers, and great explorers are no different from one another. They record their thoughts and depict sceneries as them. Travel literature is usually autobiographical and thus especially meaningful for the reader. However, as such, literature is an integration of the traveller's subjective and objective viewpoints; thus, travel accounts evoke diverse focuses and perspectives. Some have a theme on nature, others record customs, while others depict religion.

Hence, the voyages of Western explorers and travellers have inspired many a playwright and poet. Spenser, Shakespeare and Milton have often assimilated the traveller's theme into their works. Byron also has introduced the traveller's theme into his poem, *Childe Harold*.[2]

For centuries, Western prose fiction and travel literature have mutually influenced each other. If we were to compare travel literature with romance fiction of the Elizabethan period, we would find that the romantic fictitious style has substantially influenced travel literature.[3] Similarly, Mark Twain's （1835-1910） piece, *Roughing It* （1871）, has been viewed by Western critics, as a specific type of travel literature-an

---

2 See Warner Rice, "Introduction," *Ibid.*, 7-12.
3 See N.T. Jewkes, "The Literature of Travel and the Mode of Romance in the Renaissance," *Ibid.*, 31-52.

adventurous encounter. Through exaggerated humour, Twain has disguised travel literature in his satirical classic.[4]

Today, much of the West's prose fiction is built upon the plan of a journey-either by land or sea, either domestic or foreign. The journey may be fictitious or factual. Since Daniel Defoe's （1660-1731） *Robinson Crusoe* （1719） and Jonathan Swift's （1667-1745） *Gulliver's Travels* （1726）, it has been a tradition for travel literature to influence contemporary literature.[5] In the twentieth century, more and more prose fictions are built upon a journey. My personal favorites are Joseph Conrad's *Heart of Darkness* and William Golding's *Lord of the Flies*, both of which use vivid images of a journey to explore, illustrate and signify the human spirit and its development.[6]

Many classic Chinese novels have successfully transformed travel literature conventions into the means for significant literary expression. Wu Chengen's （1500?-1582?） *Journey to the West* is a typical example example. Lu Xun's favorite Qing Dynasty works also show evidences of travel literature. Among such works are Wu Jingzi's （1701-1745） *The Scholars,* Liu E's （1857-1900） *The Travels of Lao Can, and* Cao Xueqin's （1715-1763） *A Dream of Red Mansions*. The influence of travel literature is more apparent and stronger in the former two works.[7]

---

4 F. Rogers, "The Road to Reality: Burlesque Travel Literature and Mark Twain's *Roughing it,*" 85-100.

5 Warner Rice, "Introduction," *Ibid.,* 8-9.

6 For references, see Bruce Harkness （ed.）, *Conrad's Heart of Darkness and the Critics* （Belmont, California: Wadsworth Publishing Co., 1960）, James Baker and Arthur Ziegler Jr. （eds.）, *William Golding's Lord of Files: Text, Notes and Criticism* （New York: G.P. Patnam's Sons, 1964）.

7 V.I. Semanov, *Lu Hsun and His Predecessors,* tr. Charles Alber （New York: M.E. Sharpe,

For example, the opening passage of *A Dream of Red Mansions* explains that its author writers with a worthy purpose. Hoping to enlighten the readers, Cao introduces the "erotic journey." This is why Jia Baoyu is led to the Land of Illusion to "initiate him in the pleasures of the flesh." Therefore the author assimilates the traveller's theme in his narrative.[8]

In *A History of Twentieth Century Chinese Fiction and Changes of Narrative Modes in Chinese Fiction*[9], Chen Pingyuan has extensively dealt with how Chinese classical writers drew the themes of travel literature into fiction, especially the "New Fiction" of the late Qing period. He points out that since ancient times, travel literature as a genre, has been admired by many scholars, who themselves often employ this literary style at some point in their career. However, pure travel literature has been transformed, as travel themes have become popular among fiction writers. Novelists have drawn great inspiration from travel literature. Some have taken advantage of the genre to strengthen the distinctiveness and delicate feature of the natural landscape. Others have used it to disguise themselves in characters as innocent tourists on unfamiliar journeys, whose new experiences enable criticism of particular societies. Characters have become a witness of history, observing the sufferings of people, and the corruption of the upper class. They depict the writer's encounter of

---

1980） 75-119. This is a study of the influence of late Qing fiction on Lu Xun's works.

8 Wong Yoon Wah, "The Parallelism Between Arstotle's and Two Chinese Novelists' Principles of Catharsis," *Essays on Chinese Literature: A Comparative Approach* （Singapore University Press, 1989） 137-149.

9 Chen Pingyuan, *A History of Twentieth Century Chinese Fiction* （二十世紀中國小說史）, Vol. 1 （Beijing: Peking University Press, 1989）226-246; Chen Pingyuan, *Changes of Narrative Modes in Chinese Fiction* （中國小說敘事模式的轉變） （Shanghai: Shanghai People's Publisher, 1988） 196-203.

societal changes and supplement the missing parts of history. Even if the transcripts are but fictitious records, the results would nevertheless be the same.[10]

Chen Pingyuan in his above studies focuses his analysis on how travel literature affects the narrative modes of late Qing novels. Besides successfully depicting the sufferings of the people and supplementing the missing parts of history, he also points out that the most important achievement of introducing travel themes into novels is to restrict the narrator's point of view. Just as true travel accounts are largely autobiographical, novels with traveller's themes are usually written in first-person narration. In other words, the novelist links together the characters, events, and actions to the eyes, ears, and foot-steps of the traveler.[11] Late Qing travel theme novels, such as *The Travels of Lao Can, Strange Events of the Last Twenty Years, A Flower in the Ocean of Sin,* and other works of the New Fiction, are held in high esteem by Lu Xun. Vladmir Semanov's *Lu Xun and His Predecessors*[12] is an in-depth study of Lu Xun's views on these novels.

In a paper on how contemporary Chinese literature portrays itself, Lee Oufan analyzes the travel literature of Yu Dafu, Shen Congwen, and Ai Wu. He concludes that the theme of the solitary traveler, wandering on a journey in search of the meaning of life and society, can be found in a large number of fictional and nonfictional works of the May Fourth

---

10 Chen Pingyuan, A History of Twentieth Century Chinese Fiction, 236-39.
11 Chen Pingyuan, Changes of Narrative Modes in Chinese Fiction, 196-201.
12 V.I. Semanov, Lu Hsun and His Predecessors, op. cit., 42-74.

Period.[13] Chen Pingyuan, in his analysis of late Qing fiction, has also knotted that the novels of the May Fourth Period have often drawn on the travel theme, especially the theme of the returning traveler:

> The writers of the May Fourth Period have also written novels similar to travel literature, using themes like 'the home coming traveller' -an intellectual who has traveled far and long returning to his homeland witnessing its decadence and feeling despaired.⋯⋯[14]

Among the works belonging to his category, is Lu Xun's short story, "My Hometown," which is discussed in later part of this article.

The mutual influence between travel literature and Chinese literature is a complicated yet interesting subject. I hope that one day someone will conduct an in-depth study in this area. The introduction of the travel theme into Chinese literature is obvious, as has been demonstrated by Lee Qufan and Chen Pingyuan; but this also is a complicated topic. Due to the limited space, the article will only examine some stories collected in Lu Xun's *A Call to Arms* and *Wandering*. The aim is to show how the May Fourth writers use the plot of a journey to depict the darkness of society, and the sufferings of the people. Travel literature specifically limits the writer's story to what the traveller sees or hears. It injects reality into fiction, and acts as a web to tighten the plot and limit the narrative point of view. The focus of this article is to study the different types of journeys, and the meaning of the travel. This article will only consider some basic

---

13 Leo Lee, "The Solitary Traveler: Images of the Self in Modern Chinese Literature," in *Expressions of Self in Chinese Literature*, Eds. Robert Hegel and Richard Hessely (New York: Columbia University Press, 1985) 282-321.

14 Chen Pingyuan, *Changes of Narrative Modes in Chinese Fiction*, p.203.

issues, in order to reaffirm the successful transformation of travel literature conventions, into a means for significant literary expression. More specific questions-such as those concerning the particular sources influencing Lu Xun's work- are beyond the scope of this paper, and hence will not be addressed.

I Would Go Up and Down to Seek :
Lu Xun's View on Travel Literature

Before Lu Xun wrote the stories included in *A Call to Arms* and *Wandering*, he was already very interested in travel literature. For example, he translated Jules Verne's (1828-1905) adventure stories, *From the Earth to the Moon* and *Voyage to the Centre of the Earth* in 1903, and *Les Adventures du Lapitaine* in 1904. In a brief critique on *From the Earth to the Moon,* Lu Xun himself remarked:

> The author makes use of fiction to predict the Progress of the world, and express his imagination.Other elements such as scientific knowledge, human feelings, the sorrow of parting and the happiness of reunion, and adventurous experiencescan be found in the fictional works. Sometimes satire, irony and social implications are also hidden in the stories.[15]

Lu Xun was especially attracted by the mode of travel literature, in which the reader is presented with satirical attacks and human feelings.

---

15 Lu Xun's Chinese translations of Jules Verne's (1828-1905) *From the Earth to the Moon* (1865) and *Voyage to the Centre of the Earth* (1864) are now collected in *The Complete Works of Lu Xun* （魯迅全集）, Vol. 11 （Beijing: People's Literature Publisher, 1973）; Lu Xun's translation of *Les Adventures du Capitaine Hatteras* in manuscript has been lost.

For this reason, he fell in love with classical Chinese legendary accounts and novels which centered upon the plan of a journey.[16]

Through the power of fiction, especially the dramatic story of human beings, no matter beings realistic or imaginary, fictional works provide a source of interesting entertainment and enlightenment to the people. The common people may have never heard of *The Classic of Mountains and Seas, History of Three Kingdoms* and other classics, but they are familiar with legendary figures and historical figures such as Zhou Yu, Zhu Geliang. This is due to the influenceof novels *Flower in the Mirror* and *Romance of the Three Kingdoms.*……

Studies of Chinese classical literature by Lu Xun and other scholars, show that Lu Xun highly recommended works, such as *The Scholar* and *The Travels of Lao Can.* Writing fiction became the means by which he exposed the social illness and the sickness of Chinese souls. Like many writers of the late Qing period, Lu Xun continued to be obsessed with the educational function of literature and championed it as an instrument for national reform. Lu Xun even testified that he chose literature as his career because he believed it to be a more effective weapon than science or politics to fight lethargy, cowardice, and ignorance. He said his motive for writing was "to expose the disease and draw attention to it so that it might be cured.……"[17]

---

16 See Lu Xun's *"A Note on From the Earth to the Moon"* （月界旅行辨言） in *Lu Xun's Essays on Creative Writing* （魯迅論創作） （Shanghai: Shanghai Wenyi Chubanshe, 1983） 339-340.

17 "Preface to Lu Xun's Own Selection of Works" （自選集自序）, in *Lu Xun's Essays on Creative Writing*, 49.

The title of Lu Xun's first short story "Remembrances of the Past" (1911), indicates the writer's early recognition that fiction writing could be a journey into the past.[18] In the preface to *A Call to Arms* (1923), he explains that his subject matters were recollections which he "cannot forget completely."[19] Lu Xun's first collection of essays, *Dawn Blossoms Plucked at Dusk*, was originally entitled *Recollections of the Past*. In the preface written for this collection, he says: "These ten pieces are records transcribed from memory."[20] In *Wandering* (1926), Lu Xun introduced his work by quoting a few lines from Li Sao:

> In the morning, I started from my way to Cang Wu.In the evening I came to the Garden of Paradise. I wanted to stay a while in those fairy precincts, But the swift moving sun was dipping to the West. I ordered Xihe to stay the sun-steeds not go in. Long, long had been my road and far far was the journey I would go up and down to seek my heart's desire.[21]

In a short article entitled "Preface to Select Writings of Lu Xun," Lu Xun talks about the publication of *Wandering*. Here again he quotes the following two lines from *Li Sao* to express his purpose in writing fiction:

> Long long had been my road and far far was the journey;I would

---

18 There are a number of articles devoted to this short story, see, for example Jaroslav Prusek, "Lu Hsun's 'Huai Chiu': A Precursor of Modern Chinese Literature," *The Lyrical and the Epic: Studies of Modern Chinese Literature*, ed. Leo Lee (Bloomington, Indiana: Indiana University Press, 1980) 102-109.

19 *Selected Works of Lu Xun*, tr. Yang Xiangyi and Gladys Yang (Beijing: Foreign Languages Press, 1956), Vol. 1, p.1. Other quotations from Lu Xun's stories are taken from this English translation.

20 Lu Xun, *Dawn Blossoms Plucked at Dusk*, tr. Yang Xianyi and Gladys Yang (Beijing: Foreign Languages Press, 1976) 2.

21 *Ch'u Tz'u: The Songs of the South*, tr. David Hawkes, (Boston: Beacon Press, 1962) 28.

go up and down to seek my heart's desire.

It is obvious that Lu Xun considered his fiction to be a journey into old China and her social problems. Hence, most of his works were based on his childhood life in Shaoxing. He sought the symptoms of the Chinese people. He admits in "How I Wrote the Stores," "So my themes were usually the unfortunates in this abnormal society. My aim was to expose the disease and draw attention to it so that it might be corrected."[22] In addition, he wrote to draw out the "souls of the silent people."[23] Hence, he even explored the very souls of the people of China.

The Mode of Travel Literature In Lu Xun's Stories

Many of Lu Xun's stories are built upon the plan of a journey. There are three main types, namely: a journey to the native land, a visit to a remote town, and a walk in the village street. The following three tables show how successfully Lu Xun has hidden the themes of travel literature in his stories:[24]

Title of Story   Stories about Journeys to the Native Land

"Kong Yiji" ----"The wine shops in Luchen are not like those in other parts of China...twenty years ago...."

"My Old Home"----"Braving the bitter cold, I travelled more than seven hundred miles back to the old home I had felt over

---

22 *Lu Xun Selected Works*, Vol. III, tr. Yang Xianyi and Gladys Yang （Beijing: Foreign Languages Press 1980） 261.

23 Lu Xun, "Preface to Russian Translation of the True Story of Ah Q," （俄文譯本《 阿 Q正傳》序文）, in *Lu Xun on Creative Writing, op. cit.*, 9.

24 The following quotations from Lu Xun's stories are taken from the translations by Yang Xianyi and Gladys Yang in *Selected Works of Lu Hsun*, Vol. 1, op. cit.

twenty years ago."

"Village Opera" ----" I could not have been more than eleven or twelve. It was the custom in Luchen where we lived: for married women who were not yet in charge of the household to go back to their parents' home for the summer .... At such times I always went with her to stay in her parent's house. It was a place called Pingchiao Village, not far from the sea, a very out-of-the-way little village on a river...."

"The New Year's ----"New Year's Eve of the old calendar seems Sacrifice"after all more like the real New Year's Eve; for, to say nothing of the villages and towns, even in the air there is a feeling that New Year is coming. From the pale, lowering evening clouds issue fragment flashes of lightning, followed by a rumbling sound of firecrackers celebrating the departure of the Hearth God; while, nearer by, the firecrackers explode even more violently, and before the deafening report dies away, the air is filled with a faint smell of powder. It was on such a night that I returned to my native place, Luchen. Although I called it a native place, I had had no home there for some time, so I had to put up temporarily with a certain Mr. Lu, the fourth son of his family...."

"In the Wine Shop"---"During my travels from the North to the Southeast I made a detour to my home, then so S-. This town is only about ten miles from my native place, and can be

reached in less than half a day by a small boat. I had
taught in a school here for a year ... I looked for several
old colleagues I thought I might find, but not one was
there...."

"The Misanthrope"---"One autumn I stayed at Hanshishan with some
relatives also named Wei, who were distantly related to
him······" "Largely out of curiosity, perhaps, on my
way back I passed his house and went in to express
condolence ······ " "I wandered between Shanyang,
Licheng and Taiku for more than half a year, but could
find no work, so I decided to go back to S-······."

The above six stories all recount past journeys of returning natives.
Of these, "Kong Yiji," "My Old Home," and "The New Year's Sacrifice,"
are the most typical and comprehensive works with this theme returning
native. Another example is "Village Opera," with the Pingchiao Village
bearing resemblance to the Anchiao Village of Lu Xun's mother. In the
story, it is the homeland of I's mother. The other two stories, "In a Wine
Shop" and "The Misanthrope," each describe a traveller's meeting a long
forgotten friend on the way back to his native town. In his writing, Lu Xun
continues to draw upon his own childhood experiences in his own native
town, because this town itself represents the doomed mode of Chinese
existence. The village, which is backward and feudalistic, symbolizes the
larger Chinese society.[25]

---

25 I have explored the symbolic meaning of this aspect of Lu Xun's theme of "return of the
   native" in an article entitled "A Study of the Auto-Biographical Elements and the
   Antithesis Structure in Lu Xun's "My Home Town" （論魯迅〈故多〉的自傳性與對比

Title of Story   Stories about Small Towns and Cities

"An Incident"----"Six years have slipped by since I came from the country to the capital. During that time I have seen and heard quite enough of so-called affairs of state⋯⋯"

"Storm in a ---- "Although Sevenpounder lived in the village, heTeacup" had always wanted to better himself he every morning from Luchen to town, and came back in the evening⋯⋯"

"The True Story ---- "Ah Q, again, had a very high opinion of of Ah Q" himself. He looked down on all the inhabitants of Weichuang⋯⋯Moreover, after Ah Q had been to town several times, he naturally became more conceited, although at the same time he had the greatest contempt for town people⋯⋯"

"Weichuang did not see Ah Q again till just after the Moon Festival that year. Everyone was surprised to hear of his return⋯⋯"

"the revolutionaries were going to enter town and the successful provincial candidate had come to the country to take refuge⋯⋯"

"The Divorce" ---- "As Chuang Musan and his daughter Aiku stepped down into the boat from Magnolia Bridge Wharf⋯⋯"

"Not to town ⋯ ⋯ We're making a trip to Pang Village⋯⋯"

結構）, *Collected Papers on Chinese Studies* （學業論文集刊）, Vol. III （Singapore: Department of Chinese Studies, National University of Singapore, 1990） 243-270.

The travel theme is evident in "An Incident," "Storm in a Teacup" and "The Divorce". The writer opened each of these stories with prologue depicting reminiscences of the traveler. Except for "An Incident," all of the above stories do not use the first person narrative. Perhaps it is because of this that the narrators do not take the towns as their hometowns, despite the fact that the Luchen in "Storm in a Teacup " appears as his hometown in "My Old Home "and "Village Opera."

A superficial reading of "The Story of Ah Q"will not reveal evidence of the travel theme, as it is well concealed within the plot. Lu Xun develops the plot by portraying Ah Q going into town and then returning to Weichuang, while the revolutionaries enter the town and the gentry seek refuge in the country. In Chapter Two, Ah Q begins to feel pride in the fact that he has traveled to the city several times. In Chapter Six, Ah Q returns to Weichuang, surprising everyone. In Chapter Seven, the arrival of a member of the gentry in a boat causes much uneasiness in Weichuang. The Story reaches its climax in Chapter Eight, when the revolutionaries enter the town, and finally to the anti-climax in Chapter Nine when Ah Q is dragged into town for execution. It is easy to understand why Lu Xun keeps his characters in intense constant action.

The setting for the third group of stories is a street scene in a small, unknown town. Although the journey is the shortest of the three, it does not detract from the author's portrayal of what is seen, heard and felt.

Title of Story   Stories about the Street Scenes

"A Madman's" ---- "Tonight there is no moon at all, I know that Diary" this bodes ill. This morning when I went out cautiously, Mr. Zhao had a strange look in his eyes, as if he were afraid of me, as if he wanted to murder me. There were also seven or eight others, who discussed me in a whisper……"

"Medicine"   ---- "so he went out into the street. In the darkness nothing could be seen but the grey roadway……"

"The customers walked in Old Chuan's teahouse."

"Xia Yu's and Hua Xiaochuan's mothers walked to the cemetery outside the West Gate."

"The Enternal ---- San Jiaolian, Fang Ting, Zhuang Qiguang and Lamp" several other young men broke the curfew and visited the teahouses often to drink and chat. The story depicts what the group see and hear during journeys to the teahouse, the temple and the living room of Siye.

"A Warning to   ---- "On what is seen and heard on a road to the
The People" most generous part of West town."

After stepping out of his feudal-minded family into the public,the madman in "A Madman's Diary" finds out that the masses want to harm him. "Medicine" and "The Eternal Lamp" are basically dramas with their plots respective in three different stages. Backgrounds from three different places imply that there are three different journeys. "A Warning to the People" is a sketch and depicts what is seen on a journey.

In the three types of journey stories mentioned above, 'Stories of Returning to the Native Land' are not only autobiographical, realistic, and full of local colour, but they also possess the fundamental conventions of traditional travel literature. These stories are also sentimental and lyrical as the childhood events portrayed reflect the writer's own experiences. On the other hand, with the exception of "An Accident, "the second group of stories utilizes the third rather than the first person narrative, and thereby takes on a journalistic style. The third group is even more journalistic.

A Call to Arms and *Wandering* contain altogether twenty-five short stories, fourteen of which have the travel literature structure mentioned above. The other works, such as "The Comedy of the Duck" (鴨的喜劇), also imply the travel theme. Because many of his stories are built around the plan of a journey, his main characters spend most of their time travelling. Therefore we may conclude that regardless of whether the influence of travel literature on Lu Xun's writing is faint or strong, it is nonetheless apparent.

Journey Set To Explore the Sick Society and the Dark Souls

Symbolism pervades Lu Xun's six stories of returning natives. 'I' revisits towns such as Luchen, Pingchiao Village and S-town–all epitomes of Chinese villages in the past. The natives returning to their hometown signifies Lu Xun's urge to reacquaint himself with the traditional Chinese village, and perhaps, even with the old Chinese society as a whole. In "Kong Yiji," the Prosperity Tavern is a microscopic version of Luchen. The tavern represents Chinese society; the drinkers symbolize the people of China - a drunken mass. Customers of the tavern are clad in long-sleeved and short-sleeved shirts to differentiate their social ranks. The working class people are enemies of the landlords and scholars. They have a common characteristic: their love of drink. They remain in a drunken stupor, either voluntarily or by pressure from society, never to awaken to face reality. Kong Yiji should feel depressed, as he has been rejected by society for being an old style intellectual. However, the jeers and sneers of the people only represent the stupidity and ignorance of the Chinese masses. Such was the tragedy of both old China and its people.

The journeys described in"My Hometown"and"The New Year's Sacrifice"have similar symbolic meanings. They reflect the decadence, ignorance and degeneration of the villages, and illustrate the sick Chinese society and the deceased souls of its people. In the journeys described in"In the Wine Shop"and"The Misanthrope,"there are two anti-feudal intellectuals. One is Lu Weipu, who makes his living by teaching the Confucian classics; the other is Wei Lianshu, who dies a tragic death after giving into society's feudal force. With these stories, the author attempts to dig out the darkness of the souls of Chinese intellects. The S-town visited by the'I,'represents the Chinese intellectual community's uncertainties and anxieties as it gropes in the darkness during the trips. The only place in China, in which Lu Xun detects hope and happiness is Pingchiao Village in"Village Opera."However, Pingchiao Village is only a recollection of the past – the innocent and happy child and the kindhearted Old Man Liuyi have vanished. The good opera and delicious beans also have become extinct. This happy journey is different from the other five, as the'I'is only touring the hometown in a dream and is blinded to the dark side of the society. In the other trips, there is always a comparison of the past and present.

Chinese society and the Chinese soul are to be found not only in remote villages, but also in towns, cities and streets. Thus, Lu Xun has created stories about journeys through towns, cities and streets. In the former, the stories focus would be on both the city and town. For example, the'I'in"An Incident"travels from the town to the city of Beijing. Sevenpounder in"A Storm in a Teacup"travels from Luchen to the city everyday, and brings with him news and rumours of revolution. Ah Q in"The True Story of Ah Q,"has traveled to and from Weichuang to the town. Aiku in"The Divorce"has traveled from her village to Pangchuang. These works are very different from the stories based on the return of a native. The former emphasize intellectual and revolutionary matters.

The streets and lanes in Lu Xun's fiction are usually the places of extortion and the execution of the revolutionaries. In the aforementioned stories, we can see how Ah Q is dragged into the town, and exhibited in public before finally being executed. The intellect'I'of"An Incident"feels remorse and regret after he witnesses the moral character of a rickshaw man on the road. Stories focusing on trips to the streets illustrate the scenes in these streets. For instance when going for a stroll, the madman imagines the masses treating him as an enemy whom they intend to eat. In addition, Xia Yu in"Medicine"and the unidentified person in"A Warning to the People"both faced execution in the streets. Finally, the youths of"The Eternal Lamp"run into the streets, chasing a hero who wants to blow the eternal lamp out. These incidents and the streets are symbols and representations of the changing Chinese society.

Thus, the above examples can be classified into two categories: return of the native and journeys to towns and cities. The former reflect the old China, the past society, the old intellects, while the latter depict the start and illusions of China's Revolution.

Conclusion

The beginning of this article quotes *The Literature as a Mode of*

Travel, a book about the relationship between fiction and travel literature. Many of Lu Xun's stories build upon the travel theme. The first category using the return of a native, is autobiographical and employs first person narrative. The second and third categories use the more objective and contemporary reporting style of third person narration. Most of these travelers identify with the characters in the novels of the late Qing period. They act as observers on unfamiliar trips. They witness strange happenings, decadence in society, and a diseased people. These observers, e.g.'I'in"Kong Yiji," "An Incident," "In a Wine Shop"and"The Misanthrope,"suggest missing parts of history. However, their relationship with the main characters or main events is not that of an innocent party. For example, the'I'in"The New Year's Sacrifice"is an important member of a big clan. Also, the'I'in"My Hometown," "Village Opera"and"A Madman's Diary"evolves from an innocent observer to an active participant. In view of this, Lu Xun's stories with travel conventions are even more similar to travel literature by contemporary writers when we compare Lu Xun's works with *Random Notes of Xiang Xi* by Shen Congwen and *Notes on the Trip to the South* by Ai Wu.[26] The narrative and themes are quite similar. Of course, in Lu Xun's stories, the literary techniques are more complicated and superior.

 Lu Xun's expertise as a short story writer can be seen in his simple, short, yet symbolic writing style. His portrayals of journeys to hometowns, along streets, and through landscapes, all meet the constraints of a short story. The traveler in Lu Xun's stories is not like the adventurous Monkey

---

26 Leo Lee, "The Solitary Traveler: Image of the Self in Modern Chinese Literature," *op. cit.*, pp. 294-306.

God in A Journey to the West or the traveler Lao Can who is constantly on the move. The movements of his travelers are strictly restricted to the street and the farthest is to return to the hometown.

Lu Xun's stories meet the criteria of travel literature, as in extending one's knowledge and enlarging one's ideas. Lu Xun often stresses that his main motive for writing fiction is to"expose the disease and draw attention to it might be cured."In addition, he comments:"I want to write about the degeneration of the higher class and the un fortunate sufferings of the lower class and continue to expose them through short stories. My motive is to highlight these questions to the readers."[27]Hence, Lu Xun uses his stories to emphasize and expand the thoughts, as well as extend knowledge. His focus is on the"diseased old society,"and his aim is to find a"cure for it."[28]Travel literature of both the West and China uses what is seen or heard along a journey to reveal a diseased society and the degenerating people. Such literature includes Jonathan Swift's *Gulliver's Travels*, Li Ruzhen's *Flowers in a Mirror* and Liu E's *The Travels of Lao Can*. This has been studied in depth by scholars of Lu Xun for more than seventy years.

The Literature as a Mode of Travel also emphasizes that in good travel literature, the writers use their personal views and experiences to write an account filled with great ideas. Therefore, writers of travel literature often introduce symbolic images of a certain country or place. For example, Thailand is the hometown of gods, and cherry blossoms

---

27 Lu Xun, "How I Wrote the Stories," *Lu Xun Selected Works*, Vol. III, *op. cit.*, 261.
28 "Preface to Lu Xun's Own Selection of Works," in *Lu Xun's Essays on Creative Writing, op. cit.*, 49.

represent Japanese patriotism. The most surprising revelation after studying Lu Xun's works is the outstanding, striking and symbolic images in the stories. Some examples are Luchen, Jiguang Village which represent the ignorant, the backward, the conservative and the superstitious. Prosperity Tavern and Old Chuan's Teahouse and its guests are reflections of the selfish, uncaring, unrealistic, diseased and class-conscious society. If we were to compare Lu Xun to modern writers of travel literature, Lu Xun would come forth as a photographer who has taken detailed shots of landscapes and sceneries. Luchens is a microscopic view of a Chinese village. Teahouses and taverns are likewise closer views of the Chinese society. With such photographs, the images in Lu Xun's stories are more complete and concrete. It is exactly because Lu Xun's stories have this visual advantage that artists choose to put on canvas the landscapes he describes. Lu Xun's works are undoubtedly the most prominent and most sought after by fine artists.[29]

---

29 Feng Zikai 豐子愷, for instance, has sketched almost all characters and important scenes of Lu Xun's stories, see *Feng Zikai's Paintings of Lu Xun's Fiction* (Hangzhou: Zhejiang People's Publisher, 1982).

Lu Xun's Medical Studies in Japan and His Fiction: A Deconstructive Reading

From Zhou Shuren to Lu Xun: Giving Up Medicine for Literature

Lu Xun（魯迅 1881-1936） has generally been regarded as the greatest modern Chinese writer. Since his death in 1936, his fame has turned positively legendary. Almost all his contemporary writers have been purged by the Chinese Communist Government, but Lu Xun was an exception. Even Mao Zedong has paid him the highest tribute: "As commander of the cultural revolution, Lu Xun was not only a great writer, but a great thinker and revolutionary as well."[1]

When Lu Xun arrived in Tokyo in 1902, he was known only by his legal name Zhou Shuren 周樹人. He studied Japanese language at Kobun 宏文 Institute, a school that had been established to teach Chinese students enough Japanese to enable them to enter institutions of higher learning. He spent two years in learning Japanese here. Upon graduating from the Kobun Institute in 1904, Lu Xun decided to study medicine. In September 1904, Lu Xun enrolled at the Sendai Medical School 仙台醫專, which is

---

1 Mao Zedong, *Mao Zedong Xuan Ji* 毛澤東選集（Beijing ：Ren-min wenxue chubanshe, , 1952），vol. 2, pp. 668-69.

now the Faculty of Medicine of Tohoku University 東北大學 in Sendai in northern Japan. In retrospect, he and his friends had offered a variety of reasons for his choice of medicine as a field of study. [2]Among them, as he himself stated in the preface of *A Call to Arms* 吶喊（1923）, his first collection of short stories, these two reasons are most important: his father's death at the hands of traditional Chinese physicians; his understanding that medicine was somewhat associated with the rapid and successful modernization of Japan:

> From translated histories I also learned that the Japanese Reformation had originated, to a great extent, with the introduction of Western medical science to Japan.

> These inklings took me to a provincial medical college in Japan. I dreamed a beautiful dream that on my return to China I would cure patients like my father, who has been wrongly treated, while if war broke out I would serve as an army doctor, at the time strengthening my countrymen's faith in reformation.[3]

During this time, Sendai was still a relatively secluded school and unknown to most people, even among the Japanese, Sendai, hundreds of miles to the north of Tokyo, was far removed from the cosmopolitan centres of contemporary Japanese culture. Lu Xun immediately found that he was the only and the first Chinese in the school. Lu Xun's stay at Sendai, from September 1904 through March 1906, coincide with the

---

2 About Lu Xun's life in Sendai, see *The Friends of Lu Xun Society at Sendai*（compiled）, *Documents Concerning Lu Xun in Sendai* 魯迅在仙台記錄 （Sendai ni okeru Ronji no kiroku）（Tokyo：Heibonsha, 1978）。

3 Lu Xun, *Selected Stories of Lu Xun,* tr. by Yang Xianyi and Gladys Yang, （Bejing: Foreign Languages Press, 1963）, p. 21.

Russo-Japanese War which had inflated Japanese on the street occasionally. Finally he led a life of voluntary self-exile.

His first year grade average of 65.5 was just above the passing mark. The Japanese students thought it was too good for a Chinese student. Then some of Lu Xun's Japanese classmates accused him of receiving advance information as to what would be emphasized on the examination. In 1926 Lu Xun wrote what he felt:

> China is a weak country, therefore the Chinese must be an inferior people, and for a Chinese to get more than 60 marks could not be simply to his own efforts. No wonder they suspected me.[4]

In the second year, in a slide show, he saw an able-bodied Chinese about to be executed by Japanese military police with many other Chinese standing around to enjoy the spectacle. Before the term was over, Lu Xun gave up medicine for literature and left Sendai for Tokyo. As a writer, Zhou Shuren became well-known as Lu Xun, a pen-name which he first used when he published "Diary of a Madam" in 1918.Lu Xun recalls the incident in the preface of *Call to Arms:*

> This was during the Russo-Japanese War, so there were war slides, and I had to join the clapping and cheering in the lecture hall along with other students. It was a long time since I had seen any compatriots, but one day I saw a slide showing some Chinese, one of whom was bound, while many others stood around him. They were all strong fellows but appeared completely apathetic. According to the commentary, the one with his hands bound was a

---

4 Lu Xun, "Mr. Fujiro",*Dawn Blossoms Plucked at Dusk*, tr. by Yang Xianyi and Gladys Yang, （Beijing, ：Foreign Languages Press, 1985）, p. 85.

spy working for the Russians, who was to have his head cut off by the Japanese military as a warning to others, while the Chinese beside him had to enjoy the spectacle.[5]

Lu Xun explains that he gave up medical science for literature because he felt that to cure the people's spirit was more important than to cure their physical illness:

> Before the term was over, I had left for Tokyo, because after this slide show, I felt that medical science was not so important at all. The people of a weak and backward country, however strong and healthy they may be, can only serve to be made examples of, or to witness such futile spectacles; and it is not necessarily deplorable no matter how many of them die of illness. The most important thing, therefore, was to change their spirit, and since at that time I felt that literature was the best means to this end, I determined to promote a literary movement.[6]

The slide incident and Lu Xun's public-spirit explanation have been long accepted without doubt by many Chinese and Japanese scholars of modern Chinese literature as the reason why he changed from medical studies to a literary career. William Lyell says that "we ought to discount the public-spirited explanation to a certain extent", [7]while Leo O.F. Lee has pointed out that "the incident by itself was not enough to prompt Lu Xun to give up medicine for literature".[8]Recent documents recovered and

---

5 Selected Stories of Lu Xun, pp.21-22.

6 Selected Stories of Lu Xun, p.23.

7 William Lyell, Lu Xun's Vision of Reality （Berkeley: University of California Press, 1976）, p 75.

8 Leo Lee, Voices from the Iron House: A Study of Lu Xun （Bloomington： Indiana

research reports written by open-minded Japanese scholars have revealed the fact that Lu Xun suffered more serious frustrations and deeper humiliations than we expected. The militarism and anti-Chinese atmosphere of Sendai during that time must have profoundly influenced Lu Xun's sudden decision to leave Sendai for Tokyo.[9]

In 1973, a group of scholars who called themselves the "Friends of Lu Xun in Sendai" formed a committee of investigation and research to explore every detail of the private life of Lu Xun during his stay in Sendai. The findings and documents recovered were published in a book entitled *Documents Concerning Lu Xun in Sendai* （Sendai ni okeru Rojin no kiroku）. To celebrate the 90th anniversary of the arrival of Lu Xun in Sendai, Tohoku University held and international conference with "Modern China's Inter-Culture Experience" as its theme on 6-9, September 1994. Lu Xun's sudden change of interest was the focus of the conference. All participating scholars unanimously rejected the formerly well-accepted slide show incident theory that the sudden departure was entirely as he has stated in the preface of *A Call to Arms*. Abe Kenya the principal organiser of the conference, flatly denied in his paper that it was the incident that decisively changed the course of Lu Xun's life:

> We ought to discount the factors to a certain degree. The common people of the Chinese were unarmed and helpless. How could they

University Press, Bloomington）,1987）, p. 18.

9 Abe Kenya 阿部兼也, "Lu Xun and Dr, Fujiro: On Modern Scholarship" 魯迅和藤野先生 —— 關於現代的學術精神 and Izumi-Hyonosuke 泉彪之助, "Prof Fujiro and Lu Xun's Medical Notebooks" 藤野教授與魯迅的醫學筆記, *Proceedings of International Conference on Lu Xun*, 《魯迅仙台留學九十周年紀念國際學術文化研討會論文集》（Sendai： Tohoku University, Sendai, 1994）, pp.1-22; 154-173.

confront the Japanese soldiers who were brutal and barbarous? What they could do was to swallow the insults and the humiliations quietly. The theory that enlightening the people is more important than to cure the physical sickness is rather acceptable. However, looking down the body would not necessarily emphasize the spiritual values...[10]

Our question is: why did Lu Xun give us these reasons which are not convincing enough?

Racial Discrimination: Accusations of Receiving Favouritism and Miscalculation of Examination Marks

I was one of the scholars who were invited to participate in the conference held in Sendai in 1994 mentioned above.[11] As the conference was organised to celebrate the ninetieth anniversary of the arrival of Lu Xun in Sendai, a tour around the historic sites of Lu Xun was conducted on the first day of the meeting. We visited the old classrooms and other historical sites of former Sendai Medical School which is now part of the Tohoku University campus, the lodging house, and Lu Xun Memorial Room. In the Memorial Room which is part of the Tohoku University Memorial Hall, we saw the original copies of documents and records related to Lu Xun's study in Sendai. The most interesting are the academic records.

It is a well-known fact that Lu Xun made it through his first year with a cumulative average of 65.5. He was ranked 68th in a class of 142. But a

---

10 Abe Kenya, "Lu Xun and Dr. Fujiro", p. 13.

11 See *Proceedings of International Conference on Lu Xun,*, table of contents.

closer look at the academic transcripts reveals many surprises. In the First Year Academic Record, there are two arithmetic errors. Lu Xun was awarded 60 in the first term and 70 in the second in his physiology course examination. The average grade must be 65, but it was wrongly computed as 63.3. The cumulative total marks for all seven courses for the first year was 458.6 and therefore the grade average should be 65.8, but it was entered as 65.5. At the end of the first year, Lu Xun's highest grade of 83 was earned in Ethics. When 83 was converted into traditional grade system, it was given "bing" 丙 the third grade （equivalent to C grade） while it should be "yi"乙, the second grade （equivalent to B grade）.[12]

These are simple mathematics indeed. Why had they made three mistakes in calculating Lu Xun's examination marks? Professor Watanabe Jo, a native of Sendai and an important member of the special investigation team of the Sendai Friends of Lu Xun Society laments:

> I think Lu Xun was very unhappy with such errors they made. He was despised and injured by his classmates because of the leakage allegation that examination questions were disclosed to him, but he made it through for the first year by his own efforts. The examination marks were given less for computation mistake and through a grade was wrongly converted to a lower one in the academic transcripts and these mistakes were never corrected. As results of these baseless allegation and errors on the academic records, Lu Xun might think of the Sendai Medical School and its

---

12 Jo Watanabe 渡邊襄, "An Analysis of the Studies of the Documents Concerning Lu Xun" 有關仙台時代魯迅資料研究的研究） , International Conference on Lun Xun, Supplement Vol., （Sendai: Tohoku University, Sendai, 1994）, pp. 12-24

officials very differently.[13]

At the conference mentioned above, participants were presented with the Photostatted copies of seven documents of Lu Xun in Sendai Medical School, including his admission paper, timetable of classes, and class attendance record. However the academic transcripts of Lu Xun which would be most interesting to all scholars were not included in the souvenir envelope. Obviously, it was due to embarrassment.[14]

For the first year, Lu Xun ranked 68th in a class of 142. There were 30 students who were flunked and had to repeat the first year of study. As Lu Xun stated in the article entitled "Fujiro Sensei" 〈藤野先生〉（1926），soon after the announcement of the Examination results, his Japanese classmates sent representatives to check his lecture notes of Anatomy, a course taught by Prof Fujino Konkyuro 藤野嚴九郎 and another professor. At the same time he received an anonymous letter accusing him of receiving favouritism from Prof Fujiro. In correcting and supplementing Lu Xun's lecture notes, they alleged, Fujiro had given hints as to what would be emphasised on the examination. No evidence was found.

At that time probably the Japanese students knew only that Lu Xun had passed the overall first year examinations with an average cumulative grade of above 60, the passing mark. They didn't know the individual grades of all courses; otherwise they would not have been making baseless accusation and allegations. Lu Xun had not done well in Mr Fujiro's

---

13 Watanabe, 1994, p. 18.

14 Photos of Lu Xun's academic records are printed in Documents Concerning Lu Xun in Sendai, pp. 1-316

Anatomy course examination and was flunked by him. The average grade Lu Xun received in the Anatomy course was 59.3, 0.7 below the passing mark. The fact that this was the lowest grade of all courses he had taken has proved that Mr Fujiro did not help him at all. So the whole affair died a natural death. The incidents were actually triggered off by the Japanese nationalism and jingoism which were at its highest at that time. Lu Xun recalled the terrible experiences in 1926:

> China is a weak country, therefore the Chinese must be an inferior people, and for a Chinese to get more than sixty marks could not be due simply to his own efforts. No wonder they suspected me. [15]

These incidents left a deep mark on Lu Xun and decisively changed the course of his life. It was no surprise to Professor Abe Kenya who had taught in Tohoku University in Sendai for a long period that such things had happened in Sendai. He reminds us that Sendai was an army town. At that time the local Japanese were deeply involved in the Russo-Japanese War on Chinese soil. Many Sendai Medical School teachers, staffs and students were drafted and mobilised. It was in this highly charged political atmosphere that the news slides of Japanese war effort were shown when the lecture ended early. Prof Abe stresses that the strong Japanese nationalism and militarism that prompted Lu Xun to deepen his understanding and awareness of the crisis of China. These experiences also forced him to recognise the importance of changing the spirit of the Chinese people. [16]

---

15 Lu Xun, Dawn Blossoms Plucked at Dusk, 1985, pp. 85-86.
16 Abe Kenya, "Lu Xun and Dr. Fujiro: On Modern Scholarship", 1994, pp. 13-21. For a report on the social and political conditions of Sendai during Lu Xun's time, see

Lu Xun's Medical Career Was Destroyed by Fujino's Fastidiousness, Jingoism and Heartiness: The Myth of the Anatomy Lecture Notes.

During Lu Xun's first year of study in Sendai Medical School, Fujiro Konkyuro, professor in the anatomy course asked him to turn in lecture notes every week and checked them over, put in supplements, and ever corrected grammatical mistakes. Lu Xun gratefully acknowledges Fujino's effort in a number of articles. This considerate gesture toward a Chinese student during the time when anti-Chinese nationalism was at its height is really unusual. Fujino was not only Lu Xun's best model teacher, but also an exemplary man whose character he wished to emulate. Today many Chinese and Japanese scholars even make the friendship between Fujino and Lu Xun to be the national symbol of friendship between the two countries.

Surprisingly, Fujiro was not impressed by Lu Xun. Fujiro later did not have much to say of Lu Xun:

His Japanese was not all that perfect at the time he entered, and he went through a lot of effort to understand the lectures. After the lectures I would correct what he did not hear correctly or whatever mistakes he had made. He was very diligent at the lectures. He was not among the excellent students. He probably came to my house to visit, but I don't remember. [17]

Documents Concerning Lu Xun in Sendai, pp. 3-86.

17 Fujiro's recollection of Lu Xun published in Documents and Concerning Lu Xun's in Sendai, pp. 371-373, Leo Lee's English translation, see Voices from the Iron House, p. 17.

Professor Izumi Hyonosuke 泉彪之助, a professor of College of Nursing, Fukui Prefecture University is the first scholar who has studied Lu Xun's lecture notes in great detail. His paper "Professor Fujino and Lu Xun's Medical Notebooks" 藤野教授與魯迅的醫學筆記 pointed out that Fujino's corrections seem to indicate that Lu Xun had made a lot of factual and grammatical mistakes. But for a foreign student who had studied Japanese for two years, many corrections and changes related to language and grammar are not necessary. Even Fujino's comment that "this blood vessel is a little out of place" is improper and over-demanding. The remarks such as "there are many errors here" are merely expressions of xenophobia. Prof Izumi concludes that Fujino's over-demanding attitude as shown in correcting the lecture notes is a serious blow to Lu Xun's confidence. Among the courses taken by Lu Xun during the first year, anatomy was the only which was directly related to medical training. Unfortunately, it was taught by the most fastidious man, Fujino, and another professor. Lu Xun was among the one-third of students of the class who flunked. Izumi has concluded that Fujino's over-heartiness and jingoism killed Lu Xun's career as a medical doctor. [18]

From Sendai to Shaoxing: Lu Xun: As a Diagnostician and Physician-Writer

With this more accurate and fuller picture of the life of Lu Xun in Sendai, my reading of his works, especially the short stories, undertakes to subvert and undermine the claim by previous scholars that Lu Xun's home

---

18 Izumi Hyonosuke, "Prof Fujiro and Lu Xun's Medical Notebook", pp. 154-173.

town Shaoxing 紹興 was the only source of inspiration for his fiction. He has been criticised for his limitations and incapacity to draw creative sustenance from other experiences that those rooted in his childhood life in his native town Shaoxing .[19]

Many stories by Lu Xun actually contained elements which can be surely identified as Sendai Japanese experiences, but these elements have been so rearranged and transformed in his works that they have lost all their specifically personal meaning and become simply concrete human materials, integral elements of the stories. Sendai as a military town reminds us of his home town Shaoxing under the control of powerful warlords and the Manchu Government's militant rule. The image of the execution of an able-bodied but ignorant Chinese by the Japanese military police recurs frequently in his major works.

Under the influence of medical science, literature became for Lu Xun a means to diagnose the "illness" of the Chinese people and the sick society. He gave up medicine for literature because "it is not necessarily deplorable no matter how many of them die of illness". Instead of saving the physically ill, he considered changing their spirit more urgent. Therefore, his main motive in writing fiction is to "expose the disease and draw attention to it so that it might be cured." Even Fredric Jameson has pointed out that, "As a writer······Lu Xun remains as a diagnostician and a physician". [20]

---

19 C.T. Hsia, A History of Modern Chinese Fiction, (New Haven : Yale University Press, , 1961) , pp. 31-32.

20 Fredric Jameson, "Third-World Literature in the Era of Multinational Capitalism", Social Text, Vol. 15, Fall, 1986, p. 73.

Lu Xun left Japan and returned to China in 1909. He published his first short story "The Dairy of a Madman"狂人日記 in modern form in 1918. With this story and a new pen-name, "Lu Xun", he began his career as a fiction writer. His knowledge of medicine and Western literature which he learnt in Japan contributed to the writing of "The Diary of a madman". [21] He admitted such indebtedness in 1933: "To write it I drew exclusively on the hundred odd foreign works I had read and a certain amount of medical knowledge." [22] In the story, the Madman, suffering from a persecution complex, thinks that all the people around him, including his brother are going to kill him. His delusion is developed mainly by the cannibalistic horrors of feudalism which is represented by his elder brother and other gentry and landlords. Lu Xun's Madman and his mental problems are used allegorically to express the author's social criticism. [23]

In 1919, Lu Xun published two more stories "Gong Yiyi"孔乙己 and "Medicine"藥. Two young men have died differently in "Medicine." Xia Yu 夏瑜 is decapitated for taking part in the revolution against the Manchu Government. Meanwhile, in the same town, a young man named Hua 華 is dying of tuberculosis. His father buys from the executioner a roll of bread soaked with the dead revolutionary's blood. The boy dies

---

21 For English translation of Lu Xun's stories, see Selected Stories of Lu Xun,, or Diary of Madman and Other Stories, tr. William Lyell（Honolulu： University of Hawaii Press, 1990.）。

22 Lu Xun, "How I came to Write Stories?" 〈我怎麼做起小說來〉 Complete Works of Lu Xun, 《魯迅全集》Vol. 4,（ Beijing Ren-min chu-ban-she, 1957）, p. 393.

23 For detailed discussion, see my article "The Influence of Western Literature on China's First Modern Story", in Wong Yoon Wah, Essays on Chinese Literature: A comparative Approach,（Singapore： Singapore University Press, Singapore, 1988）, pp. 52-66.

after eating the bread soaked with blood. The story reminds us of the account of Lu Xun's father's suffering and death from tuberculosis at the hands of traditional Chinese physicians. [24]

These early stories are enough to show that Lu Xun's primary ambition as a writer was to serve as a spiritual physician, though he is always content to probe the disease with out prescribing a cure.

The Executed and the Onlooker:
The Ignorant Chinese in the Slide and Lu Xun's Fiction

Lu Xun's best stories are contained in *A Call to Arms* 吶喊（1923）and *Wandering* 彷徨（1928）, his first and second collections. Many of these stories by Lu Xun are devoted exclusively to the portraits of cruel and senseless crowds. When ordinary people appear in these stories, either in minor roles or as members of a crowd surrounding the main action, they are the able-bodied but ignorant people whom Lu Xun had seen in the slide in the classroom in Sendai Medical School. After seeing a crowd of senseless Chinese who were watching with joy another Chinese about to be executed by the Japanese military police, Lu Xun realised that "the people of a weak and backward country, however strong and healthy they may be, can only serve to be made examples of, or witness to such futile spectacles." Returning to China, Lu Xun saw similar scenes everywhere he went: "Later when I came back to China I saw idlers watching criminals being shot, who also cheered as if they were drunk." [25]

The able-bodied Chinese executed by the Japanese military police

---

24 For a discussion of these stories, see Leo Lee, Voices from the Iron House, , pp. 49-88.
25 Lu Xun, Dawn Blossoms Plucked at Dusk, 1985, p. 86.

who was not aware of the absurdity of the political situation reminds us of Xia Yu in "Medicine". Although he is a revolutionary who is attempting to save his persecutors and the crowd, they are incapable of understanding his intention. Instead, they provided information to the tyrant authorities to have him imprisoned, robbed, beaten and executed. The onlookers at the scene of execution of Xia Yu and the noisy, senseless customers at the tea-shop of the Huas are images reminiscent of that of the news slide.

Ah Q in "The True Story of Ah Q" is a healthy and hard-working young man living in the Wei Village. His bad characteristics and national traits which include greed, ignorance, spinelessness, fence-sitting, and a slave mentality, make him a man to be executed as a warning to others. He is accused by a member of the gentry and finally sentenced as a criminal. He is paraded before he is executed. Leo Lee therefore remarks: "It is clear that Lu Xun's portrait of Ah Q is a fictional fleshing-out of the able-bodied Chinese spy in the news slide incident". [26] Before his death, Ah Q himself is also a regular member of the crowd at the execution ground. In the opening paragraphs of another story entitled "A Warning to the People"示衆, a man is being paraded along the streets as a warning to the people. Nobody knows what crime the prisoner has committed. He is nameless and faceless and he himself does now know why he has been sentenced to death. He is one of the ignorant majorities, the so called slumbering crowd.

The motif that masses are always spectators at executions was developed more fully in his stories. Almost all his stories describe the

---

26 Leo Lee, Voices From the Iron House, p .77.

ignorance of the masses and the sorrow of the revolutionaries caused by the unawakened crowd. There is a gathering of onlookers at the scene of execution of Xia Yu in "Medicine":

> Before too long, he notices some soldiers moving about... When they marched past him on the way to the intersection... there is a chaotic flurry of footsteps, and in the twinkling of an eye a small crowd forms. The people who had been pacing back and forth in twos and threes suddenly flow together to form a small human tide that rushes toward the intersection. Just before reaching the head of the T, the tide breaks and forms a semicircle.
>
> Hua Lao Shuan 華老栓 also looks toward the intersection but can see nothing except the backs of the crowd. Their necks are stretched out long, like ducks whose heads have been grabbed and pulled upward by an invisible hand...[27]

The people who sit about the tea-shop of the Huas are mindlessly conformist. They symbolise all that is wrong with Chinese society. Lu Xun's second story, "Kong Yiji" depicts the crowd's insensibility to a member of its own kind. Kong Yiji, an old intellectual, suffers in the midst of the customers at the Prosperity Tavern who tease and mock him as if he were a clown in a circus. When he has been beaten into a cripple he has to crawl to the tavern, and the crowd shows no sign of compassion. Kong Yiji's suffering and humiliations are their entertainment. Therefore the death of Kong Yiji is a kind of execution while jeering customers are the callous masses who appeared in the slide before. Another example of the

---

27 Diary of Madman and Other Stories,, pp. 50-51.

crowd similar to that in the slide appear in "A Warning to the People". When the two policemen escorting a criminal appear along a street in the Western suburb of the Capital, the people compete with each another to occupy a place to watch the show:

> In no time at all, the trio is partly surrounded by a large semicircle of spectators. By the time a bald-headed old man adds himself to the group, there are already very few places left. There are occupied straightaway by a red-nosed fat man who is so wide that he takes up space enough to accommodate several people, forcing the straggling latecomers to content themselves with position in a second row······[28]

The theme of persecution and masses who are always spectators also can be found in "New Year Sacrifice"祝福. The death of Xianglin Sao 祥林嫂 is caused by her fellow villagers, including both gentry and commoners. These villagers are acting as both persecutors and spectators. Lu Xun has hidden this theme in many other stories such as "Tomorrow" 明天 in which the helpless and solitary window is in sharp contrast with the revelers in the nearby tavern.

Conclusion

Many stories by Lu Xun are built upon the travel theme. The travellers who are also the narrators play the role of observers when they take a trip to their home town. [29]Lu Xun often stressed that his main

---

28 Diary of Madman and Other Stories, , p. 292
29 Wong Yoon Wah, "A Journey to the Heart of Darkness: The Mode of Travel Literature in Lu Xun's Fiction", Tamkang Review, Vol. XXIII, Nos 1-4, Autum 1992-Summer 1993, pp. 671-92.

motive for writing fiction was to "expose the disease and draw attention to it so that it might be cured". His focus is on the "diseased old society", and his aim is to find a "cure for it". Therefore he uses what is seen or heard along a journey to reveal a diseased society and degenerating people. The most interesting revelation after studying Lu Xun's fiction as a mode of travel literature is the symbolic image of village towns like Lu Zhen. These towns represent the ignorant, the backward, the conservative and the superstitious. The people on the streets and customers of the Prosperity Tavern or the Hua Lao Shuan's teahouse are reflections of the selfish, uncaring, callous and ignorant people. Teahouse and taverns provide likewise intensive views of Chinese society. The jeers and sneers of the people represent the stupidity and ignorance of the Chinese masses. Such was the tragedy of both China and its people at the turn of the twentieth century.

The Beginning of Modern Chines Fiction: The Influence of Western Literature on China's First Modern Story

Zhou Shu-ren 周樹人 (1881-1936) wrote "The Diary of a Madman" in 1981.[1] With this short story and a new pen-name Lu Xun 魯迅 , he began his literary career[2]. It is not only his first story, but also the first modern story written in China.[3] The term "modern story" means that it is written in modern colloquial Chinese and in the modern Western story form. "The Diary of a Madman" not only brought something new to a literary tradition, but it is also, perhaps, the only short story in the world written by a writer at his first attempt that has been so widely read and discussed.

"Influence" is used in this study to de⁻ ⸱te the ideational and formal

---

1 "Kuangjen riji" 狂人日記 was written in April 1, 1918 at the request of Qian Xuantong 錢玄同 (1887-1939) , one of the editors of *New Youth* (Xin Qingnian 新青年) , the most influential magazine during the May fourth Movement. It was first published in the May 1981 issue of the *New youth* and was collected in *Call to Arms* (Na-han 吶喊), Lu Xun's first collection of short stories which was published in 1923.

2 Lu is his mother's family name, while Lu Xun is a character derived from a pen-name Xun- Xing 迅行 which he signed to an essay of 1907. It was the first time that he wrote under this pseudonym.

3 Lu Xun wrote a short story "Huai Jiu" 懷舊 in literary language in the winter of 1911 and was published in *Xiaoshuo yuebao* 小說月報 under the pseudonym Zhou Chuo 周趨 For a study of this story, see "Lu Xun's 'Huai Jiu': A Precursor of Modern Chinese Literature," *Harvard Journal of Asiatic Studies* (1969) , pp. 169-176.

consequences that certain internal relations had had on a work of literature. To suggest an author's literary debts does not diminish his originality. Influence is not imitation; it shows the influenced author producing work which is essentially his own. "Literary influence," wrote Joseph Shaw, "appears to be most frequent and most fruitful at the times of emergence of national literatures and of radical change of direction of a particular literary tradition in a given literature. In addition, it may accompany or follow social or political movement or especially, upheavals."[4] This is particularly true to what was happening in China during the first half of this century. Closely interrelated with the political upheavals and Westernization movement, Chinese literature has undergone a revolution. It is Western literature that served as a direct stimulus to the movement. Never before in the history of China has literature been so pervasively influenced by Western authors. As China's first modern short story, "The Diary of a Madman" exemplifies the birth of a new literature.

The purpose of this paper is to study the juxtaposition of Western influences in the short story. My attention is not confined to the location of sources, borrowings in and so on. It is to investigate such questions as: what was retained and what was rejected, and why, and how was the material absorbed and integrated? I have restricted my analysis to three European influences in the story. [5] The influence of literary works upon

---

4 J.T. Shaw, "Literary Indebtedness and Comparative Literary Studies," *Comparative Literature: Method and Perspective,* eds. New P. Stallknecht and Horst Frenz (Carbondale: Southern Illinois University Press, 1961) p. 66.

5 About the medical knowledge and Nietzsche's philosophical ideas in the story, see J.D. Chinnery, "The Influence of Western Literature on Lu Xun's 'Diary of a Madman'," *Bulletin of London University, School of Oriental &African Studies,* vol. X X III (1960), pp. 309~922.

literary works is the most convincingly demonstrable type and aesthetically the most interesting. This is a case in point. It is hoped that this study may contribute not only to our knowledge of literary history in modern China, [6]but also to our understanding of the creative process and of the story as a piece of work of art.[7]

Lu Xun's Account of His Literary Indebtedness

In 1898 when Lu Xun was eighteen years old, he left his home town Shaoxing 紹興 for Nanking. He spent about a year in Jiangnan Naval Academy. Dissatisfied with the institution, he transferred to Nanking Railways and Mines Academy in the following year. [8] It is during this period that he was exposed to Western knowledge and literature for the first time. He studied many "foreign subjects" in the second school:

I went to N- and entered K- School; and it was there that I heard for the first time the names of such subjects as natural science, arithmetic, geography, history, drawing and physical training.[9]

---

6 For instance, Bonnie S. McDougall's *The Introduction of Western Literary Theories into Modern China* (Tokyo: The Centre for East Asian Cultural Studies, 1971) is a study closely related to the history of modern Chinese literature.

7 "The Diary of a Madman" has been highly valued for its social value. It is regarded as an important document in the intellectual history of modern China. As evinced by the bibliography appended at the end of this paper, this aspect of the story has been considerably emphasized.

8 These institutions were set up with an aim to speedily modernize China. The Chinese names are: 江南水師學堂, and 南京路礦學堂。

9 " Preface to *Call to Arms*" 魯迅全集(*The Complete Works of Lu Xun*)(Peking: Ren-min chu-ban-she, 1957) , vol. 1, pp.3-4. All English translations of Lu Xun's writings in this study are quoted from *Selected Works of Lu Xun,* tr. By Yang Xianyi and Gladys Yang (Peking:Foreign Languages Press, 1956) . Those which are not available in the Yang's translation are my own.

He was greatly impressed by Thomas H. Huxley's（1825-1895）
Evolution and Ethics in Yan Fu's 嚴復（1835-1921）translation. It is said
that he could recite in long paragraph in his later day. During his four-year
（1899-1902） stay in Nanking he almost exhausted the whole of the
available supply of Yen Fu's translation of Western philosophical and
political works. Besides, he spent much time in reading newspapers
published by the reformists. [10]

It was in Japan during 1902-1909 as a student of medicine that Lu
Xun discovered the existence of such revolutionary poets such as Byron,
Shelly, Heine, Pushkin and Petofi. He also widely read in Western fiction.
Wishing to introduce Western Idea and literature to China, he started
writing essays on Western literature. [11] He also translated a couple of
Western short stories.[12] His contact with medical knowledge and Western
literature contributed to the writing of "The Diary of a Madman." He
himself admitted such indebtedness in 1933:

> I started to write stories not because I felt I had any special talent
> as a story-writer. It was merely that I was at that time living in a
> hostel in Peking and had neither reference books with which to
> write articles nor original foreign works to translate. I had to make

---

10 Xu Shou-chang 許壽裳 and others, *Writers' Views of Lu Xun* 作家談魯迅（Hong
   Kong: Wenxue yenjiushe 文學研究社 , 1966）, pp. 10-11. For a list of Yen Fu's
   translations and the reformists' newspapers, see J.K. Fairbank and K.C. Liu, *Modern
   China, A Bibliographical Guide to Chinese Works, 1898-1937*(Harvard University Press,
   1950）, pp. 138, 445, and 503.
11 The essays written at this time are now collected in *Complete Works*, vol. 1, pp.
   153~360.
12 Collected in *Anthology of Short Stories from Foreign Countries*（ 域外小說集）, a joint
   venture by Lu Xun and his brother Zhou Zuoren. It was first published in Tokyo in two
   volumes in 1909, and it was reprinted in 1920 by Shanghai's 羣益書社。

do by writing something of a quasi-fictional character. This was "The diary of a Madman." To write it I drew exclusively on the hundred off foreign works I had read and a certain amount of medical knowledge. Apart from this I had no other equipment.[13]

Referring to the writing of "Madman" in 1935, Lu Xun particularly singled out the influence of N. Gogol's (1809-52) "The Diary of a Madman" and F.W. Nietzsche's (1844-1900) *Thus Spake Zarathustra:*

> In 1834 the Russian, N. Gogol, had written "Diary of a Madman"; in 1883 F.W. Nietzsche had put into Zarathustra's mouth the words: "Ye have trod the way from worm to man, and much in you is yet worm. Once ye were apes, and even yet man is more ape than any ape"... But the later "Diary of a Madman" aimed to expose the evils of the family system and the doctrine of Propriety and was much more bitter than Gogol's. Neither had it the vagueness of Nietzsche's Superman. [14]

Besides these two stories, V. Garshin's (1855-1888) "The Scarlet Flower" also can be demonstrated to have produced upon Lu Xun's story an effect. In the following I will first examine the relationship of Lu Xun's story to Gogol's. Following is an investigation of the influence of Garshin's "The Scarlet Flower" on Lu Xun's story. Finally the stylistic parallels between Nietzsche's and Lu Xun's will be compared.

---

13 "How I came to write Stories", *Complete Works*, vol. 4, p. 393.
14 "Introduction," *A Corpus of Modern Chinese Literature* (中國新文學大系), Zhao Jiabi 趙家璧 ed. (Shanghai: Liangyou Books Company 良友圖書公司, 1936), pp. 1475-6. See also *Complete Works*, vol. 6, p. 190. Both Nietzsche's and Gogol's names were mentioned in the essays "文化偏至論," "摩達詩力說," and "人之歷史," which were written in 1907 in Japan.

The Influence of Gogol's "The Diary of a Madman"

Both Gogol's and Lu Xun's stories are entitled "The Diary of a Madman." Both are diaries written by a madman. But the central ideas and pattern of narrative are different. Gogol's story is a record of a gradual invasion of a man's mind by insanity - more specifically, by delusion of grandeur. The madman in Gogol's story is a down-trodden "little man," a copying clerk at a government office. In spite of his insignificance and poverty, he entrenches in his wishful thinking:

> I'm a gentleman! And I can be promoted too. I'm only forty-two, an age when one's career is really just beginning. Wait, my friend, I'll go higher than you yet, and, god willing, very, very much higher. Then I'll have a social position beyond your dreams. Do you imagine you're the only to have dignity? Give me a fashionable new coat, let me wear a tie like yours, and you won't be worthy to shine my shoes. My lack of means - that is the only trouble. [15]

He even dares to fall in love with the daughter of his Division Chief. When he learns from the dogs that his idol has been betrothed to a guard-officer, he finds a refuge in imagining grandeur. He thinks that he is the king of Spain. At the end of the story he is taken to the asylum where he suffers from tortures of the warders.

---

15 N. Gogol, *The Diary of a Madman and Other Stories,* trans. A. MacAndrew (New York: New American Library, 1960) , p. 12. The Chinese translation of Gogol's madman was first done by Geng Jizhi 耿濟之 and was published in Xiaoshuo Yuebao, vol. 12, no. 1, （Oct. 1, 1921） . It is entitled "Fengren riji"瘋人日記。

Gogol's "madman" is a realistic portrayal of a portrayal of a petty clerk who becomes mad because of his feelings of inferiority and of his dream of vanity. On the other hand, Lu Xun's "madman" is to be used allegorically to express the author's social criticism. There is social criticism in Gogol's story, but Gogol's social criticism that emerges from the narrative is weak. The ideas expressed in Lu Xun's story, particularly those related to the author's outlook on Chinese society and understanding of Chinese problems are too complex to be merely derivative. For instance, the reasons which drive Lu Xun's madman to madness imply the Chinese social problems. His delusional system has been developed mainly by the horror of cannibalism of feudalism which is represented by his elder brother, Zhao Gueiweng 趙貴翁 and others. On the other hand, the mental breakdown of Gogol's madman is due to the feelings of inferiority and jealousy of his superiors, particularly the Chief of the Division, and the young man who takes away his girl.

The influence indeed had not been absorbed into Lu Xun's psyche without leaving any demonstrable trace. When the two texts are placed side by side, the reader's attention is attracted by certain parallels. The formal and ideational data that they present convince us of the importance of Gogol's story in helping to mould the content and form of Lu Xun's.

There are nineteen entries n Gogol's story, all dated. There are thirteen undated entries in Lu Xun's, plus one introductory note. [16] In the first entry of Gogol's story the madman meets two dogs on the street. He remarks that "dogs are a clever race" and "know all about intrigue." [17]

---

16 In the introductory note Lu Xun states that the "original diary" is dated.

17 Gogol, *The Diary of a Madman*, p. 15.

the same thing happens in Lu Xun's first entry in which the madman meets a dog on the road, about which the madman remarks that it is in the plot. Both Gogol's and Lu Xun's madmen have a servant （Marva and Chen Laowu）. These servants are the people who witness the madmen most clearly. Gogol's story closes with a plea of saving "the wretched son". [18] Surprisingly enough, Lu Xun ends with strikingly similar words which urge the people to save the children.

The following quotations show some of the correspondences which are clearly discernible Eben at first glance. For the purpose of comparison I quote Lu Xun's texts both in English and Chinese. [19]

1. Gogol: I saw Madgie and a dog that had been following the two ladies sniffing at one another······I must say I was quite surprised to hear her （dog） talking. （1）

   Lu Xun:Why should that dog at the Zhao house have looked at me twice?

   那趙家的狗，何以看我兩眼呢？（1）

2. Gogol: a dog is an extraordinary politician and notices everything, every step a human takes. （5）

   Doges are a clever race. They know all about intrigue······（6）

   Lu Xun: the other day the dog in the Zhao house looked at me several times; obviously it is in the plot too and has become their accomplice.前天趙家的狗，看我幾眼，可見他也同謀，早已接洽。（7）.

---

18 Gogol, The Diary of a Madman, p. 18.

19 The Arabic number at the end of each quotation indicates the number of entry of the story.

3. Gogol: I've heard that in England, a fish broke surface and uttered a couple of words in such an outlandish language that scholar have been trying to work out their meaning for three years⋯⋯I read in the newspapers about two cows who went into a store and asked for a pound of tea. （1）

Lu Xun: and I have copied out a part to serve as a subject for medical research.今撮錄一篇以供醫家研究。（Introductory note）[20]

4. Gogol: But today something suddenly became clear to me when I recalled the conversation between the two dogs. （5）

Lu Xun: Only today have I realized that they had exactly the same look in their eyes as those people outside. 今天才曉得他們的眼光，全同外面的那伙人一模一樣。（3）

5. Gogol: So I went out for a walk to think it all over. Now, finally, I'll find out everything about these intrigues and plots; I'll understand all the little wheels and springs and get to the bottom of the matter. These letters will expiain. （6）

Lu Xun: Everything requires careful consideration if one is to understand it⋯⋯I tried to look this up, but my history has no chronology, and scrawled all over each page are the words:"Virtue and Morality."凡事總須研究才會明白⋯⋯我翻開歷史一查，這歷史沒有年代，歪歪斜斜的每頁都寫著「仁

---

20 According to Chou Zuoren, this phrase was derived from a stereotype of journalists. In the 1910s, newspapers in China were fond of publishing strange news such as a cow with two heads. The news often ended with such words "to serve as a research subject for the students of natural sciences" （以供博物家研究）. See Zhou Xiashou 周遐壽 （Zhou Zuoren）, *The Characters in Lu Xun's Short Stories* （魯迅小說裏的人物）, （Shanghai: Shanghai chuban gongsi 上海出版公司）, pp. 8-9.

義道德」幾個字。(3)

6. Gogol: Mother, save your wretched son!······There is no room for him in this world. They are chasing him. Mother, take pity on your sick child······ (19, last entry)

Lu Xun: Perhaps there are still children who have eaten men?

沒有喫過人的孩子，或者還有？

Save the children······救救孩子······ (13, last entry)

The Influence of Garshin's"The Scarlet Flower"

Certain passages in the story show parallels with those of Garshin's"The Scarlet Flower."Garshin wrote mostly in the forms of diary, confession and letter. He was one of Lu Xun's favorite writers during his days in Japan. He did read"The Scarlet Flower"in Japan, though he did not translate it. [21] His translation of Garshin's other stories which were collected in *Yuwai Xiaoshuo Ji* was done in Japan. [22]

The madman in"The Scarlet Flower"tries to pluck the two flowers outside the window of the lunatic asylum. For him the red flowers are the roots of evil. Despite of the warder's effort to stop him with every means, he does not give up the self-appointed heroic mission. He regards the act as a deed of valour of which he is obliged to perform. One night when the watchman at his bedside has fallen asleep, he breaks the strait jacket and the window bar. He has completed the mission, but due to over-exhaustion,

---

21 Zhou Xiashou （Zhou Zuoren）, *Lu Xun's Old Home* (魯迅的故家)（Hong Kong: Datong Book Store 大東書局, 1962）, p.163.

22 He translated Garshin's "Four Days" and "Meeting" which were collected in *Yuwai Xiaoshuo Ji.*

he dies in the following morning. The influence of "The Scarlet Flower" on another Lu Xun's story "Everlasting Lamp" (Changming Deng 長明燈) is deeper than its influence on "The Diary of a Madman." Both the plot and theme of "Everlasting Lamp" are indebted to "The Scarlet Flower." It is also about a madman who wants to extinguish a lamp in a Buddhist temple. For him putting out the flame is to abolish all the evil of the world. The stern and cruel action of the villagers can no longer stop him.[23]

"The Scarlet Flower" is written from a second person point of view. However, the narrative and events develop as a journal. The two red flowers in Garshin's story symbolize the evil in the world, while Lu Xun's cannibalism represents wickedness of the feudal system and the degenerate individual. Those who try to abolish the "evil" are treated rather cruelly by the people. This is the important message of both stories.

Garshin's madman cannot sleep at night. Some new idea comes to his mind and he decides to pluck the red flowers outside the window. Lu Xun's madman's "initiation" also takes place in a moonlight night. Compare the following passages:

Garshin: The moonlight poured into the room through the barred window······he awoke for several seconds perfectly sane and seemingly healthy.

He did not sleep all night... he had come at last to realize what his task was in his world.24

---

23 For this reason I think Prof. Huang Sung-K'ang's statement that "'The Diary of a Madman' was the only story in which traces of foreign influence can be clearly detected" is doubtful. See Huang Sung-K'ang, *Lu Xun and the New Culture Movement of Modern China* (Amsterdam: Djambatan, 1957), p. 53.

24 Garshin, *The Scarlet Flower*, tr. B. Issacs (Moscow: Foreign Languages Publishing

Lu Xun: Tonight the moon is very bright.

I have not seen it for over thirty years, so today when I saw it I felt in unusually high spirits. I begin to realize that during the past thirty-odd years I⋯⋯

I can't sleep at night⋯⋯[25]

今天晚上，很好的月亮。

我不見他已是三十多年，今天見了，精神分外爽快，才知道以前三十年全是發昏，然而須十分小心。

⋯⋯⋯⋯⋯

晚上總是睡不著，凡是須得研究才會明白。

Garshin's madman accuses that the doctor is an executioner in disguise. In the eyes of the madman the patients are men of great idea and innocent victims. Lu Xun's madman is revolutionary and he pours out the attack on the doctor in a same vein:

Garshin: Why are you doing evil? Why have you herded together all these unfortunate people?⋯⋯Why these tortures? To a man who has had a great idea....[26]

Lu Xun:⋯⋯Actually I knew quite well that this old man was the executioner in disguise! He simply used the pretext of feeling my pulse to see how fat I was; by so doing he would receive a share of my flesh⋯⋯[27]其實我豈不知道這老頭子是劊子手的扮的!無非借了看脈這名目，揣一揣肥瘠:因為這功勞，也分

House, n.d.）, pp. 73, 165, and 173-4.

25 *Complete Works,* vol. 1, pp. 9-10.

26 *The Scarlet Flower,* p. 166.

27 *Complete Works*, vol. 1, p. 12.

一片肉吃⋯⋯

Despite of these similarities, the social implications are rather different. Garshin's madman who has had a great idea is "tortured" only by the doctor. The "evil" that he is trying to get rid of represents the wickedness of human nature and the injustice of his time. Lu Xun's madman is to be eaten by people. Cannibalism has a special reference to the Chinese feudalism and Confucian morality. Lu Xun's doctor also has a specific reference to the Chinese herbalistic doctor, a component of the old society. The vision of Garshin's story is limited to the final action of the madman. However the story of Lu Xun says so many significant things that today we regard it as the general introduction of his later works.

The Influence of Nietzsche's "Zarathustra's Introductory Discourse"

There is also satisfactory external evidence that the story must have been influenced by Nietzsche's *Thus Spake Zarathustra*. Lu Xun came into contact with Nietzsche's philosophical writings in Japan. During his stay in Japan as a medical student he read Nietzsche with tremendous excitement. The number of the essays that he wrote after returning to China gives testimony of this.[28]

Among the philosophical works of Nietzsche, Lu Xun was particularly attracted by *Thus Spake Zarathustra*. In 1918, almost at the

---

28 See Cao Juren 曹聚仁, *A Critical Biography of Lu Xun*（魯迅評傳）（Hong Kong: Sanyu Book Store 三育書店, 1967）, pp. 50-56. See also note 11. Lu Xun's second foreign language was German. However there were only a few books in German on his bookshells when he was in Japan. Nietzsche's *Thus Spake Zarathustra* was one of the few books that were on his bookshell. See Zhou Zuoren, *Lu Xun di gujia*, p. 207.

same time that the madman was written, Lu Xun translated the first three sections of the "Zarathustra's Introductory Discourse" into literary Chinese. Due to whatever reason we do not know, it had never been published in his life time.[29] About two years after the "Madman" was written, he translated the "Introductory Discourse" into modern Chinese in complete form. Translator's notes were added. It was published in the *New Tide* 新潮 magazine in 1920.[30]

Lu Xun himself not only admitted Nietzsche's influence, he even paraded the indebtedness to *Thus Spake Zarathustra*. Biography convinces us of the existence of such relations; however, the essential test must be within the works themselves. Did Zarathustra really provide the ideational and formal inspiration for the story? For this purpose, a careful examination of both texts is necessary: Parallels as to atmosphere, setting, images, theme, pattern of narration, mannerisms, etc. The following examination will focus on the "Introductory Discourse" only, because the indebtedness is limited to this part of *Thus Spake Zarathustra*.

At the age of thirty-nine, Nietzsche lived in unusual solitude. It was on the lonely heights of the Alps et Sils-Maria in the Upper Engadine that came the inspiration of Zarathustra. He said: "I could sing a song there of,

---

29 Friedrich W. Nietzsche's *Thus Spake Zarathustra* is divided into four parts. The first part is "Introductory Discourse" which consists of ten sections. Lu Xun's earlier partial translation entitled 察羅堵斯德羅緒言 is now included as an appendix in *Lu Xun Yiwen Ji* 魯迅譯文集 (Peking: Renmin wenxue chubanshe 人民文學出版社, 1959), vol. 10, pp. 773-778.

30 Lu Xun used Tang Si 唐俟 as pen-name when the full translation was published in New Tide (June 1920). He mentioned in a note that he wanted to continue to translate the whole book. But he never realized his promise. See *Ji wai ji shiyi* 集外集拾遺, vol .3 of *Lu Xun sanshi nian ji* 魯迅三十年集 (Hong Kong: Xin wenyi chubanshe 新文藝出版社, 1970), pp. 33-59.

and will sing it, although I am in an empty house, and must sing it to my own ears." [31] He lamented that he had no hope of waking up the people in deep slumber. [32]

Curiously enough Lu Xun was thirty-seven in 1918 when he wrote the story. He was also leading the loneliest period of his life when he perceived the story of the madman. Like Nietzsche, he also lived in an "empty house".[33]

> Imagine an iron house without windows, absolutely indestructible, with many people fast asleep inside who will soon die of suffocation.   But you know since they will die in their sleep, they will not feel the pain of death. Now if you cried very aloud to wake a few of the lighter sleepers, making those unfortunate few suffer the agony of irrevocable death....
>
> But if a few awake, you can't say there is no hope of destroying the iron house.

Nietzsche found the figure of Zarathustra to be at once the exemplar and spokesman of his new gospel. Lu Xun chose the madman to express his revolutionary ideas. Zarathustra sings into his "own ears" with obscure language because there is no hope of waking the people in deep slumber. However, the madman wants to shout with angry voice, wishing to destroy the iron house and wake up the people in deep sleep. Yet both messages are disregarded by the people.

---

31 Friedrich W. Nietzsche, *Thus Spake Zarathustra,* trans. A. Tille and rev. M.M. Bozman （London: J.M. Dent & Sons, 1950）, III, p. 172.

32 *Thus Spake Zarathustra* , IV, p. 286.

33 Preface to *Call to Arms, Complete Works*, p. 7.

"Zarathustra's Introductory Discourse" is divided into ten sections. Both stories are of the same length, about twelve pages. For the great part, the discourse consists of interior monologues which reflect the contents of Zarathustra's minds. Thus both methods of narration are quite close to each other.

The madman's "career" parallels Zarathustra's to some extent. Zarathustra, aged thirty, is enlightened and renounces the world. He goes to the mountains where he spent for ten years in meditation. After his spirit has been undergone completely changed, he returned to his own town again. The "Introductory Discourse" begins with this passage: [34]

> When Zarathustra was thirty years of age he left his home and the lake-side where he dwelt and went into the mountains. There he possessed his spirit in solitude and for ten years wearied not thereof. But at length his heart changed, — on a day he arose with the dawn stood before the presence of the Sun, and spake thus into him……
>
> 察拉圖斯忒拉三十歲的時候，他離了他的鄉里和他鄉里的湖，並且走到山中間，他在那裏受用他的精神和他的孤寂，十年沒有倦，但他的心終于變了，……他和他的曙光一齊起，進到太陽面前對他這樣說……

The madman is also in his thirties when many things come to light in his mind. Zarathustra emerges in the morning before the sun, while the madman appears at night with the moon. Compare the following opening passages [35] with the above quotation:

---

34 *Zarathustra*, p. 5. Lu Xun's translation is also provided.
35 *Complete Works*, p. 7.

Tonight the moon is very bright.

I have not seen it for over thirty years, so today when I saw it I felt in unusually high spirits. I begin to realize that during the past thirty-odd years, I have been in the dark; but now I must be extremely careful……

今天晚上，很好的月光。

我不見他，已是三十多年；今天見了，精神分外爽快。才知道的以前三十年多，全市發昏；然而須十分小心……

Zarathustra condemns traditional Christian morality as the code of the slavish masses and preaches the superiority of the will of man when he is "awakened." The madman denounces the traditional family and social systems when he begins to "understand"（ming bai 明白） the cannibalism of the old institutions. Nietzsche's Europe, after the cultural and industrial revolution, was in its heyday. The sun image probably suggests this meaning. Lu Xun's China was still in the most chaos and darkest period. For this reason I think, the madman has been arranged to be appeared in darkness. He is enlightened by the moonlight which may symbolize the beginning of the new tide of thoughts. The change from "sun" to "moon" is necessary and appropriate for Lu Xun's own consciousness and time.

The second movement of both stories is also very much alike. In order to spread the news that "God is dead" and teach people to be Superman, Zarathustra leaves the mountains and goes into the city. When he reaches the woods he comes across an old hermit who talks to him about5 God. Later, the crowd in the marketplace greets him with laughter. As he preaches, the crowd, including the children, turn away from him to see a rope walking performance.He meets several kinds of people as he continues on his road, all of them greeting him with hostilities. The grave-diggers mock him sorely. The shepherd calls him "robber". The following are some sketches of the scenes:

1、When Zarathustra had thus spoken... And all the people laughed at Zarathustra.（p. 7）

察拉圖斯忒拉這樣說了的時候...於是所有羣眾都笑察拉圖斯忒拉。

2、When he had spoken these words Zarathustra looked again on the people and was silent. There they stand, he said within his heart, they laugh: they understand me not: I am not the mouth for these ears……（p. 8）

查拉圖斯忒拉說了這句話的時候，又看著羣眾而且沉默了。「他們在這裡站著」，他對他的心說，「他們在這裡笑：他們不懂我，我不是合于這些耳朵的嘴……」

3、How they look on me and laugh: and while they laugh they hate me. There is ice in their laughter. （p. 10）

現在他們瞥視我而且笑：而且他們正在笑，他們也仍嫌忌我。這有冰在他們的笑里。

4、At the gate of the city he met with the grave-diggers. They held their torches to his face, and knowing Zarathustra, mocked him sorely... And they laughed and put their heads together.

在市門口，他遇見了掘墳人：他們用火把照在他臉上，認識察拉圖斯忒拉而且對于他很嘲罵……他們大家都哄笑而且將頭湊在一起。

Lu Xun also begins his story with the madman walking in the street where he meets hostilities of the people. He first meets Mr. Zhao, an old gentry. Then he sees a crowd who are discussing him "in a whisper." The people, both old and young run away in panic. The children and the young man about twenty years old look at him "fiercely." His own brother calls him "madman." Compare these passages with those just quoted above:

1、This morning I went out cautiously, Mr. Zhao had a strange look in his eyes, as if he were afraid of me, as if he wanted to murder me. There were seven or eight others, who discussed me in a whisper. And they were afraid of my seeing them. All the people that I passed were like that. The fiercest among them grinned at me……（Entry 2）

早上小心出門，趙貴翁的眼色便怪：似乎怕我，似乎想害我，還有七八個人，交頭接耳的議論我，又怕我看見。一路上的人，都是如此。其中最凶的一個人，張著嘴，對我笑了一笑……

2、The most extraordinary thing was that woman on the street yesterday who spanked her son and said, "Little devil! I'd like to bite several mouthfuls out of you to work off my feelings!" Yet all the time she looked at me. I gave a start, unable to control myself; then all those green-faced, long-toothed people began to laugh derisively……

最奇怪的是昨天街上的那個女人，打他兒子，嘴里說道：「老子呀！我要咬你幾口才出氣。」他眼睛卻看著我。我出了一驚，遮掩不住；那青面獠牙的一伙人，便都哄笑起來……

3、When I interrupted the tenant and my brother both stared at me. Only today have I realized that they had exactly the same look in their eyes as those people outside.（Entry 3）

我插了一句嘴，佃戶和大哥便都看我幾眼。今天才曉得他們的眼光，全同外面的那伙人一模一樣。

4、all the words spoken by our tenant, gaze at me strangely with an enigmatic smile. （Entry 3）

佃戶說了這許多話，卻都笑吟吟的睜著怪眼看我。

5、And I am afraid he has already taught his son: that is why even the children look at me so fiercely. （Entry 8）

還怕已經教給他兒子了；所以連小孩子，也都惡狠狠的看我。

Both Zarathustra and the madman find out that the people are degenerated and are dangerous. The former says it vaguely: "More perils found I amongst men than amongst beast." But the madman points out their sin precisely and boldly:

Wanting to eat men, at the same time afraid of being eaten themselves, they all look at each other with the deepest suspicion...

自己想吃人，又怕別人吃了，都用著疑心極深的眼光，面面相覷……

At least in one case, Lu Xun imitated Nietzsche's both idea and language very closely:

Nietzsche: Ye have trod the way from worm to man, and much in you is yet worm. Once were ye apes, and even yet man is more ape than any ape. （p. 5）

（Lu Xun's translation: 你們已經走了從蟲豸到人的路，在你們裏面還有許多份是蟲豸。你們做過猴子，到了現在，人還尤其猴子，無論比那一個猴子。）

Lu Xun:Brother, probably all primitive people ate a little human flesh to begin with.

Later, because their outlook changed, some of them stopped, and because they tried to be hood they changed into men, changed into real men. But some are still eating—just like reptiles. Some have changed into fish, birds, monkeys and finally men; but some do not try to be good and remain reptiles still. When those who eat men compare themselves with those who do not, how ashamed they must be. Probably much more ashamed than the reptiles are before monkeys.

大哥，大約當初野蠻的人，都吃過一點人。後來因為心思不同，有的不吃人了，一味要好，便變了人，變了真的人。有的卻還吃 —— 也同蟲子一樣，有的變了魚鳥猴子，一直變到人。有的不要好，至今還是蟲子。這吃人的人比不吃人的人，何等慚愧。怕比蟲子的慚愧猴子，還差得很遠很遠。

Many things cannot simply be borrowed from another language, but must be reshaped in order to be fitted into the native literary tradition, or the author's own time and national history. The changes from "morning" to "night" and from "sun" to "moon" are cases in point. Nietzsche's main messages are "the God is dead" and "I teach you to be Superman." For Lu Xun his revolutionary announcements are: "Down with the man-eating morality of the old society" and "the man-eaters should change from the bottom of their hearts." In the age of Nietzsche, "blasphemy against God was the greatest of blasphemies."[36] In Lu Xun's story, we find that the unpardonable offence is an attack on the long history of feudalism. The madman is being persecuted because he once "trod on Mr. Ku Chiu's（Gu Jiu）account sheets for many years past"（history of feudal oppression in

---

36 Zarathustra, p. 6.

China).

The different use of animal images also reflects how well Lu Xun digested and transmuted the sources and borrowing s for his own purposes. In the "Introductory Discourse," there are lions, eagle, serpents, wolves, and monkey. As the translator's notes show, Lu Xun himself was well aware of the significance of these symbols. However, in "The Diary of a Madman" Lu Xun turns these animals into allegorical figures with different meanings.

Conclusion

In conclusion, a precise evaluation of the importance of these influences is difficult to assess. It is simply because it is all but impossible to follow a specific influence through the unique and subtle transformation which had undergone in the author's mind. Besides, the number of works in which an author can find inspiration is theoretically unlimited. There might be some other sources which still remain unknown. Therefore there are limitations in such an investigation of the way in which the borrowings from other texts have been employed in the story and of how they have actually contributed to its structure and qualities.

However, a comparative study of the obvious borrowings and surface similarities shows that the three pieces of literary work concerned did help Lu Xun to fulfill himself by the ways as shown above. Despite of the fact that there is a juxtaposition of influences in the story, the total work is Lu Xun's own creation. He succeeded in incorporating them into the story. Thus the influences are integral elements of the story, and the story is enriched by the influences utilized.

Madness and Death in the May Fourth Era Fiction:A Study of the Theme of Anti-Traditionin Modern Chinese Literature

The Chinese literary revolution began in 1917. The achievement of this revolution's first decade is substantially represented in the 10-volume *A Comprehensive Anthology of Chinese New Literature.*[1] In this anthology, there are three volumes devoted to prose fiction. A long time ago, as I carefully read each of the anthology's stories, I was drawn to a number of stories that have been useful in fashioning a cohesive purview of Chinese tragedy. A great many of the fictitious characters, many of them being principal protagonists, find themselves faced with mental illness, a tragic death, or a combination of both.

For the purpose of comparison, I have also examined the three volumes of short stories contained in *A Comprehensive Anthology of Chinese New Literature: Supplementary Volumes,*[2] which are

---

1 .Zhao Jiabi 趙家璧 ed. *Zhongguo xin wenxue daxi* 中國新文學大系 (Shanghai: Liangyou Publishing Co. 良友圖書公司, 1935-1936) , 10 vols. Works of fiction appear in vols 3-5

2 *Zhongguo xin wenxue daxi xubian* 中國新文學大系續編 (Hong Kong: Hong Kong Literary Study Society 香港文學研究社, 1968) Works of fictions are included in vols.2-4

representative of the revolution's second decade of development. However, the three stories, written between 1928 and 1938, the tragic elements under study decreased to an insignificant low level. It seems to me that the line of continuity as a theme of anti-tradition broke down rather abruptly.

For the past 16 years, I have been teaching a course dealing with major writers in modern Chinese literature. My teaching and research in the past have compelled me to expand my reading beyond the three volumes of prose fiction mentioned above. As I have researched what both distinguished and little known writers have said about the dead and the insane, the fiction of the Chinese literary revolution has taken on new meaning for me. The cases depicted are not merely isolated ones, in which the writers simply described the general suffering of a human being. I have noticed that among the many symbolic cases of insanity and death there are recognizably cohesive threads, which imply larger meanings of the May Fourth Movement.

The Insane and Death in Lu Xun's Fiction

In the early stage of research, my study of Lu Xun's 魯迅 （1881-1936） stories gave some knowledge of their complexities. I was surprised to find that the death rates is very high in Lu Xun's stories which are explicitly anti-tradition. Very few of his characters are healthy, mentally or physically. In the end they usually find it difficult to escape death or insanity. Because I noticed that by 1986 there had been no study attempting to view these tragic stories as s series of cohesive works, I asked a student Lee Soo Tuan to write a thesis on the subject. He related the prevailing anti-tradition thinking of the May Fourth era to Lu Xun's fiction. The conclusion of his thesis, entitled "A Study of the Madness and Death in Lu Xun's Fiction and Their Social Significance", supports my observation that death and madness are related to the condemnation of old tradition.[3] In studying of Lu Xun's tragic figures against the intellectual background of the May Fourth period, we find that the ultimate causes of death and madness are social and political injustices, rather than the environment of fate.

At about the same time, I noticed that scholars in China were also paying some attention to this aspect of Lu Xun's fiction. In 1984, Peng Dingan published an article to study the geneology of the insane in his fiction. He traced the roots of madness to social illness and revolution. [4] In 1988, Zhang Hongsheng wrote a paper on the death of forerunners in Lu Xun's stories. These intellectuals either died from disillusionment or persecution.[5] Because of these studies, Lu Xun's tragedy as a mode of narrative fiction began to attract wider attention.

Madness and death are two of the many unavoidable sufferings all human beings have to face. The pains of all kinds of illness, loss, death and other forms of suffering, of course, have always been the great themes of literature. During the May Fourth period, most writers generally held

---

3 Li Shuduan 李樹端（. Lee Soo Tuan）, "A Study of the Madness and Death in Lu Xun's Fiction and Their Social Significance" 魯迅小說人物的"狂"與"死"及其社會意義, unpublished academic essay in Chinese, Department of Chinese Studies, National University of Singapore, 1988.

4 Peng Dingan 彭定安"The Geneology of the Madmen in Lu Xun's stories"論魯迅小說中的狂人家族, *Journal of Modern Chinese Literature Studies* 中國現代文學研究叢刊, No.4, June 1984, pp. 158-179.

5 Zhang Hongsheng 張鴻聲, "From Madman to Wei Lianshu: A Study of the Death of Forerunners in Lu Xun's Fiction" 從狂人到魏連殳—論魯迅小說先覺者死亡主題 *Journal of Modern Chinese Literature Studies*, No 3, March 1988, pp. 275-282.

the view that literature is primarily an imitation or representation of life, particularly of social life. The sociological approach to literature is especially cultivated by the leftist and realistic writers. Those who wrote about the nature world and the inner or subjective world of the individual are not considered to be part of the mainstream, but rather seen as part of the minority.

Any attempt to view Lu Xun's tragic stories as a cohesive genre may find the tragic elements not only has social relevance, but they also root themselves in the anti-old values campaign of the May Fourth Movement. The portraits of madmen or madwomen are born out of the anti-Confucius, anti-tradition thinking. The death of his characters is designed with ideological purposes.

Until now, study of the death and insane in the May Fourth era has been individual and piecemeal. An attempt to view the Chinese tragedy of the May Fourth period as a "genre" may yield fresh meaning. Therefore, I expand my examination to the works of other writers belonging to different schools or literary movements. My choice is, of course, rather random and arbitrary. In addition to Lu Xun, the works of Lu Yin 盧隱 (1898-1934), Yu Dafu 郁達夫 (1896-1945), Wang Luyan 王魯彥 (1901-1944), Xu Qinwen 許欽文 (1897-1984), Jian Xianai 騫先艾 (1906-), and Tai Jingnong 台靜農 (1902-1991) are discussed individually and placed in the perspective of the May Fourth tragedy. With these various groups of writers, I hope I can avoid to distort the cases to prove my points.[6]

---

6 The selection of works for analysis in this paper is indebted to these two books: Yang Yi 楊義, *A History of Modern Chinese Fiction*, Vol.1 (Beijing: People's Literature

Lu Xun's short stories, excluding those in *Old Tales Retold* 故事新編 (1936), all of which are included in two collections entitled *Call to Arms* 吶喊 (1923) and *Wandering* 彷徨 (1926). Out of these 25,[7] there are 11 pieces in which 19 characters become insane or dead. Among the 19 characters, three are mad, ten dead, and six suffering mental illness and finally dead. For the sake of convenience, I provide some of the relevant details of the stories under study. The titles of the tragic stories, the identities of the characters, the symptoms and signs of mental disease or abnormality, are indicated in the following table:

	Title of story	character	Sign of madness	Cause of death
Family Members of the Mad	"Madman's Diary" 狂人日記	Madman 狂人 (an intellectual)	Suffering from schizophrenia; accusing that gentry's scholars and feudal systems are man eaters.	
	"The Eternal Lamp" 長明燈	Madman 瘋子 (an intellectual)	Trying to below out the eternal lamp of the temple	
	"Tomorrow" 明天	Fourth Shan's wife 單四嫂子 (a widow)	Driven to madness by sadness from the death of her son	
Characters Who Are Mad And Dead	"In the Wine Shop" 在酒樓上	Shungu 順姑 (a young country woman)	Tortures after refusing to marry a stranger; she hides her illness	Unknown sickness

Publishing House 人民文學出版社, 1986) and Qian Liqun 錢理群, WuFuhui 吳福輝 and others, *Thirty Years of Modern Chinese Literature* (Shanghai: Shanghai Literature Publishing House 上海文藝出版社, 1987)

7 *Old Tales Retold* (Shanghai: Cultural Life Publisher 文化生活出版社, 1936); *Call to Arms* (Beijing: New Tide Society 新潮社, 1923); *Wandering* (Beijing: Beixin Bookstore 北新書局,1926)

	"Medicine" 藥	Xiayu 夏瑜 （a revolutionary）		Jailed and beheaded Blood spitting
	"The Misanthrope" 孤獨者	Wei Lianshu 魏連殳 （a deviationist）	Wants the old system to be abolished	Executed be firing squad
	"The Story of Ah Q" 阿Q正傳	Ah Q 阿Q （a peasant）	Involved in robbery and revolution	
	"The White Light" 白光	Chen Shi-Cheng 陳士成 （an old-style scholar）	Trying to dig for treasures after repeatedly failing an examination	Drowned in a lake
	"The New Year's Sacrifice" 祝福	Xianglin's Wife 样林嫂 （a country woman）	Living in terror because she is worried about her life after death	Committed suicide
	"Kong Yiji" 孔乙己	kong Yiji 孔乙己 （an old-style scholar）		Hardships and poverty
	"Regret for the Past" 傷逝	Zijun 子君 （an educated young woman）		Unknown
Family Members of the Dead	"Tomorrow" 明天	Bao Er 寶兒 （son of Shan-Shi's wife）		Killed by maltreatment of a quack doctor
	"Medicine" 藥	Little Hua 華小栓 （son of teashop owner）		Contracted TB and killed by malpractice）
	"The New Year's Sacrifice" 祝福	A Mao 阿毛 （son of Xianglin's wife）		Eaten by a wolf

	"In The Wine Shop" 在酒樓上	Three-Year-Old brother（younger brother of Lu Weifu 呂緯甫		Unknown
	"The Misanthrope" 孤獨者	Grandmother 祖母（a country folk）		Suffered an epidemic disease
	"Madman's Diary" 狂人日記	Little Sister 小妹（sister of Madman）		Eaten by the oldest brother
	"The Eternal Lamp" 長明燈	A peasant beaten to death in the Lucky Light Village		Punishing for taking part in antifeudalism movement
	"Madman's Diary" 狂人日記	A peasant beaten to death in the Wolf Village		Revolting against the landlords

The table above shows the tragic characters can be divided into three categories:（1）family members of the insane,（2）characters who gave gone mad and have later died for various reasons, and （3） family members of the dead. I use the term "madness" or "insane" in a loose and broad sense, including real mental illness and deviation from traditional political or culture thinkings. In China, people are considered "mad" if they are radical in action or speech.

In "The Madman's Diary", Lu Xun described an intellectual who is considered mad because he attacks "the feudalistic systems that eat people"（吃人禮教）. He survives at the end of the story simply because he had surrendered by his Big Brother, a landlord and the rook physician. The madman in the story symbolizes the abortive revolution of modern China. This revolution is characterized by awakening intellectual joining the revolutionary movement with zeal, but later compromising to the old power after being set back by some frustrations. In "The Eternal Lamp", a young man repeatedly attempts to extinguish the lamp in a temple. Because the superstitious villagers regard the lamp as a guardian of their well beings, they want the young man to be killed. However, for the young man, the lamp is a symbol of superstition, and the Chinese old traditions. Before he has carried out his heroic mission, he is locked up by the villagers, who plan to execute him. Both of these two so-called madmen are actually carried away by enthusiasm for overthrowing the old system of Chinese culture. They are not mad in the sense of developing mental illness.

It is not necessary to discuss in detail all the cases included in the table above. The characters, who are suffering, mentally or physically, are representing four different social groups. The first group consists of the old-style scholars who are the products and victims of the old educational and social systems. As represented by Kong Yiji and Chen Shicheng, they rejected by society. The tragic fates of these people are symbolic of the pending death of the past tradition, which is an important theme in many stories of Lu Xun.

I may the new intellectuals and the forerunners of the revolution into the second group of characters. The Madman in "The Madman's Diary", Xia Yu in "Medicine", and the insane in "The Eternal Lamp" are awakening and critical intellectuals. They dare to condemn the old values, the old ethical and political systems. Together with Lu Weifu in "In the Wine Shop" and Wei Lianshu in "The Misanthrope", they are representing the abortive revolution in modern China.

There are five children who died in Lu Xun's stories. The Little

Sister is eaten by his Big Brother and his accomplices and Little Hua is killed by swallowing blood-soaked mantou 饅頭. Baoer is the only hope of Fourth Shan's wife, but he dies in the hands of a crook physician. The children's death symbolizes the disappointment of Lu Xun who once expected a better future for the younger generation of people. Children are not able to grow up healthily, mentally or physically. Even worse, many of them die very young.

The common people who are insane or dead in the fourth group are Ah Q, Shungu, Zijun, Xianglin's Wife, Fourth Shan's wife, and two unnamed peasants. The tragedy of these country folks is brought about by social and political injustice.

From above observations, we may conclude that the ancestors of these Chinese tragic heroes are not those of the Greeks or modern Western tragic heroes. These people, whether intellectuals or country folks, are all used by the author to express his anti-tradition and anti-establishment feelings.

The Insane and Dead Female Characters in Lu Xun's Fiction

Lu Yin was a contemporary of Bing Xin 冰心 （1900- ）. Not only did the two write during the same period, but they also both attracted readers with short stories depicting social problems. Bing Xin's first story, "Two Families" 兩個家庭, was published in *Morning Post* 晨報 in 1919.[8] It is about a scholar Chen Huamin 陳華民, who has just returned from England to find himself alienated in his old society still ruled by a

---

8　The story appeared on 18-22 September 1919 in the *Morning Post's* literary supplement.

war-lord government. He condemns the life-style of his wife, who as the daughter of a gentry-official indulges in idleness. Disappointment and frustration have changed Chen Huamin totally, even to the point of developing an inferiority complex and withdrawal himself from all of society. In the end, he drowns his sorrows in drinking and commits suicide. About a year later, Bing Xin's "The Last Peace" 最後的安息 （1920） depicted a child-daughter-in-law who is tortured to death by her mother-in-law.[9] Both stories contain a hidden attack on the old Chinese society. Lu Yin's fiction was more concerned with social ideas than Bing Xin's. Before 1922, Lu Yin wrote a large number of stories attacking the old traditions. Of the 14 short stories in her first collection of works, *Old Friend by the Sea* [10] the image of the insane and/or dead occurs in five. These five stories, written 1921-1923, are among her early works. Relevant data of these stories are provides in the following table:

Title of story	Characters	Sign of Madness	Cause of Death
"A Writer" 〈一個著作家〉	Shao Fuchen 邵浮塵（a young man in love）	Suffering from mental disorder	Killed herself with a broken bottle
"A Writer" 〈一個作家〉	Qinfen 沁芬（a young woman in love）	Emotionally unstable）	Blood splitting
"A Letter" 〈一封信〉	Meisheng 梅生 （a country girl）		Tortured to death by husband's family
"Tears" 〈餘淚〉	Bai Wuxing 白吾性 （a woman teacher of a missionary school）		Killed in civil war of the war-lords while working as nurse for the Red Cross

---

9 The story was first published on 11-13 March in the *Morning Post's* literary supplement.

10 *Old Friend by the Sea* （Shanghai: Commercial Press, 1925）.

"The Sorrow of a Girl Depressed" 〈或人的悲哀〉	Yaxia 亞俠（an educated young woman）	Suffering from spiritual depression and neuroticism	Drowned herself in the lake
"Lishi's Diary" 〈麗石的日記〉	Lishi 麗石（an educated woman）	Suffering from mental disorder	Unclear-doctors claimed death by heart attack, but friends claimed death from mental illness

As shown in the table above, all but one of the tragic characters are so-called "awakened new females" 覺醒的新女性. Most of Lu Yin's female characters are suffering from some kind of mental disorder prior to committing suicide. The common cause of their tragedies is the pressure received from conservative families and a feudalistic society. The death of these new females is designed to be a kind of protest because they are victims of the old ethics.

Shortly after Lu Yin's stories were published, Mao Dun 茅盾 remarked that Lu Yin's writing has a very close kinship with the May Fourth Movement. He even pointed out that one can "breathe the air of the May Fourth era whenever we read her stories." 11 This may explain why Lu Yin put her characters to death so easily and let them be tortured by mental disease so often. She obviously wrote in line with the current thinking and fit her works into the "problem fiction"問題小說, a chief mode of narrative fiction in her day.

The Insane and Dead Male Characters in Yu Dafu's Fiction

---

11 Mao Dun " on Lu Yin"盧隱論, *Selected Works of Lu Yin* 盧隱選集（Fuzhou: Fujian People's Publishing House 福建人民出版社, 1985）, p. 1.

Yu Dafu claimed that all his works of fiction are a kind of confession, a revelation of his inner feelings. He opposed the popular literary views of his time that literature mirrors life and society. "Literary works are authors' autobiographies," he said. Images of the insane and /or dead also appear in some of his stories, particularly those written during the early period of modern Chinese literary revolution（1917-1927）. His first story, "The Silver Colour of Death"銀灰色之死, portrays a young Chinese man who suddenly dies at the front gate of a Women Medical College in Tokyo. This story carries the same didactic message as those of other realistic writers. In "The Sinking"沉淪, the title story of his first collection of stories, a young man commits suicide by drowning himself in the sea of Japan, he blames old China for being weak and refusing to reform and change. In "Sacrifice"薄奠, the rickshaw man is dead because of the poverty brought about by social injustice. In "Snowing Morning" 微雪的早晨, Zhu Yaru 朱雅儒 has been driven to insanity because he has lost his fiancée to a military officer. The following is a brief summary of the relevant facts involved in each of the above stories:

Title of story	Character	Signs of Madness	Cause of Death
"The Silver Colour of Death" 〈銀灰色之死〉	Y （a young man studying in Japan）	Has a split personality and is living in a fantasy world	Sudden death at the main gate of a Women Medical College
"The Silver Colour of Death" 〈銀灰色之死〉	Y's wife		Tortured by mother-in-law and died of pneumonia

"The Sinking" 〈沉淪〉	He 他（a young man studying in Japan）	Has a split personality and is living in a fantasy world	Drowned himself in the sea, because he saw himself as a victim of a weak nation
"Simple Sacrifice" 〈薄奠〉	He 他 （a poverty-stricken rickshaw man）		Drowned in a river, either by accident or suicide
"Green Smoke" 〈青烟〉	A man in distress	Suffering from depression	Drowned himself in a river
"A Snowing Morning" 〈微雪的早晨〉	Zhu Yaru 朱雅儒（a student from the countryside）	Suffering from mental disorder, attacking the military war-loads	Died of sickness after losing his fiancée to a military officer

Compared with Lu Yin's characters, Yu Dafu's tragic characters are predominantly male, but the fact of his characters remains the same: most of them commit suicide after having been driven to insanity. Because these stories thematically portray victims of an unjust society, Yu Dafu later claimed himself to be one of the pioneer writers of proletarian fiction. However, he, as a writer, is more widely associated with his insistence that one should write about the inner, the subjective world of the individual.

The Insane and the Dead in Regional Fiction

Fiction about one's native homeland which is also called "regional fiction" （鄉土小說）is neither a school nor a movement, but merely a group of works vivid with local colour or regionalism. The writers of regional literature are presumably less involved in ideological campaigns and the literary thoughts of the May Forth era. However, this is not true as we look into the works of Jian Xianai, Tai Jingnong, Wang Luyan, and Xu Qinwen. The reason is that they wrote their stories to explore their memories of the life in the remote villages even though they were living in big cities which were sub-merged by anti-tradition campaign.12 It is not surprising that the themes of anti-tradition pervade their stories. The following table provides relevant contents of some of the stories under study:

Author and Title	Characters	Signs of Madness	Cause of Death
Wang Luyan, "Autumn Night" 王魯彥 〈秋夜〉	I 我(an intellectual)	Has hallucinations, regards all oppressed people as his brothers; the dogs of Zhao Family attack from all sides	Dreamed of drowning by accident
Wang Luyan, "Pamelo" 王魯彥 〈柚子〉(1924)	Baldhead Wang 王禿頭		Beheaded for the crime of demanding payment from local government
Wang Luyan, "Juying's Marriage" 王魯彥 〈菊英的出嫁〉 (1926)	Juying 菊英(died at 18, 10 years ago)		Sickness
Same as above	Juying's husband-to-be (died 10 years ago)		Sickness

---

12 For a brief introduction and anthology of regional fiction, see Yan Jiayan 顏家炎, *Modern Chinese Fiction of Various Schools*, Vol. 1 (Beijing: Beijing University, 1989), pp. 1-11. See also Ho Jiquan 何積全 and Xiao Chenwang 蕭沉網 ed., *Anthology of Chinese Regional Fiction* 中國鄉土小說選, 2 vols. (Guiyang 貴陽:Guizhou Renming Chubaneshe 貴州人民出版社, 1986).

Xu Qinwen, "The Mad Woman" 許欽文〈瘋婦〉(1923)	Shuanxi 雙喜（wife of a young country folk）	Tortured by mother-in-law results in madness	Mentally sick from being continuously tormented by her mother-in-law
Xu Qinwen, "Grave Yard" 許欽文〈石岩〉(1926)	Homeless workers		Seven workers are buried alive in an accident
Xu Qinwen , "A Er, the Running Nose" 許欽文〈鼻涕阿二〉(1927)	Juhua 菊花（a woman who is sold to a man as a concubine, after her husband passes away）		Impoverished after losing the favor of her husband
Jian Xianai "Water Burial" 蹇先艾〈水葬〉(1926)	Luomao 駱毛（a pretty thief）		Executed by village officials who drown him alive
Jian Xianai, "The Village Tragedy" 蹇先艾〈鄉間的悲劇〉(1934)	Qi Dama 祁大媽（a hardworking woman）	Suffering from mental illness, after being deserted by her husband	Committed suicide by jumping into the well
Jian Xianai, "On the Road to Guizhou" 蹇先艾〈在貴州道上〉(1931)	Zhao Shishun 趙世順（a vagabond）		Arrested and beheaded by soldiers while working as a footman
Tai Jingnong, "The Flame of Candle" 台靜農〈燭焰〉(1926)	The son of the Wu 吳 family（who, despite his critical illness, has arranged his marriage to a young beautiful girl Cuigu 翠姑）		Died from critical illness, three or four days into his marriage

Tai Jingnong, "New Grave" 台靜農〈新墳〉（1926）	The Fourth's Wife 四太太（a widow, who becomes a beggar after her children are killed by the army and her property is taken away）	Begging along the street, she cries: "Daughters and sons are married."	Burns herself to death
Tai Jingnong, "Red Lantern" 台靜農〈紅燈〉（1926）	Deyin 得銀（he sells dumpling to make a living, but is forced to join the bandits later）		Arrested and beheaded by the army

The people in the rural areas suffer because old customs, superstitious practices, landlords, and warlords are terrible man-eaters. Although "The Village Tragedy" by Jian Xianai was written during a later period, it deserves special attention. In this story, Qi Daniang 祁大娘 is a woman labourer who has worked very hard to support her family. She is happy and healthy, until she learns that her husband is living with another woman. She discovers that the woman is an award given to her husband by a city landlord, who wishes to keep her husband in the city. The thought of this disgrace drives her to sanity. In the end, she commits suicide by jumping into a well. This suicide is implicitly blamed upon the landlord, a symbol of the old tradition.

"The Village Tragedy" was originally written in 1934, but was revised sometime after 1949. this revision was later named "A Strong Willed Woman"倔強的女人. As indicated by the change in title, the end of the new story is no longer tragic: Qi Daniang wants to live and take good care of her children. She firmly believes that poor people will stand up to be the master of the land in the near future.[13]

The different ending changes the tone and theme of the story. The revised version of the above story carries the popular theme and tone of the fiction from 1940s to 1970s. After 1949, attack on traditional values and cultures no longer attracts writers. Therefore, tragic endings are replaced by positive ones. This is because the communist authorities have not allowed tragedy to be depicted under their rule.

"Water Burial", also written by Jian Xianai, is an interesting piece as well. In the original version, Luomao is arrested for stealing and sentenced to death by drowning. In the first version, we are not told what exactly Luomao has stolen, nor do we know whom he has stolen from. However, after1949, the author changed the original story by indicating that Luomao has stolen something from a landlord. The leftist writers in Mainland China are familiar with Gorky's famous saying, "Stealing from the rich in the past is a protest by the poor".[14] Likewise Luomao, a victim of the old and disordered society, has become a hero of the country folk. While the earlier version of this story is an expression of the anti-old tradition campaign of the May Fourth period, the later version is a promotion of the people's revolution.

Conclusion

The May Fourth period witnessed the crucial conflict between old and new intellectuals — between the old faith and the renaissance mind.

---

13 See Song Zhibang 宋贊邦 and Wang Jiehua 王介華(eds.), *Research Materials for Jian Xianai and Liao Gongxian* 蹇先艾廖公弦研究合集 (Guiyang: Guizhou Renmin Chubanshe 貴州人民出版社, 1985).

14 See note 4.

The influence of the May Fourth anti-tradition thought is evident in the works of Lu Xun, Yu Dafu, Lu Yin, and many others, including those less involved in the intellectual movement. For the *xiangtu* writers, intellectual elements appear, at first sight, to have had little bearing upon their works of regionalism. However, these writers were equally shaped by their contemporary "climate of opinion."

Influenced by the Chinese intellectual movement that totally rejected Confucianism and old Chinese cultures and systems, writers of the 1920s and early 1930s were attracted to using realistic fiction primarily as a tool for social regeneration. While this type of writing may not represent the maturity displayed in the same writers' later works, their purpose was to prove their commitment to destroying Confucian ideology and the old institutions. The rebels, the reformers, the radicals, the awakening intellectuals, and the revolutionaries in the stores were considered mad, in the eyes of establishment. However, their deaths, no matter caused by execution or by suicide, reveal the writers' condemnation of the old society. They all wrote for a similar purpose: to expose the evils of society in order to enlighten the people, and to shock them into action towards reform.

Therefore, we can understand that tragic writing as a mode of fiction was popular specifically during the first ten years of modern Chinese literature. Among the stories I have discussed above, I notice that many of them were the first literary attempts by the authors. Lu Xun's "Diary of Madman", Yu Dafu's "The Silver Colour of Death", Lu Yin's "A Writer", and Bing Xin's "Two Families" were all maiden works. The rest were among their earliest works if not the first. The reason is not difficult to understand. When a writer begins to write his first story as an apprentice, he is usually more easily influenced by the form or theme which is flourishing and popular at that time. Writing without a personal vision, and lacking originality and individuality, the writers usually adopt the forms of writing most easily learned, which usually stereotyped forms of writing are. Therefore, the rhetoric of anti-tradition thinking pervaded most of the early writings of the May Fourth writers.

Most of the works discussed above have been the subjects of literary analysis. Since this paper is a synthetical study of the anti-tradition theme, the artistic and technical aspects are not my concern here. In the case of Lu Xun and other *xiangtu* writers, philosophical and ideological contents seem to enhance their artistic value. However, this is not so in all cases. The stories by Lu Yin and Yu Dafu are obviously hampered by too much unassimilated ideology.

I agree that in interpreting works of art a scholar cannot simply categorize them into ideological camps. Such a blanket categorization would be disastrous to understanding the uniqueness of each work of art. However, my purpose here is simply to point out that the May Fourth confrontation between the old and the new finds compelling expression in the works of many fiction writers. This is one of the many types of writings produced at this time. I must also point out that there are differences as well as similarities within the theme of anti-tradition.

The Impact of Dream of the Red Mansions on Lu Xun and other Modern Chinese Writers

The scholars who study literary indebtedness notice a common phenomenon: literature influence seems to be most apparent in times when literary forms and aesthetics appear to be outworn and the direction of a particular literary tradition is undergoing radical change. When classical literature cannot provide an answer to the authors' needs, they may discover in foreign countries what they seek in terms of form or ideology which they can adapt or transmute to their own consciousness, time and society. The seed of literature influence will be affected by the particular quality of the soil and climate where it takes root.[1]

The influence of foreign literary works on Chinese literature in the May Forth era is perhaps the most obvious example of this kind. The Chinese literary revolution, begun in 1917, represented a complete break from the native tradition. The forces that gave impetus to the new literature came from abroad. As pointed out by Wang Yao 王瑤 in his article " The Relation Between Modern Chinese Literature and Native Tradition"中國現代文學和民族傳統的關係, almost all writers who

---

1 J.T Shaw, "Literary Indebtedness and Comparative Literary Studies", in Newton Stallknecht and Horst Frenz（eds.）, *Comparative Literature : Method and Perspective*（Carbondale: Southern Illinois University Press,1973）, pp.91-93.

advocated literary revolution were against old literature. They denounced traditional Chinese literature as a dead literature, and wanted the new literature to break away from the Chinese literary tradition. Only those who opposed literary reform held the view that the evolution of an indigenous literary tradition was equally indispensable for the formation of a new literature. Many writers, including Lu Xun, even urged the people not to read classical literature.[2]

Although writers of the new literature strongly criticised traditional literature, they were all schooled in the literary traditions of China. Most of the leading new intellectuals during the early period who adopted an uncompromising attitude towards traditional literature were deeply influenced by Chinese traditional liberal arts education. In 1919, the year when the May Fourth Movement took place, Lu Xun 魯迅, the oldest among them, was 38, Guo Moruo 郭沫若 27, Mao Dun 茅盾 23, Ye Shaojun 葉紹鈞 25, Zhu Ziqing 朱自清 21, Wen Yiduo 聞一多 20 and Pin Xin 冰心 19. In their early years they were all schooled in the rigid and orthodox style of traditional education. But they all complained that traditional culture had become intellectually stifling.[3]

Traditional Chinese literature however, did not altogether lose its position of eminence and value even during the May Fourth era. Influenced by Western literary theory and concept, a sudden revolutionary change in the literary hierarchy occurred. Fiction and drama have never

---

2 The essay is collected in Ma Liangchun 馬良春（ed.）, *On Modern Chinese Literary Trends* 《中國現代文學思潮流派討論集》（Beijing: People's Literature Press 人民文學,1984） pp.139-56.

3 *Ibid.*,p.141

been regarded as important literary genres because they were considered pure entertainment with no didactic value. However, ever since fiction was elevated to its highest stature after 1917. *Dream of the Red Mansions* 《紅樓夢》 began to be recognised as a great novel. As Lu Xun observed, "In China, fiction was excluded from literature." He also added: "Fiction and drama were never regarded as proper literature. They have now been accorded the highest positions after the introduction of Western literary theory. Therefore *Dream of the Red Mansions* and *The Romance of the Western Chamber* 《西廂記》 are occupying an equally important place as *Book of Poetry* 《詩經》 and *Li Sao* 《離騷》 in the history of literature. "[4] *Dream of the Red Mansions* had also received great attention because it was used as an example that great works in the vernacular language had been in existence for a long time. It therefore unexpectedly enjoyed enormous popularity and had a great impact on the modern Chinese writers and their works.

The *Dream of the Red Mansions* appeared in Beijing in the middle of Qian Long's 乾隆 reign, around 1765. In the last two centuries, it has become extremely popular and has exerted a great deal of influence. There have been many sequels. The original novel first appeared with only 80 chapters. The present popular version of the novel in its standard 120-chapter form was not published until almost 30 years after Cao Xueqin's 曹雪芹 death. It is generally believed that the last 40 chapters were recovered later and had been edited by Gao E 高鶚.[5] Many later

---

4 Lu Xun, *Complete Works of Lu Xun* 《魯迅全集》, Vol.6 （Hong Kong:Literary Study Society 文學研究社,1973）, p.231

5 Zhou Cezong（ChowTse-tsung）周策縱，*Essays on Dream of the Red Mansions* 《樓夢

sequels were published and some twenty of them have become quite popular: *The Second Dream of the Red Mansions*《後紅樓夢》, *Sequel to Dream of the Red Mansions*《續紅樓夢》, *Awakening from the Dream of Red Mansions*《大紅樓夢》,and so forth.[6] All these sequels to the novel are designed to continue the love story and give it a happy ending. To satisfy the demands of readers for more romance, many novelists started writing in the style of *Dream of Red Mansions* about actors and prostitutes. Thus the popularity of the novel led to the emergence of a new type of novel. Numerous plays, opera and movie produced in the past were based on the story of the novel. Their impact on Chinese culture and society is beyond our assessment.[7]

The study of *Dream of the Red Mansions*' impact on modern Chinese literature is most interesting and of great value. Since many writers and their works have been influenced by this classic Chinese novel, the complexity and importance can be used as theme of an international conference. It would be exciting to see such a conference on *Drama of the Red Mansions*, in which the writers themselves were invited to discuss their own creative process of works which have been influenced by the novel.

As too many writers and works are involved to go into detail in this paper, I will limit my discussion to four modern Chinese writes: Lu Xun

---

案》(Hong Kong: Chinese University Press,2000）.

6 Xing Zhiping 邢治平, *Ten Lectures on Dreams of Red Mansions* 紅樓夢十講（ Honan: Zhongzhou Shuhua 中洲書畫, 1983）, pp.208-215

7 Lai Chunquan 賴春泉, "Lu Xun and Dream of The Red Mansions", *Collection of Essays on Lu Xun on His One Hundred Years of Birthday* 《魯迅誕辰百年文集》,Vol.2 (Guangdong Lu Xun Study Group 廣東魯迅研究小組,1981),pp.372-86; Xing Zhiping, *Ten Lectures on Dream of the Red Mansions*, pp.211-14.

魯迅, Ba Jin 巴金, Cao Yu 曹禺 and Bai Xianyong 白先勇. They represent writers of various periods in modern China. Lu Xun emerged in the 1920, Ba Jin and Cao Yu in the 1930s, and Bai Xianyong in the 1960s. A brief discussion of the literary indebtedness shows that the literary influence of the novel on modern Chinese writers has been pervasive and fruitful.

Lu Xun and the Realistic Tradition
of *Dream of the Red Mansions*

Like the other leading writers of modern Chinese writing during the early period, Lu Xun adopted an uncompromising attitude toward the "bad traditions" of classical Chinese literature. He was undoubtedly one of the most influential and effective critics of Chinese tradition. He urged the young people to "read a few only" or "not to read" Chinese classics, fearing that they would be poisoned by the old culture. When he was young, he himself was especially interested in Chinese classical fiction. From 1920 to 1924 when he was inspired to write short stories, he wrote *A Brief History of Chinese Fiction* 《中國小說史略》 and *The Historical Development of Chinese Fiction* 《中國小說的歷史變遷》 [8] Lu Xun was one of the modern Chinese writers who developed many of their own ideas and techniques to suit their own purposes. [9] Lu Xun was probably

---

8 *A Brief History of Chinese Fiction* （first published in Beijing, Vol. I in 1924, Vol. II in 1925）, *The Historical Development of Chinese Fiction* （written in 1924）. For the English translation, see *A Brief History of Chinese Fiction*, translated by Yang Hsien-yi and Gladys Yang （Beijing: Foreign Language Press, 1976）.

9 Wang Yao 王瑤, "Lu Xun's Writings and Chinese Traditional Literature" 《論魯迅作品與中國文學的歷史聯系》,Essays on Lu Xun's Writings 《魯迅作品論集》（Beijing:

the earliest writer to value the realistic approach of the author of *Dream of the Red Mansions*. In *The Historical Development of Chinese Fiction*, he observed:

> As for the novel itself, it is one of the gems of Chinese literature. The author's greatest virtue is that he dares to describe life realistically without subterfuge or concealment, unlike earlier writers who made their characters either black or white. Hence all the people in this book are real. The most significant thing about this work is that it put an end to the traditional view of novels and how to write them, the beauty of the language is only of secondary importance.[10]

Lu Xun thus valued the novel for its realism, a tradition which he applied to his own fiction. About his stories, he once remarked: "Through the short stories I wrote about the degeneration and crime of the upper classes and the misery of the lower classes."[11] He also said, "Sometimes I also exposed the sickness of the old society, by drawing the attention of the people to it and hoping that it may be cured." [12] Cao Xueqin in Chapter 1 of the novel says: "All that my story narrates the meeting and partings, the joys and sorrows, the ups and downs of fortune, are recorded exactly as they happened. I have not dared to add the finest bit of

---

People's Literature 人民文學,1984）, pp.1-39.

9 *The Complete Works of Lu Xun* 《魯迅全集》, Vol.8 （Hong Kong: Literary Study Society 文學研究社,1957）p.350.

10 *The Complete Works of Lu Xun* 《魯迅全集》, Vol.8 （Hong Kong: Literary Study Society 文學研究社,1957）p.350.

11 "Author's Preface to English Translation of His Short Stories", *The Complete Works of Lu Xun,* Vol.7,p.632

12 *The Complete Works of Lu Xun,* Vol .4.pp 347-48.

touching-up, for fear of losing the true picture."[13] Lu Xun noted that *Dream of the Red Mansions* is an autobiographical novel of Cao Xueqin: "The author's life seems to fit the incidents in the novel very well." He went further to say that" The work is based on the author's own life. [14] What he meant was that the author not only wrote the novel with realism but also made great use of his personal experience. As we know, Dream of the Red Mansions was the first Chinese novel to draw liberally on autobiographical experience. Similarly Lu Xun also admitted that his stories were all based on unforgettable experiences, and referred to his memory as "dream":

> When I was young I, too, had many dreams. Most of them came to be forgotten, but I see nothing in this to regret. For although recalling the past may make you happy, it may sometimes also make you lonely, and there is no point in clinging in the spirit to lonely by bygone days. However, my trouble is that I cannot forget completely, and these stories have resulted from what I have been unable to erase from my memory.[15]

Zhou Xiashou's 周遐壽 *The Characters in Lu Xun's Fiction* 魯迅小說裡的人物 fully demonstrates that Lu Xun's home town Shaoxing 紹興 was the principal source of his inspiration. The experience, deeply rooted in his native home, symbolised the old Chinese way of life.[16]We can see

---

13 *Dream of the Red Mansions*,Vol.1 （Beijing: People's literature,1972）,p.3.

14 Lu Xun, T*he Historical Development of Chinese Fiction, in The Complete Works of Lu Xun*, Vol.8, p.350.

15 "Preface to *Call to Arms*"《吶喊自序》, *The Completed Works of Lu Xun*, Vol.1,p.3.

16 Zhou Xiashou, *The Characters in Lu Xun's Fiction* （Hong Kong: Zhong Liu Publisher 中流出版社,1976）. Zhou Xiashou （ Zouren 作人） is a brother of Lu Xun

that both writers felt drawn towards greater realism and the use of personal experience.

Lu Xun would have also learned many other literary lessons from *Dream of the Red Mansions*, especially as a form of art and social criticism. It's difficult to assess these influences because they have undergone subtle transformations to suit his individual consciousness, time and society. Furthermore, the number of works are unlimited, both Chinese and Western, in which he had found inspiration.

Lu Xun seldom deals with love in his stories, "Regret for the Past"傷逝 being the only exception. He never wrote a long novel, all his works of fiction are short stories notwithstanding these differences, there are many other similarities. Like D*ream of the Red Mansions*, Lu Xun's short stories are realistic descriptions of the Chinese Society in a period of transition. The People and village symbolized the old Chinese way of life. Four Uncle 魯四老爺 in Lu Xun's " The New Year's Sacrifice"祝福 is hypocritical gentleman as represented by Jia Zheng 賈政. The old man Gao 高老夫子,a Confucian moralist and an universal hypocrite bears some resemblance to many characters in the novel.[17] " The New Rear's Sacrifice" is a tragic tale about Xianglin Sao 祥林嫂 a peasant woman, hounded to death by feudalism and superstition. She is no way like 林黛玉. Runtu 閏土"My Old Home"故鄉 is different from Jia Baoyu 賈寶玉 because the former is a weather-beaten peasant burdened with family cares while the latter is born with a silver spoon in his mouth. Runtu is an

---

17 Yang Yi 楊義, *Studies of Lu Xun's Fiction* 《魯迅小說縱論》(Xian : Shanxi People's Publisher 陝西人民出版社,1984) ,pp.251-54; see also Wang Yao, "Lu Xun's Writings and Chinese Traditional Literature", *Essays on Lu Xun's Writings*, pp.29-30.

inlliterate son of a poor peasant and Boa-yu, a spoilt son of a distinguished gentry family. Characters such as these in lu Xun's stories are drawn from people he met in the early part of his life .Thus Lu Xun's autobiographical and realistic approach reflects his observation that "the author's greatest virtue or concealment, unlike earlier writers who made their characters either black or white. Hence all the people in the book are real:[18]

> Lu Xun was particularly impressed by the artistic achievement of the dialogue in *Dream of the Red Mansions*:
>
> Gorky deeply admired Balzac for his wonderful dialogue in his fiction. Balzac , without using description, has enable his reader to see the real person by reading by his dialogue······In China we don't have such an excellent novelist yet, but in *Water Margin* 水滸傳 and *Dream of the Red Mansion* we can find such successful dialogue which reveals to us a great deal about how a character looks.[19]

In Lu Xun's short story "Tomorrow"明天,the conversation between Fourth Shan's Wife 單四嫂子 and Doctor Ho Xiaoxian 何小仙, though very brief, reveals the latter's true character. The empty rhetoric of the doctor reflects his apparent inabliity to cure and the moral character of a quack doctor:

> "What's wrong with my Bao Er, doctor?"
>
> "An obstruction of the digestive track."
>
> "Is it serious? Will he······?"
>
> " Take these two prescriptions to start with."

---

18 Yang Yi, Studies of Lu Xun's Fiction, p.301
19 The Complete works of Lu Xun, Vol.5, p.429.

"He can't breathe, his nostrils are twitching."

"The element of fire overpowers that of metal······"[20]

The characterizations of Doctor Ho reminds us of doctor Hu 胡庸醫 in *Dream of the Red Mansions* who wrote out a prescription before knowing the sex and identity of his patient. The character such as graybeard 花鬚子"Medicine"藥 and He Daotong 何道統 in "Soap"肥皂 are revealed through their dialogues, not by direct description."[21]

Cao Xueqin is a good psychologist and his masterpiece is a supreme work of psychological realism. The finest of other Chinese novels cannot compare with *Dreamm of the Red Mansions* in probing the deeper psychological truths about the characters. Lu Xun and some of his contemporary writers' interest in exploring the mental activities of the characters in their works of fiction may be attributed to the influence of *Dream of the Red Mansions.*[22]

Like modern fiction writers in the west, Cao Xueqin skillfully employs the point-of–view technique in the novel. He uses both the first-person and third person narrator in the novel. At some points in his narrative, the omniscient narrator simply describes externals, assuming the objective viewpoint, but at other moments, the narrator would present a scene to us from the view of one of the characters such as Baoyu, Daiyu and even Liu Laolao 劉姥姥, therefore using the first person limited

---

20 "Tomorrow", *The Complete Works of Lu Xun* （Beijing: Foreign Languages Press, 1972）.

21 Lai Chunquan, "Lu Xun and *Dream of the Red Mansions*", *Collection of Essays on Lu Xun on His One Hundred years of Birthday*, Vol.2,pp.379-80.

22 Sun Huaizhong 孫懷中, *Lu Xun and Chinese Classical Chinese Novels* 《魯迅與中國古典小說》（Shanxi People's publish, 1982）,pp.304.305.

narration. The novel contains many characters' view points and we see the action in one of each tern.[23]

Lu Xun is the earliest master of the point- of -view technique. After careful examination of his 25 short stories that we find that a clear distinction can be made between the employ that the first-person narrator or third-person narrator The 12storeis told in the first person are: " Dairy of a madmen"狂人日記, " Kong Yiji" 孔乙己 "Regret for the Past"傷逝, "An Incident" 一件小事, "The Story of Hair"頭髮的故事,"The New Year's sacrifice", " In the Wineshop"在九樓上, " My old home"故鄉, "The Isolate"孤獨者,"My Old Home"故鄉, "Some Rabbits and a Cat"《兔和貓》, "A Comedy of Ducks" 鴨的喜劇,and "Village Opera" 社.Thirteen of the twenty-five sties are presented from the third-person point of view. These are: "Dragon Boat Festival" 端午節, "Happy Family"幸福的家庭, "Soap"肥皂, "Schoolmaster Gao", 高老夫子 "Medicine"藥 , "Tomorrow", "Storm in a Teacup"風波", "The White Light "白光, "The Eternal Lamp"長明燈"A Warning to the People"示眾, "and "Divorce"離婚.[24]

The point-of-view chosen has formal, moral and philosophical significant. It is not merely a matter of technique but part of the meaning of fiction. For this reason, the same story cannot be told from another point of view. In "Kong Yiji", the story of a marginal member of the literati who has turned to a thief is told by an uninvolved but sensitive boy

---

23 Hu Juren 胡菊人," An Interview with Bai Xianyogn on the Art of Fiction"《白先勇論小說藝術》, *The Art of Fiction*《小說技巧》, (Taipei: Yuanjing Publisher 遠景出版社,1978),pp.173-80.

24 Yue Daiyun 樂黛雲 (ed.), *The Studies on Lu Xun by Foreign Scholars* 《國外魯迅研究論集》(Beijin: Peking University Press, 1981), pp.334-65.

whose job is to warm the wine. Thus, the story has an economical and restrained character, and is more powerful in repudiating the old Chinese way of life.

Dream of the Red Mansions and Ba Jin's Novels of Old Families

Ba Jin who was from a conservative patriarchal family, emerged as a prominent writer in the 1930s. He was a famous for his critical attitude is always the conviction in his novels that "the System" is alone responsible for the existence of all kind of evil, a belief to which many of his contemporaries also subscribed. Ba Jin was also a professed anarchist as indicated by his pen-name which is formed from the syllabus of two anarchists' name, Bakunin and Kropotkin. He was in the1930s, the most well-known advocate or anarchism as well as the greatest authority on the revolution and anarchistic literature of the West among modern Chinese writers.

Born into a large traditional Chinese gentry family in Chengdu 成都, Shichuan 四川 province, he receive a traditional education. He is therefore deeply rooted in classical literature. As a small boy, he was deeply impressed by the story of Dream of the Red Mansions. He remembered that in his childhood days, his elder brothers and sisters always got together for a drink and their conversation topics always included a discussion of the characters of the novel. Members of his family, except for Ba Jin and other children of his age, had all studied the novel well. His father bought a wood-printed. The family later bought a modern edition published by the Commercial Press 商務印書館. Ba Jin admitted that even before he began to read the novel, he was well-informed of the characters and incidents of the novel.[25]

The best known of Ba Jin's novel is the trilogy *The Torrent*《激流》, comprising *The Family*《家》, *Spring* 《家》and *Autumn*《秋》 which tells a story of the disintegration of the traditional Chinese society and Chinese and old family system. It is the longest and most ambitious piece of modern Chinese fiction before the Second World War. Ba Jin admitted that he drew upon his family life he knew his adolescent years in Chengdu for his novel:

> *The Family* is a true story, in that its characters represent people I loved or loathed. Some of the events I personally witness or experience the same suffering. The third brother Juehui 覺慧 ,the youngest rebel in The Family was like opening memory's grave. Even as a child I frequently witnessed the ruination of the lives of lovable young people who were driven to tragic end. When writing this novel, I suffered with them and, like them, struggled in the grip of a demon's talons. It is replete with my deep love, my intense hate.[26]

In *The Family*, juexin and Juemin were modeled after the author's two eldest who had experienced the same suffering .Then third brother Juehui 覺慧, the youngest rebel in *The Family*, was a self-portrait of BA

---

25 *Collected Works of Ba Jin*《巴金文集》,Vol.10 （ Hong Kong: Nan guo Publisher 南國出版社,1970） pp.56-57.

26 " Notes on *The Family*"《關於家》,*The Family*《家》(Beijing: People's Literature 人民文學出版社, 1980,1980）, p.467,see also *The Family,* translation by Sidney Shapiro （Beijing:: Foreign Languages Press,1958） , pp.I-II.

Jin, who admitted the similarity of their characters and backgrounds.[27] The head of conservative patriarchal family Grandfather Gao 高老太爺, the ill-fated maids many other characters in the novel are compared the cousin Qin 琴 with Xichun 惜春 in *Dream of the Red Mansions.*[28]

Ba Jin's other best know novels include *Fire*《火》(1940-450) , *Leisure Garden* 憩園 (1944) and *Cold Nights* 寒夜 (1947) These works all deal with the life of the traditional Chinese extended family. One cannot help but think of *Dream of the Red Mansions* on reading these works and most scholars find it hard to avoid mentioning this classis novel whenever they discuss Ba Jin's works, especially *The Family.* Liu Wu-Chi in a brief analysis of Ba jin's trilogy, says:[29]

> The complete trilogy is more immense in length and than the *Dream of the Red* Mansions and more sophisticated in its treatment of youthful love and rebellion······But in the novel the flaming passion of youth in its insurrection against family bondage burns much more violently than Jia Baoyu's······

In another paragraph, he also remarks:

> Insofar as he drew his material from his own experience, the novel, again like the *Dream of the Red Mansions* , may be regarded as autobiographical······[30]

---

27 Ibib.,p.476
28 Ibid.
29 Liu Wu-chi, *An Introduction to Chinese Literature* (Bloomington: Indiana University Press, 1966) , p.272.
30 *Ibid.*,p.273

Cao Yu's Beijing Man and
Dream of the Red Mansions

C.T. Hsia's *A History of Modern Chinese Fiction, 1917-1957*, published in 1961, remains the most important authority on this subject. In 1980, C.T. Hsia remarks that "all the modern Chinese gentry family has been influenced by *Dream of Red Mansions*. Cao Yu is no exception"[31]. The remark refers to modern fiction writers and playwrights. As a contemporary of Ba Jin., Cao Yu is another Chinese writer who wrote a number of plays dealing with degenerate family life of the well-to-do, some belonging to old gentry family on its way to dissolution, other to the newly-risen group of financier-industrialists. Cao Yu's plays are the best examples of the influence of foreign models.[32] Although he borrowed many techniques from abroad, he also absorbed this kind include *Thunderstorm*《雷雨》(1934), *Sunrise*《日出》(1936),*Beijing Man* (1940) and *The Family* 《家》(adapted from Ba Jin's novel ,1941) . *Beijing Man* has been influenced by the plot and characterisation of *Dream of the Red Mansions.*[33]

Born to a scholar official family in Tianjin 天津 in1910, Cao Yu was familiar with the life of the feudal family. He recalled that among the four members of his family, his father, mother and brother were opium

---

31 C.T Hsia,"Cao Yu's Visit to Columbia University and Comment on *Beijing Man*" 《曹禺訪哥大紀實兼評北京人》, *Ming Bao Monthly*《明報月刊,》No.174(June 1980):53-66; C.T. Hsia, *A History of Modern Chinese Fiction* (New Haven: Yale University Press,1961)

32 S.M.Lau, *Tsao Yu* (Hong Kong University Press, 1970) .

33 Tian Benxiang 田本相,*On Cao Yu's Drama* 《曹禺劇作論》(Beijing:China's Drama Publisher,1981) ,pp.225-41

smokers. He received a traditional education when he was young. However, he was fascinated by *Dream of the Red Mansion* and other classic novels in those days. These inspired him to be a writer.[34]

Readers of *Beijing Man* find that the content and spirit of the play are more Chinese and relatively less influenced by the Western drama than are Thunderstorm and Sunrise. Written in 1940, *Beijing Man* is study of the disintegration of the already impoverished Zeng 曾 family in Beijing in the early 1930s. The Zengs had been powerful and wealthy a generation ago. After the downfall of the Manchu Dynasty in 1911, both the fortunes of this scholar-official family and Zeng Hao's 曾皓 authority as patriarch of the family suffered a blow.

Divided into three acts, the play starts with Chen Laima 陳奶媽 ,arriving from the countryside to visit her old master, Zeng Hao. Chen Laima, the formal wet noise of Wenqing, the spoilt son of Zeng Hao, bring along her daughter's son Xiaozhuer 小柱兒. The first thing she seems is the number of creditors demanding payment of debts from the Zengs. The second thing she seems is the degeneration of Wenqing, who is lying on his bed smoking opium. The readers, through the eyes of Chen Laima, come to know immediately the disintegration of a big family. This is the most economical way to introduce the downfall of the Zeng family to the readers. It is very likely that such a plot is influenced by a scene describing the visit of the Daguangyuan 大觀園 by Liu LaoLao 劉姥姥 in *Dream of the Red Mansions*.[35]

---

34 *Ibid.*, p2

35 C.T. Hsia ,"Cao Yu's Visit to Columbia University and Comments on *Beijing Man, Ming Bao Yue Kan*, No.174,pp.56-60.

The readers who are well read in *Dream of the Red Mansions* should also be able to recognize that Sufang 愫方 is in many ways similar to Lin Daiyu:

> Sufang is about thirty years old. She was born to a prominent family in the South. Her father was a famous scholar-official. After his death, the family became very poor. Soon after her mother died, she was bought to Beijing by her maternal aunt. Since then Sufang has been living with the Zengs' family in Beijing, never returning to her old home in the south.[36]

Arriving in Beijing, Sufang discovers that Zeng Wenqing has been married to Siyi 思懿 ,thought he is actually in love with his cousin Sufang. As we know, Jia Baoyu and his cousin Lin Daiyu who is also from the South are in love with each other, but Jia Baoyu is married to Xue Baochai 薛寶釵 .There are many other characters from *Dream of the Red Mansions* with a parallel in *Beijing Man*: Wenqing's father Zeng Hao. the last patriarch of the Zeng family, looks like Baoyu's father Jia Zheng 賈政.The domineering Siyi is a sister of Wang Xifeng 王熙鳳.[37]

The Influence on Bai Xianyong and His Short Stories

Among the Chinese writers living outside mainland China who emerged after1949, many were influenced by *Dream of The Red Mansions*. They are represented here by Bai Xianyong because its influence on his works is perhaps the most obvious and aesthetically the most interesting.

---

36 *Ibid.*,pp58-60
37 Tian Benxing, *On Cao Yu's Drama*, pp.226-27

C.T Hsia in an essay written in 1971 considered Bai Xianyong as one of the most talented few short story writers ever produced in China since the May Fourth era. He pointed out that the artistic achievement of his best works is comparable to those of Lu Xun, Zhang Ailing 張愛玲 and a few others.[38]

Bai Xianyong is different from the writers of the May Fourth era in his attitude towards Chinese literature and culture. He is a Western-trained Chinese writer who has benefited from the great writings of both the West and China. He has never, even in theory, criticized traditional Chinese literature. He openly admits to being indebted to it, especially *Dream of the Red Mansions*.

Bai Xianyong's most detailed discussion of his view of *Dream of the Red Mansions* and its influence appeared in an interviewed article "Bai Xianyong on the Art of Fiction." In his opinion, a novel dealing with the most complex subject matter and themes needs to employ the most sophisticated techniques. *Dream of the Red Mansions* is a work with such qualities. Cao Xueqin turned his unforgettable people and their lives into a novel with universal meanings. Bai Xianyong admits that he writes in such a tradition:

> My interest in literature began to grow in my high school days when I read tradition Chinese poetry. My language has been influenced by these works. I read *Dream of the Red Mansions* at the age of eleven. I read it again and during high school. Even now I still enjoy the novel and it has influenced the language of my

---

38 C.T. Hsia, "On Bai Xianyong ", *Taipei People* 《臺北人》(Taipei: Morning Bell, 1971) pp.231-52.

stories.

Among the many techniques employed by *Dream of the Red Mansions*, Bai Xianyong paid special attention to the narrative point of view, dialogue, the symbolic drama and symbolic scenes. He is particularly impressed by the themes about joy and sorrow, partings and reunions — the vicissitudes of life which are fully reflected in the novel. The quest for the meaning of human existence in the tragic world also has a long lasting influence on his stories.[39]

In one of Bai Xianyong's earliest short stories entitled "Mrs Jin"金大奶奶, there is a scene describing Mrs Jin committing suicide by drinking poison because her husband wanted to marry a songstress as his second wife. The scene of Mrs Jin's death is obviously influenced by the scene in Chapter 98 of *Dream of the Red Mansions* in which Daiyu dies in fulfillment of an ancient debt. [40] Bai Xianyong also admitted that the story of "Thinking of the Past"思舊賦, which is told from the point of view of two servants, is similar to the novel's technique of telling a story from different points of view. In "Song of Liang Fu"梁父吟, the contents of the couplet, the arrangement of books and the chess game are symbolic, and he acknowledges indebtedness to the techniques used in *Dream of the Red Mansions*.[41]

Bai Xianyong was invited to participate in the 1980 International Conference on *Dream of the Red Mansions* which was held at University of Wisconsin in Madison. He presented a paper entitled "The Influence of

---

39 Hu Juren, The Art of Fiction, p..202

40 C.T.Hsia, "On Bai Xianyong", Taipei People, p237

41 Hu Juren, The Art of Fiction, p.202.

Dream of the Red Mansions on 'Wandering in a Garden'遊園驚夢. In this study, Bai Xianyong explained that in Chapter 23 of *Dream of the Red Mansions*, the opera *Romance of the Western Chamber,* suggests the tragic love affair of Jia Baoyu and Lin Daiyu, while *Peony Pavilion* recalls the tragic ending of Lin Daiyu. He suggested that the opera performed within the novel served to develop the plot or give meaning to the novel. He pointed out that *Peony Pavilion* played an important role in his story "Wandering in a Garden", the plot and characters of one closely relating to the other. Influenced by *Dream of the Red Mansions,* "Wandering in a Garden" also deals with the theme of human events（being） as uncertain as the weather" or "Life （being） like a dream".[42]

---

42 Chow Tse-tsung, *Proceedings of First International Conference on Dream of the Red Mansions* （Hong Kong : Chinese University of Hong Kong Press,1983）, pp.251-52

The Study of Lu Xun and other Modern Chinese Writers in Japan: From Political Mirror to Scholarship

Introduction

The importance of Japanese scholarship in modern Chinese literature is recognized by scholars through the world. Even in mainland China, Japanese scholars' achievements in the field of modern Chinese literature have received special attention. For instance, *A Collection of Essays on Lu Xun by Foreign Scholars 1960-1981* 國外魯迅論集, a book published by Beijing University Press, reflects the increasing importance of Japanese scholarship. Japan is the only country which has five of its scholars' articles selected and translated in the book. There are four by American scholars, three by overseas Chinese scholars, and two by Czechoslovakian scholars. There is only one essay selected from each of the following countries: Soviet Union, Holland, Australia and Canada. In "A Bibliography of Important Studies on Lu Xun in Foreign Countries During the Last Twenty Years" 近二十年國外魯迅研究論著要目, an appendix in the book, 200 entries of books and articles in Japanese are included. There are only 37 entries in English and 48 in Russian.[1] The bibliography

1 Yue Daiyun 樂黛雲 (ed.), *A Collection of Essays on Lu Xun by Foreign Scholars 1960-1981*, (Beijing: Peking University Press, 1981), pp.508-521.

suggests the importance of Japanese scholarship in modern Chinese literature today. Many scholars in both East and West agree that one cannot be a good scholar of modern Chinese literature if he is totally ignorant of the Japanese scholarship.

I was invited by the Japan Society for the Promotion of Science（日本學術振興會）in May and June in 1985 to visit Japan's major universities. The visit's main object was to study the main teaching and current research trends in modern Chinese literature at Japan's universities today. Before my visit, I wrote to Professor Onoe Kanehide 尾上兼英, Director of Institute of Oriental Culture, University of Tokyo （東京大學東洋文化研究所）, for advice. I asked him to serve as my "host scientist" in the Tokyo area and advise me on the universities and scholars I should visit. He replied my letter in Chinese promptly by saying: "You are welcome to visit Tokyo University, and there are many scholars in Tokyo who study modern Chinese literature." He then drew up a list of the universities and scholars he thought I should visit:[2]

Tokyo University: Professor Maruyama Noboru

丸山昇教授

Professor Ito Keiichi

伊藤敬一教授

Tokyo Capital University:Professor Matsui Hiromitsu

松井博光教授

Professor Iiteru Souhei

飯倉照本教授

---

2 In Professor One's letter dated 23 April 1985. Professor One's recent interest includes Chinese literature in the 1930s. The list would be very different in 2006.

Tokyo Christian University:Professor Ito Toramaru

伊藤虎丸教授

Waseda University:　　　Professor Sugimoto Tatsuo

杉本達夫教授

In addition to these established scholars, there are many other young ones, including:

Hokkaido University:　　Professor Nakano Miyoko

中野美代子教授

Assoc. Prof. Maruo Tsuneki

丸尾常喜教授

Kyoto University　　　: Professor Takeuchi Minoru

竹內實教授

Osaka University of Foreign :Professor Aiura Takashi
Studies　　　　　　　　相浦杲教授

Kobe University:　　　　Professor Yamada Keizo

山田敬三教授

Kansai University:　　　Professor Kitaoka Tomoyuki

北岡正子教授

Kansai University:　　　Professor Katayama Tomoyuki

片山智行教授

Kyushu University:　　　Akiyoshi Shikio

and others.（2）秋吉久紀夫教授 Professor Onoe

Kanehide is one of the leading scholars in the field of modern Chinese literature in Tokyo. The list he suggested points to the fact that Tokyo University is no longer the only centre where modern Chinese literature is taught and studied. The teaching and research of modern

Chinese literature have been brought to other universities in Tokyo and other areas. For example, after his retirement from Tokyo University, professor Ono Shinobu 小野忍 joined Wakoh University. Professor Takeuchi Minoru 竹內實 and Professor Matsueda Shigeo 松枝茂夫 taught modern Chinese literature in Tokyo Capital University for some years before. Professor Takeda Taijun 武田泰淳 brought the beginnings of research in Chinese literature of the modern period to Hokkaido University. Because of his pioneering effort, Hakkaido University has become an important place for the study of modern Chinese literature. [3] Professor Masuda Wataru 增田涉 taught modern Chinese literature first in Osaka City University and then in Kansai University. His early effort and achievement may be one of the important reasons which has made Kyoto the second important centre for the study of modern Chinese literature in Japan today.

In order to understand the current study of modern Chinese literature, I think it is necessary to visit various universities throughout Japan. To trace its historical development, I decided to visit the universities in Tokyo with Tokyo University as my host university. From Tokyo I proceeded to Yokohama City University and Hokkaido University. I then visited universities in the Kansai areas such as Kyoto University and Osaka University of Foreign Studies. My last visit was to Kyushu where I visited North Kyushu and Shimonoseki City University.

---

3 The scholars involved in the teaching and research of modern Chinese literature include Professor Maruo Tsuneki   丸尾常喜, Sudo Yoichi 須藤洋一, Nakano Miyoko and others.

The Birth of the Study of Modern Chinese Literature in Tokyo

I went to see Professor Onoe Kanehide and Maruyama Noboru soon after my arrive in Tokyo.[4] They are not only the most established scholars in the field of modern Chinese literature, but are also the most influential leaders in the Tokyo area. Professor Onoe Kanehide arranged a meeting for me with the scholars who are involved in both teaching and research in the universities in Tokyo on 13 June 1985. Professor Onoe thought this was the most direct approach to the study of modern Chinese in Japan today. The following scholars were invited to participate in the seminar which was held at the institute of Oriental Culture, University of Tokyo.[5]

1. Onoe Kanehide 尾上兼英（1927）,Tokyo University　東京大學
2. Ito Keiichi 伊藤敬一（1927）, Tokyo University　東京大學
3. Ito Toramaru 伊藤虎丸（1927）, Tokyo Christian University 東京女子大學
4. Ashida Takaaki 蘆田孝昭 （1928）,Waseda University 早稻田大學
5. Tatsuma Shosuke 立間祥介（1921）
6. Matsui Horimitsu 松井博光（1930）, Tokyo Capital University 東京都立大學

---

4 Professors Onoe and Maruyama were the leaders of the Lu Xun Study Society and now lead the study group Leftist Literary Movement in the1930s. Professor Maruyama's publication include *Lu Xun and Revolution Literature* （1972） and *Lu Xun :His Works and Revolution Activitie*s （1965）.

5 According to Professor Onoe, it is the Japanese practice not to indicate a woman;s year of birth. Professor Sugimoto Tatso's name was added at the end of the list because he thought could not come for meeting.

7. Maruyama Noboru 丸山昇（1931）,Head of Department of

8. Chinese Literature, Tokyo University 東京大學

9. Inouchi Akira 井口晃（1934）, Central University 中央大學

10. Litera Souhei 飯昌照平（1934）, Tokyo Capital University 東京都立大學

11. Kiyama Hideo 木山英雄（1934）, Ichishi University 一橋大學

12. Kamaya Osamu 釜屋修（1936）, Wakoh University 合光大學

13. Maeda Toshiaki 前田利昭（1941）, Chuo University 中央大學

13. Kojima Hisayo 小島久代（　）, Gakushuin University 學習院大學

14. Ashida Hajime 蘆田肇（1942）, Kokugakuin University, 國學院大學

15. Sachi Toshihiko 佐治俊彦（1945）, Wakoh University 和光大學

16. Kondo Tatsuya 近藤龍哉 （1946）, Saitama University, 埼玉大學

17. Ozaki Fumiaki 尾崎文昭（1947）, Meiji University 東京大學

18. Egami Sachiko 江上幸子（　）, Tokyo University 東京大學

19. Shiramizu Noriko 白水紀子（1952）,Wakoh University 和光大學

20. Shirota Tomoaki 代田智明（1952）,Ibaragi University 茨城大學

21. Shimode Tetsuo 下出鉄男 （1952）, Wakoh University 和光大學

22. Kato Miyuki 加藤三由紀（　）, Ochanomizu University 御茶水女子大學

23. Hiraishi Yoshiko 平石淑子（　）

24. Karima Fumitoshi 刈間文俊（　）, Komazawa University 駒澤大學

25. Mizoguchi Yizo 溝口雄三（1933）, Tokyo University 東京大學

26. Koshio Emiko 小鹽惠美子（　）, Ochanimizu University 御茶水女子大學

27. Sato Mifuko 佐藤普美子（　）, Daito Bunka University 大東

28. Sugimoto Tatsuo 杉本達夫（1937）, Waseda University 早稻田大學

Almost all the scholars of the first and second generations in Tokyo were invited. Unfortunately, many did not turn up because there was a thunderstorm and several areas in the city were flooded that afternoon.

Modern Chinese literature was introduced to Japan in the late 1920s. Soon after that works by Chinese writers began to be read and studied by the Japanese. Japanese Sinologist Aoki Masaru 青木正兒 (1887-1964) wrote an article entitled "Hu Shi and the Chinese Literature Revolution" published in *Chinese Study* (支那學) in 1920.

In this article, Aoki Masaru predicted that "Lu Xun would become a great writer".[6] Lu Xun's writing was the earliest works to be translated into Japanese. In the 1930s and 1940s the Japanese scholars who had made important contributions in translation and studies of modern Chinese literature included Aoki Masaru 青木正兒(1887-1964), Takeuchi Yoshimi 竹內好 (1908-1977), Sato Haruo 佐藤春夫 (1892-1964), Kaji Wataro 鹿地亘 (1903), Oda Takeo 小田嶽夫 (1900), Masuda Wataru (1903-1977), Matsueda Shigeo 松枝茂夫 (1905-　　　), Takeda Taijun 武田泰淳(1912-76), Kuraishi Takeshiro 倉石武四郎(1897-1975), Ono Shinobu 小野忍 (1906), Ogawa Tamaki 小川環樹 (1910), Hatano Taro 波多野太郎 (1912) and others. These scholars are what we call today the first generation of researchers in modern Chinese literature in Japan. Among the Chinese writers, Lu Xun, Lao She and Mao Dun were most often studied in terms of having the largest number of translations and

---

6 *Chinese Study* , No.3(1920). Quotation taken from Liu Boqing 劉柏青 , "The Study of Lu Xun in Post-War Japan" 《戰後日本魯迅研究概觀》 *Study of Lu Xun* 《魯迅研究》 , No.6 （December 1984）, pp.58-60.

studies. These are in-depth and systematic studies.[7]

The Society for the Study of Modern Chinese Literature 中國文學研究會, the first organization devoted to the research of modern Chinese literature, was founded by a group of students who were studying in Tokyo University in 1934. The important members of this society were Takeuchi Yoshimi 竹內好, Takeda Taijun 武田泰淳, Matsueda Shigeo 松枝茂夫, Masuda Nataru 增田涉, and Ono Shinobu 小野忍. These scholars became the most influential scholars of the first generation. Among them, Takeuchi Yoshimi was generally considered the greatest scholar among his contemporaries. His works on Lu Xun and other writers are among the best research works written in his time. (8)[8]Takeuchi's favorite research subject was Lu Xun. He stressed that the study of Lu Xun and other Chinese writers could be used as a mirror, a criticism of Japan's modernisation. The study of modern Chinese literature can help Japanese to understand China and recognize the mistakes that Japan made during their process of modernisation. Takeuchi considered Lu Xun a great teacher and his Western approach to learning, which is critical and selective, should be followed by the Japanese. Takeuchi's way of studying modern Chinese literature influenced the other Japanese scholars very

---

7 About the study of Lu Xun in Japan, see Liu Xianbiao 劉獻彪 and Lin Zhiguang 林治廣(ed.), *Lu Xun and Sino-JapaneseCultural Exchange* 《魯迅與中國文化交流》(Hunan: Renmin chu-ban-she, 1981) .For the study of Mao Dun, see Furutani Kumikotz 古久美子 (ed.), "A Bibliography of Studies on Mao Dun Published in Japan " 《日本所出版茅盾研究參考資料目錄》*Yi Ya*, Nos. 18-19 (1984),pp. 94-106. About Lao She's studies , see Kusaka Tsuneo 日下恒夫 and Kurahashi 倉橋幸彥 (ed.), *Studies of Lao She in Japan* 《日本所出版老舍關係文獻目錄》(Kyoto: Friendship Bookstore, 1984)
8 Takeuchi Yoshimi's important publications include Lu Xun (1944), *Introduction to Lu Xun* 《魯迅入門》(1953), *Notes on Lu Xun* 《魯迅雜記》(1949) .

deeply. This may explain why the Japanese scholars in the past had been paying their attention selective to a few Chinese writers only.[9]

The Japanese scholars of the second generation emerged in the 1950s and 1960s.During this period, a great number of students in Tokyo University, Tokyo Capital University and Universities in Kansai area such as Kyoto University began to show keen interest in modern Chinese literature. A group of students in Tokyo University organized the Lu Xun Study Society 魯迅研究會 and published a journal called *Studies of Lu Xun* 魯迅研究. Another group of students in Tokyo Capital University published a journal called *The Big Dipper* 北斗. These two periodicals became the most important outlet for the young scholars to publish their research papers. Among the most distinguished scholars who emerged at the same time in Tokyo and Kansai areas were Takeuchi Minoru , Imamura Yoshio 今村與志雄, Once Kanehide, Takata Atsushi 高田淳, Maruyama Noboru, Kiyama Hideo 木山英雄 , Tekeuchi Noboru 竹內晃, Ito Toramaru, Matsui Hiromitsu 松井博光, Iitera Souhei 飯倉昭平, Ito Masafumi 伊藤正文, Aiura Takashi 相浦杲,Nakasawa Toshi 中川俊,Yamada Keizo 山田敬三,Kitaoka Masako 北岡正子,Sugimoto Tatsuo 杉本達夫,Ito Keiichi 伊藤敬一 and others. These second generation scholars are now about 50 years old and have become the leading scholars in the study of modern Chinese literature in Japan today. Many first generation leaders such as Takeda Taijun 武田泰淳,Takeuchi Yoshima 竹內好,Masuda Wataru 增田涉,and Ono Shinobu 小野忍 have passed away in the 1970s.

---

9 See Liu Boqing, "The Study of Lu Xun in Post-War Japan ", *Study Of Lu Xun*, No.6 （December 1984）, pp.64-66.

On the list of scholars invited to participate in the seminar held at the Institute of Oriental Culture, the first 11 scholars and Professor Sugimoto Tatsuo 杉本達夫（listed as No.28 only because he told the organizers he could not make it） are second generation scholars. If the other names mentioned in Onoe Kanehide's letter whom he suggested I should visit outside Tokyo area are added to these 12 scholars, they would represent the most important scholar in the field of modern Chinese literature in Japan today. Those listed from No.12 to No.27 are third generation scholars. Their average age is about 35 years old. Unlike their teachers, theses younger generation scholars tend to study various topics and writers, thus greatly expanding the research areas and scope of study. Most of them have their own specialized areas of research. For example, Kojima Hisayo 小島久代 studies Shen Congwen, Ashida Hajime 蘆田肇 comparative study of Chinese and Japanese literary relationship, Sachi Toshihiko 左治俊彦, Leftists' literature in the 1930s,Kondo Tatsuya 近藤龍哉, Hu Feng 胡風, and the 1930s literature, Ozaki Fumiaka 尾崎文昭, Zhou Zuoren, Egami Sachiko 江上幸子, Ding Ling 丁玲, Shimode Tetsuo 下出鐵男, Xiao Jun 蕭軍, Sato Mifuko 左藤美普子, new poetry of the 1920s. I mention their individual fields of research interest because it may indicate a breakaway from the traditional areas of scholarship in modern Chinese literature established by the first generation leaders.

The second generation scholars in Tokyo area are still carrying on the tradition of their teachers. Their best scholarship is shown in their studies of Lu Xun. Maruyama Noboru's 丸山昇 two books on Lu Xun, *Lu Xun: His Works and Revolution* 魯迅－他的文學與革命 *and Lu Xun and Revolutionary Literature* 魯迅與革命文學 are considered the most important works after Takeuchi Yoshimi's study on Lu Xun. Other scholars such as Onoe Kanehide,Ito Toramaru, Iitera Souhei 飯倉昭平, Kiyama Hideo 木山英雄 have also published very good books on Lu Xun. Some of the scholars have already broken away from the tradition of studying Lu Xun and begun extending their research to other writers .Ito Keiichi 伊藤敬一 wrote extensively on Lao She and Ito Toramaru 伊藤虎丸 is a leading scholar on Yu Dafu. Matsui Hiromitsu 松井博光, Ashida Takaaki 蘆田孝昭, Iiteru Souhei 飯倉昭平 are interested in Mao Dun, Ba Jin ,Zhou Zuo-ren and others .These writers have not been studied by their predecessors.[10]

The Society for the *Study of Chinese Literature in the 1930s* 中國卅年代文學研究會, an organization with Maruyama Noboru, Ito Toramaru, Kiyama Hideo, and Onoe Kanehide as the leading members, is the most respected and influential society promoting the study of modern Chinese literature in Tokyo. Their achievement is evidenced by the three collections of research papers published in *Oriental Culture* 東洋文化 as a special feature.[11] At present, there is a study group in the Institute of Oriental Culture called *Leftist Literary Movement in the 1930s* (一九三〇年代左翼文藝活動). With Professor Onoe Kanehide as its leader, the members meet every week at the Institute. Each member of the group takes turns to present a paper. In Tokyo there are many other bodies devoted to the study of modern Chinese literature. The Youth Society 新

---

10 The section dealing with modern Chinese literature in *Index to Publications on China* 《中國關係論說資料索引》,Nos.1-20（1964-1978）（Tokyo,1982）suggests that the areas of research had been greatly expanded.

11 The numbers and dates of publication of three issues of Oriental Culture are ：No.52 （March 1972）, No.56 （March 1976） and No.65 （March 1985）.

青年讀書會 is one. It holds regular discussions on modern Chinese literature and publishes a magazine called The Owl 貓頭鷹 which has become an important forum for the graduate students and young scholars to publish their papers.[12] Another society called The Drum 邊鼓社, publishes an annual bibliography of periodical articles and books publisher in Japan. The first volume contains books and articles published in 1977 to 1980, and the second volume contains those published in 1981-82.[13] Both are very exhaustive for the periods covered. The Lao She Study Society 老舍研究會, under the leadership of Shibagaki Yoshitaro 柴垣芳太郎 and Ito Keiichi, was formed in 1984.

Kansai：Second Centre for the Study of Modern Chinese Literature

After Tokyo, I visited Professor Suzuki Masao 鈴木正夫 at Yokohama City University and Professor Maruo Tsuneki 丸尾常喜 at Hokkaido University in Sapporo.[14] Both of them are closely related to the scholars in Tokyo and were graduates from Osaka City University. Professor Takeda Taijun 武田泰淳 and Professor Onoe taught modern Chinese literature in Hokkaido before. For this reason, modern Chinese literature is an important field of research for both students and staff

---

12 For example, No.3 of The Owl （June 1984） was devoted to the Studies of Ba Jin.

13 A Bibliography of Books and Articles on Modern and Contemporary Chinese Literature Published in Japan 《日本現代當代中國文學研究文獻目錄》,Vol.1（1981）,Vol.2（1983）.

14 Professor Suzuki Masao is co-editor of the volumes of Source Materials for the Study of Yu Dafu 《鬱達夫資料》,published by the Institute of Oriental Culture, Tokyo University in 1969, 1973 and 1974 respectively. Professor Maruo Tsuneki is a scholar of Lu Xun.

members. The *Hot Win* 熱風, a journal on modern Chinese literature, had become very important before it ceased publication a few years ago.

Professor Simizu Sigeru 清水茂, Head of Department of Chinese Language and Literature, Kyoto University served as my host scientist for Kyoto and Osaka. I was first scheduled to see Professor Takeuchi Minoru 竹內實, at Research Institute for Humanistic Studies 京都大學人文科學研究所, Kyoto University. Professor Takeuchi is a bit older than the other second generation writers. He has published extensively on modern Chinese literature and his important books include *Literature in China Today*《現代中國文學》,*On Lu Xun*《魯迅的遠景》 and *Lu Xun and His Friends*《魯迅周邊》. He is now completing *The Complete Work of Lu Xun* and *An Annual Chronology of Important Events in Modern Chinese Literature Since 1840*《中國現代文學年表》. Professor Takeuchi Minoru joined Kyoto University in 1973 and his presence has been helpful in developing Kansai as another centre for the study of modern Chinese literature.

Professor Simizu Sigeru 清水茂 also arranged for me to visit the Department of Chinese Literature of Osaka University of Foreign Studies where I met Professor Aiura Takashi 相浦杲（1926-1990 年）, Head of the Department , and his colleagues Professors Nakasawa Toshi 中川俊 and Korenaga Shun 是永駿. Professor Aiura Takashi is one of the second generation scholars whom I mentioned before. He has been actively promoting the teaching and research of modern Chinese literature. As a second generation scholar, Professor Aiura does not stick to Takeuchi Yoshimi's tradition. He has written on many writers of both modern and contemporary periods, as well as a number of comparative studies on the

Chinese-Japan literary relationship. Nakasawa Toshi is an authority on Ding Ling and Xiao Hong and Zhao Shu-li. Korenaga Shun has more articles published than any other third generation scholars in Japan. Most of his recent papers deal with Mao Dun 茅盾. As pointed out by Professor Onoe, there are many other established scholars in this region. Among them, Yamada Keizo 山田敬三, Kitaoka Masako 北岡正子, Katayama Tomoyuki 片山智行 and Akiyoshi 秋吉久紀夫 are widely published scholars.

In the Kansai area, I was surprised to find many third generation scholars. This is evidenced by the periodicals devoted to the study of modern Chinese literature. There are more journals for publication of studies in modern Chinese literature in Kansai than in Tokyo. In Kyoto, in addition to the academic journals like *Journal of Oriental Study* 《東方學報》, *Bulletin of Chinese Literature* 《中國文學報》, *The Whirl Wind* 《颱風》 is an important outlet for the scholars to publish their research papers outside the university. *The Whirl Wind* is the main organ of Whirl Wind Society 颱風之會 which was organized by a group of scholars with research interest in modern and contemporary literature.[15]

The most important journal devoted to modern Chinese literature is *The Wild Grass* 《野草》, an organ of the Association for the Study of Modern Chinese Literature 《中國文藝研討會》. The Association has a membership of 200 scholars, with the office established in the Research Centre of Modern Chinese Language and Literature at Osaka Economics University 大阪經濟大學. Professor Aiura Takashi of Osaka University

---

15 *The Whirl Wind* , up to 1985, has publishe 18 issues.

of Foreign Studies is the leader of the group. *The Wild Grass* was first
launched in 1970 and has now published 35 issues. Each issue of the
journal of about 200pages carries special features such as "Literature in
the May Fourth Era" or "Literature in the Liberated Areas".

As shown by the articles published in the past issues, topics cover
various writers and problems including modern, contemporary and Taiwan
literature. The contributors include the second and third generation
scholars from various institutes and places of Japan. Almost all
well-known scholars in modern Chinese literature have published papers
in the *Wild Grass*. The Association for the study of Modern Chinese
literature also publishes another magazine called *Bulletin of Association
for the Study of Modern Chinese Literature*《中國文藝研討會會刊》. It has
now published 50 issues. The bulletin includes articles and newsletters.
Other magazines, devoted to the study of modern Chinese literature ,
including *Yiya*《咿啞》,the *Unnamed*《未名》*Bulletin of Taiwan Literature
Society*《台灣文學研討會會報》and *Bulletin of Mao Dun Society*《茅盾
研究會會報》are playing an important role in recent year.[16]

The Teaching Programmes of Modern Chinese Literature in Japan's Universities

Most of the major universities in Japan today offer courses in modern
Chinese language and literature. In the graduate programme, the study of

---

16 *Yi Ya* , a journal published by the Yi Ya Society 咿啞之會. It has, up to 1985, published
20 issues of the journal. *Unnamed,* was launched in1982 , under the leadership of
Professor Katayama Tomoyuki . *Bulletin of Taiwan Literature Society* was first launched
in1982, 10 issues were published by July 1985. The first and second issue of *Bulletin of
Mao Dun Society were published* by July and November 1984 .

modern Chinese literature also occupies an important place. The universities in Tokyo such as Tokyo University, Waseda University, Tokyo Capital University, Toyo University 東洋大學, Wakoh University 和光大學 and Tokyo Christian University , have good teaching and research programmes for the study of modern Chinese literature.

Elsewhere, for examples, Kyoto University, Osaka University of Foreign Studies, Kobe University, Kansai University, Osaka City University, North Kyushu University, Kyushu University, the study of modern Chinese literature is fast growing. More and more students are taking Chinese as major subjects. Students taking modern Chinese literature out-number those who opt for classical Chinese literature. I paid special attention to the contents of courses dealing with modern Chinese literature when I visited the universities. My meeting with the teachers of the courses was very helpful in understanding the syllabi of the courses. The following is a list of courses dealing with modern Chinese literature offered in the respective universities. The lecturer and main topic of each course are indicated within the brackets:

（a） Department of Chinese Literature, Tokyo University

1. Chinese Literature in the 1930s（Professor Maruyama Noboru , with special reference to Lu Xun）.

2. Study of Modern Chinese Literature（Professor Maruyama Noboru , with special reference to Leftist Writers）.

3. Complete Works of Lu Xun, Vol II （Professor Maruyama Noboru）.

4. Special Topic on Modern Chinese Literature （Professor Ito Keiichi, with focus on Lao She）.

5. Special Topic on Modern Chinese Literature （Professor Maruyama,

with focus on Zhu Ziqing 朱自清）．

6. Study of Zhou Zuoren 周作人 （Professor Kiyama Hideo）

（b）Department of Chinese Literature, Waseda University.

1. Study of Modern Chinese Literature （Professor Sugimoto Tatsuo, with special reference to autobiographical writings）．

2. Source Materials Related to Lao She and Literary Movements during the War of Resistance Period（Professor Tatsuo）．

3. History of Chinese Fiction （Professor Ashida Takaaki, dealing chiefly with modern Chinese fiction ）．

（c）Department of Chinese Language and Literature, Kyoto University.

1. Topics in Modern Chinese Literature （Professor Takeuchi Minoru, dealing mainly with Lu Xun.

2. Selected Readings in Modern Drama.

3. Chinese Essay Writing（on Lao She's Zheng Hong Qi Xia）．

（d）Department of Chinese Language, Osaka University of Foreign tudies.

1. History of Modern Chinese Literature（Professor Korenaga Shun, dealing with Literary debates）．

2. Seminar on Modern Chinese Literature （Professor Korenaga Shun, dealing mainly with the works of Mao Dun）．

3. Study of Chinese Literature: Comparative Study of Sino-Japanese Literature（Professor Aiura Takashi with special reference to the relationships of Lu Xun, Guo Moruo and Yu Dafu to Japanese literature）:

4. Seminar on Chinese Literature: Study of Contemporary Chinese Literature（Professor Korenaga Shun, selected reading of works published in literary magazines published in China）．

（e）Department of Chinese Literature and Philosophy, Toyo University-

1. Introduction to the History of Modern Chinese Literature（Professor Nakamasa Masaharu 中下正治 ）.

2. Seminar on Modern Chinese Literature （Professor Kanaok Shoko 金岡照光, dealing mainly with the works of Lao She ）.

（f）Department of Chinese Literature, Hokkaido University

1. Seminar on Chinese Literature（Professor Maruo Tsuneki,1979 to 1985 lecture topics [one topic each year]: Cao Yu's 曹禺 *Family* 《家》, Chinese Literature in the 1930s ,Lu Xun's "The True Story of Ah Q"阿Q正傳 and "Village Opera " 社戲, Lao She's *Gu Shu Yi Ren* 《鼓書藝人》and Ai Wu's 艾蕪 , *A Trip to the South* 《南行記》）.

2. Seminar on Chinese Literature（Professor Fujimoto Kozo 藤本幸三, topics in recent years include: Chinese DramaIn the 1930s, Modern Chinese "Local-colour" LiteratureSelected Readings in Contemporary Chinese Literature.

A selected list of curriculums for modern Chinese literature offered by five universities shows that almost all professors lectured on very specialized topics. There are very few introductory courses which are comprehensive, although this may be suggested by some of the course titles. Instead, the professors actually lecture on a topic of which they have done in-depth study. For instance, Professor Aiura Akira told me that he discussed the influence of Kuriyagana Hakuson's 櫥川白村 *Going out of the Ivory Tower* 《出了象牙之塔》and *The Symbolism of Depression* 《苦悶的象徵》on Lu Xun's *The Wild Grass* in the class of "Comparative

Study of Sino-Japanese literature".[17] I was even more surprised to learn that Professor Maruo Tsuneki of Hokkaido University spent a semester to lecture on Lu Xun's "Village Opera" in a course entitled "Seminar on Chinese Literature". Professor Maruyama Noboru of Tokyo University and Professor Takeuchi Minoru of Kyoto teach a course called "Study of Modern Chinese Literature". Because both of them are experts on Lu Xun, they used to lecture only on Lu Xun .Professor Korenaga Shun's current research interest is in Mao Dun, and he teaches Mao Dun's works only in a course called "Seminar on Modern Chinese Literature".

The close relationship between the individual's research interest and what he teaches is the most important reason why Japanese scholars can produce research work without being interrupted by their teaching responsibilities, thus enabling Japanese professors to be very productive in publication. The curriculums listed above also show that Lu Xun and the literature of the 1930s do not occupy an important place in the universities as in the past. Many modern Chinese writers, who have been neglected completely in the past, have become subjects of study in the classrooms. Contemporary Chinese writers and their works have been receiving more and more attention. In the Osaka University of Foreign Studies, Professor Korenaga Shun teaches a course dealing with the most recent works chosen from current periodicals published in China.

---

17 Aiura Akira , "A   Study of Lu Xun's   *Wild Grass* from a Comparative Perspective "
《從比較的角度來分析魯迅散文詩〈野草〉》, *Study of International Relation*《國際
關係論的綜合研究》(Osaka, 1982) ,pp. 1-48. "Lu Xun and Kuriyagana Hakuson"《魯
迅與櫥川白村》,*Wild Grass,* No 29 （1981）,pp.5-51.

The Study of Modern Chinese
Literature in Japan Today: New Directions

Yen shaotang 嚴紹璗 has included about 400 biographies of established scholars in the field of Chinese language and literature in *Scholars of Chinese Studies Japan*《日本的中國學家》.[18] The researchers who are interested in modern Chinese literature have greatly increased in recent years. Following the increase in the number of scholars and journals are new developments in the study of modern Chinese literature.

1、From Lu Xun to Taiwanese Literature

The first significant change is that Japanese scholars have extended their study to all periods, including contemporary literature in China and Taiwan. The scope of research of the first generation scholars was very narrow. They focused on a few selected writers and their works. This research tendency of the past is reflected in existing bibliographies in *Index to the Publications on China*, 1964-1978《中文關論文資料索引》, 200 entries of studies of modern Chinese literature are included, of which about 70 entries are studies of Lu Xun. The second most studied writer is Mao Dun but there are only 15 entries. Lao She comes third with nine entries. The other writers such as Ding Ling and Zhao Shuli each have only three entries. *A Bibliography of Studies of Modern Chinese Literature*《日本中國現代文學研究主要文獻索引》covers 1970-81 and it includes 240 entries, Lu Xun has 100 entries, Mao Dun 24, Yu Dafu 13, and Lao She eight.[19]

The appearance of the large number of so-called third generation

---

18 Yen Shaotang 嚴紹璗 , *Scholars of Chinese Studies in Japan* （Beijing: China's Social Sciences Publisher, 1980 ）.

19 Edited and published by Institute of Social Science, Beijing, in two parts.

scholars has brought about drastic change in research areas. The articles published in the past 34 issues of *The Wild Grass* and 20 issues of *Yi Ya* fully reflect this latest development. *A Bibliography of Books and Articles on Modern and Contemporary Chinese Literature published in Japan* is an exhaustive bibliography for the years 1977-81.It reflected the new development in which scholars of the young generation problems. The scholars in Kansai are paying increasing attention to contemporary Chinese literature in China and Taiwan.

2、From Politically-oriented Scholarship to Degree-oriented Scholarship

The second significant change lies in the motivation and rationale underlying the research and teaching. As upheld by Takeuchi Yoshimi, the main purpose of studying modern Chinese literature in the past was to learn through literature, the Chinese experience in modernization. It is not easy to find a writer like Lu Xun whose work can throw light on social reformation in Japan. With this social and political orientation in choosing a writer, the first and second generation scholars found very few Chinese writers worthwhile studying.

As for the third –generation scholars, their considerations are more personal, for so long as their research can earn them a degree or increase their academic importance, they are willing to study a subject. Thus, the study of modern Chinese literature is now for the sake of academic achievement, not for revolution or social reform. For the younger scholars, there is a tendency to study those writers and works which have been relatively neglected by past scholarship. They are also freer to explore problems because they are less influenced by scholarship from China.

3、Changes in Methodology

After breaking away from the politically-oriented tradition, the younger generation scholars began to study modern Chinese literature from different angles and perspectives. They give more attention and emphasis to analytical and critical approaches than historical and biographical ones. They are less influenced by Chinese scholars in China. Some of the leading scholars, though they belong to the second generation, have contributed a great deal to the comparative study of modern Sino-Japanese literature. There are quite a number of good studies using the comparative approach. Hiyama Hisao's *Lu Xun and Sohseki*《魯迅與漱石》, Ito Toramru's *Lu Xun and the Japanese*《魯迅與日本人》and Aiura Takashi's " A Story of Lu Xun's Wild Grass from a Comparative Perspective"〈從比較的角度來分析魯迅散文詩野草〉represent the change in methodology in recent years.

4、The Study of Modern Chinese Literature Outside Universities

The attention of my research trip was directed to the scholars affiliated to the research institutions. I did not have the time and opportunity to meet scholars living and doing research outside the universities. Takeuchi Yoshimi, preeminent scholar of the first generation, spent almost all his life outside the university. At present, there are many promising young scholars who are not related to any academic institutions. In the past, journals published by universities were the only outlet to publish papers dealing with modern Chinese literature. Today the situation has changed. Journals such as *The Wild Grass, The Whirl Wind* and *The Owl* are not published by universities but are well recognized by all scholars of modern Chinese literature.

5、The Study of Malaysian and Singapore Chinese Literature

Among the scholars I visited, Professor Imatomi Masami of Tokyo University, Professor Yamamoto Tetsuya of Kyushu University, Professor Suzuki Masao of Yokohama City University and Professor Hirofumi Ogi of Shimonoseki City University are interested in modern Chinese literature in Malaysia and Singapore. They have published many articles on modern Chinese literature from Malaysia and Singapore.[20] Professor Sakurai Akiji 櫻井明治 of Aichi College University 愛知學院大學 has translated a number of Chinese and English works from Singapore into Japanese. Professor Chen Chunshun 陳俊勳 of Tsukuba University 筑波大學 and Tominaga Hei 福永平, a journalist with Mainichi Daily are co-translators of the Japanese translation of *Anthology of Singapore Short Stories*（1985）and Miao Xiu's 苗秀 *Can Ye Xing*《殘夜行》（1985）.

Conclusion

Japan has been considered as one of the important centers in the world for the study of modern Chinese literature. Many Japanese scholars such as Takeuchi Yoshimi, Masuda Nataru, Maruyama Minoru and Takeuchi Minoru are recognized as some of the top scholars in the field. Japanese scholarship in modern Chinese literature has become so important that many research topics cannot be completed if Japanese source are not consulted. There are two centers for the study of modern Chinese literature in Japan, namely, Tokyo and the Kansai area. Professor in Tokyo University played a leading role in Tokyo in the study of the literature of the 1930s and 1940s. The scholars in Kyoto University, Osaka University of Foreign Studies, Kobe University and Kansai University on the other hand, are more interested in the study of contemporary Chinese literature than of the early periods.

---

20 A society called Nanyang Chinese Study Society 南洋華文學會 was formed by these scholars to promote the study of Chinese language and literature in Singapore and Malaysia.

附　錄：

王潤華著〈魯迅詩抄〉

一、在仙台醫專第六教室

九十年後

我回到仙台醫專第六教室

坐在魯迅的座位上

幻燈片仍然無聲放映著

日軍槍斃中國偵探

子彈突然發出刺耳的爆炸聲

驚醒了我

發現學者們已悄悄離去

我匆忙追趕出去

魯迅在校園一棵松樹下

滿臉困惑的

望著前面仙台醫專校史展覽館

世界各國的學者

正低頭爭論魯迅的成績單

爲什麼有三種分數計算錯誤？

爲什麼誣告藤野先生在筆記裏留下暗號

而偏偏解剖學卻不及格？

1994 年作

二、重訪魯迅寄宿的佐藤屋

夏季最後的一日

佐藤屋在綠樹中午寐

樓上右邊魯迅寄宿的屋子

玻璃窗緊閉著

從後院廚房升起的炊煙

從水井中飛出的小鳥

都在尋找

魯迅今天有沒有回來

再與宮城監獄的犯人

共吃同一鍋裏的飯菜？

> 後記：魯迅於一九零四年九月赴日本仙台醫專，二年級中途退學，因為
> 救中國人的靈魂比肉體重要。今年為魯迅留學仙台九十周年（現屬東北
> 大學）為此邀請國際魯迅學者前往出席一國際研討會。

1994 年 9 月

三、訪魯迅上海故居

1.

整整一個下午

我站在且介亭門口

等待魯迅

踏著滿街的落葉回家

2.

吶喊之後

我開始感到彷徨

因爲我疲倦的影子
吵著要離我而去

3.

路邊一株野草抬起頭
很有耐心的說：
這就是上海山陰路大陸新村九號
魯迅在這屋子裏
翻譯過《死靈魂》
寫了《花邊文學》、《且介亭雜文》
編選《中國新文學大系》小說二集
又寫完《故事新編》
在一九三六年十月十九日清晨
咳嗽、抽煙之後
便披衣出去散步

4.

我突然聽見
魯迅在樓上咳嗽
便立刻上一樓尋找
瞿秋白沒有匿藏在客房裏
魯迅臥房書桌上壓著一篇未完成的
〈因太炎先生而想起的二三事〉原稿
煙灰缸還發出美麗牌香煙的煙味
那枝傾斜立著的毛筆
聆聽了五十年樓梯的聲音

等待著魯迅回家寫完它

5.

我匆匆走進附近的內山書店
正在聊天的不是魯迅和內山完造先生
而是中國人民銀行的職員
他們正在點算鈔票
門口那棵法國梧桐告訴我：
它認識魯迅
如果他從山陰路回家即刻通知我

6.

我沿街向每一棵法國梧桐樹查問
它們都說
常常看見阿Q、閏土、祥林嫂等人經過
短鬚撇在唇上的魯迅
五十年來卻未曾出現過

7.

下午五點
在靜謐的虹口公園
我終於找到魯迅
他沉默的安坐在園中的石椅上
草木都枯黃了
只有他身上的綢袍還是那樣綠

註：一九八六年十一月一日訪上海山蔭路魯迅故居、內山書店及魯迅墓之後
　　作。魯迅自稱這故居為且介亭，瞿秋白曾居樓上客房。內山書店原址目
　　前已改成為銀行。